METEOR BOYS

METEOR BOYS

TRUE TALES FROM THE OPERATORS OF BRITAIN'S FIRST
JET FIGHTER – FROM 1944 TO DATE

STEVE BOND

GRUB STREET • LONDON

First published in hardback in 2016 by
Grub Street
4 Rainham Close
London
SW11 6SS

Copyright © Grub Street 2016
Copyright text © Steve Bond 2016

This paperback edition first published in 2020

A CIP record for this title is available from the British Library

ISBN-13: 9-781-911621-90-4

Printed and bound in India by Replika Press

DEDICATION

To my darling wife Christine
July 1947 – October 2015
Who always encouraged me in my writing but sadly did not live to see this book completed

CONTENTS

PREFACE

THE RIGHT HONOURABLE LORD TEBBIT C.H.

More than one book has been written about the Gloster Meteor and rightly so, since it was the first jet-engined aircraft to enter RAF service and the only one to see action on the Allied side during the Second World War. However, in *Meteor Boys* Steve Bond looks at the men (and it seems that there were no women) who flew the Meteor. In doing so Bond reminds us of a century in which the value put on human life in war or the preparation for war was very different from that of today, in Western circles at least.

The First World War had cost the lives of nine million combatants and seven million civilians, a rate of about four million a year. At Verdun and on The Somme over 600,000 men died in a matter of weeks. Thirty years later the nuclear weapons used against Hiroshima and Nagasaki cost around a quarter of a million mainly civilian lives, bringing to a close a conflict which had taken the lives of something between 50 and 85 million people worldwide – again the majority of whom were civilians. Those two Great Wars of the first half of the twentieth century had between them claimed between 65 and 100 million lives, mostly civilians. In London we had experienced the Blitz in 1940 which killed 40,000 during a time when many of my generation did our homework in air raid shelters and became accustomed to walking to school past the un-cleared debris of the previous night's bombing. Within two or three years the tide of war had turned and the skies of London and the East of England were darkened as the overwhelming might of Bomber Command and the US 8th Army Air Force headed out to all but obliterate several great German cities initially taking terrible casualties themselves as they did so. It is all but impossible to estimate the number of casualties during the Cold War, which closed the twentieth century, but they were simply accepted as part of the price of peace. However, perhaps under the remorseless growth in the capacity of the media to bring the horrors of war into our living rooms, it has now become *de rigueur* for the prime minister to extend his condolences in the House of Commons to the families of any British serviceman lost in action. Indeed we have begun to mark the deaths of those murdered by the Isil terrorists with a minute's silence in the Palace of Westminster, a tribute not given to those murdered earlier by their IRA/Sinn Fein terrorist predecessors.

Such things were not thought of in the times related by Steve Bond. The 'Meteor Boys', of whom I am proud to be one, flew from the last months of World War Two, through some of the hot spots of the Cold War, notably Korea and indeed there are still just a few of us left flying the last few surviving Meteors today. We were a very mixed bunch, from Cranwell graduates, short-service commissioned and non-commissioned officers, regulars and auxiliaries, day fighter, night fighter, ground attack and reconnaissance pilots and navigators.

It took a lot of us to fly the total of 3,922 Meteors ever built. Now there are only five still flying and a few more living on in museums or as gate guardians. There were times when the Meteor had a slightly dodgy reputation because of the number which were being written off, often with their pilots, but readers of this book may well reach the conclusion that although the aircraft had weaknesses, such as its very high fuel consumption, many of the losses were down to the aircraft being operated in weather conditions in which its late 1930s-style instrumentation and lack of navigation systems were a frequent cause of losses. Another factor which these tales bring out, was the fall in the standards of training brought about largely by the sudden increase in the annual output of pilots from 300 to 3,000 a year as the Attlee government responded to the threat of soviet Russia and the Warsaw ·Pact forces from 1950.

Now, like the Meteor itself, we 'Meteor Boys' (many of whom were part of that re-armament programme) are gradually fading away too, but some of us still meet up in the bar, toasting absent friends and sharing our memories of days together, some boring, some exciting, some tragic but many funny too. Steve Bond spent many hours listening to our ramblings and bringing them back to life. They all make great reading but let me confide that although there are some which left me very subdued, far more brought smiles to my lips and not a few which earned the writer's greatest accolade, of outright laughter.

I particularly enjoyed reading the piece by Alan Colman (p.23) who was a contemporary of mine on No.36 Pilot course as a National Service pilot in June 1949. It was a pretty successful course as we all got our wings and suffered only two casualties, one killed during our jet conversion at Middleton St. George and the other at OCU on a ground-attack detail. Alan was not commissioned then and left the RAF, but subsequently re-joined on a short-service commission and flew for some years with 74 Squadron at Horsham St. Faith. As the North Weald and Horsham Wings often exercised together, we must at times have been not far apart. He describes the flying life and ground-based pranks which left all of us so often either roaring with laughter or sweating with fear. That runs on to a wonderful account (p.35) of how one of his colleagues on 74 Squadron Derek Morter, determined to give a fright to some Welsh TA infantrymen sheltering beneath a tree during a training exercise near Thetford, gave himself one too, bringing back home part of the top of the tree. Chris Strong recounts some of his airborne flirtations with the deadly reaper, but sets the tone of those days with his tale of being posted to the Aircrew Transit Unit at RAF Driffield awaiting his pilot training course to find that his principal duty was to attend aircrew funerals, scoring three funerals in his first fortnight in the RAF. Indeed, he quotes Churchill's concern that in 1954 Fighter

Command lost 515 aircraft and 308 pilots, which the chief of staff described as "normal". George Black (on p.52) tells of being one of a course of 13 students at Driffield AFS in 1952 of whom five were failed and three killed which, even for those days, was somewhat below par.

Of so many remarkable stories I have no doubt that my favourite is that of Peter Greensmith (p.108) who was on a Meteor squadron in Egypt in 1953. During a simulated dogfight with a Venom he performed an unorthodox manoeuvre and lost the tail section of his aircraft. The Venom pilot did not see him bale out and he was posted missing, presumed dead. In fact he landed safely but in the middle of the Sinai Desert. It would be a shame to reveal the end of this adventure, but that alone is worth more than the price of this extraordinary compendium of the lives of the 'Meteor Boys'.

INTRODUCTION
AND
ACKNOWLEDGEMENTS

As with any aeroplane it is the aircrew and ground crew who are the people best placed to tell the story of the Gloster Meteor's remarkable career and a good many of them have stepped forward here to recount their experiences. Many are exciting, some are sad, quite a few are humorous, but they are all typified by a great underlying affection for the type.

The Meteor has a secure place in history as not only the Royal Air Force's first operational jet-powered aeroplane, but the first such to serve with any of the Allied powers during the Second World War, its rival the de Havilland Vampire not joining a squadron until 1946. The first Meteors reached 616 Squadron (Sqn) in July 1944 and on 4 August the first success against a V1 flying bomb was achieved by Fg Off 'Dixie' Dean. WO Sid Woodacre, a fellow pilot on 616 Sqn, described his own victory thus:

> "I was among the first to shoot down a V1 flying bomb. This was on 17 August 1944, when I was on an anti-Diver patrol under Biggin Hill control. I saw a V1 coming in south of Dover and caught up with it about three miles south of Canterbury. A Mustang was already sitting behind it but for some reason he didn't open fire. I was flying at about 400 mph and had no difficulty in overtaking both the Mustang and the V1 and then attacked and fired three short bursts at a range of about 200 yards. I saw strikes on its starboard wing and it then rolled over and went straight down. I saw it blow up when it hit the ground south of Faversham and explode harmlessly in fields below me, but the blast was enough to throw my Meteor about, even at 1,500 feet. If you were unlucky enough to hit the bomb itself, it would blow up and you could be in considerable danger."

Patrols against the V1 continued until 31 August by which time the Meteors had accounted for 11 of them and shared in the destruction of a further three. Although the squadron moved onto the Continent in March 1945, no Meteor versus Me 262 encounter ever took place, despite 616 Sqn's best endeavours to try and flush the German jets out in the closing days of the conflict. After the war, the aircraft embarked on a remarkably varied and lengthy career which continued long after the final operational unit gave it up when 60 Sqn at Tengah retired its final NF.14 night fighters in favour of Javelins in the summer of 1961.

From an early stage in its career, the type had begun to move into other roles beyond its original day fighter use and its versatility was to prove to be the key

F.1 EE217 YQ-B 616 Squadron, Manston, July 1944. [via Peter Arnold]

to its longevity. In addition to the night fighter variants developed and built by Armstrong Whitworth (largely because Gloster was heavily engaged in Javelin work), the Meteor saw extensive service as a pilot (and later navigator) trainer, a fighter/photo-reconnaissance aircraft, target tug, communications aircraft and, in the twilight of its career, as a pilotless drone to be shot at by guided missiles.

Following the proof of jet-powered flight by the Gloster E.28/39, the company was encouraged to push ahead with an operational fighter and it was largely the original requirement for a six 20-mm cannon armament that resulted in the Meteor having twin engines, primarily due to the modest thrust available from the early production power plants. In fact, the armament required was subsequently reduced to four cannons, but the design (under the leadership of George Carter) was already decided. First to fly was actually the fifth of eight unnamed F.9/40 prototypes, doing so on 3 March 1943 from RAF Cranwell in the hands of Michael Daunt. Much discussion went on between Glosters and the Ministry of Aircraft Production (MAP) about what to call the production aeroplane. The ministry preferred Thunderbolt until someone pointed out that the Republic P-47 had got there first, which raises an intriguing possibility. Since the Meteor became universally known to its pilots and ground crew as the Meatbox, had the earlier name been adopted would it have been known as the Thunderbox!?

The initial production F.1 was only ever considered by the company to be an interim operational Meteor with just 20 being completed. The F.2 was intended to use the Halford H.1 engine, but as this was needed in its production form as the Goblin to power de Havilland's Vampire, only a single F.2 was built. The rather more developed F.3 was what Glosters felt was a combat-worthy aeroplane, the first of which joined 616 Sqn in December 1944 and which, like the F.1, was fitted with the Welland engine. A total of 210 of these were built before being followed by 490 examples of the F.4, a higher performance variant taking advantage of an uprated Derwent engine while also introducing shorter span wings for improved manoeuvrability. Production was undertaken at the company's Huccelcote factory near Gloucester and flight testing from the former RAF airfield at Moreton Valence.

Next in line numerically was the FR.5, a fighter reconnaissance aircraft the sole prototype of which was written off on its first flight killing the pilot, Rodney Dryland. The mark was then abandoned (in favour of the later and much improved FR.9) as was the F.6 which was, in effect, the next step forward towards the F.8, but which never got off the drawing board.

In the meantime, it was the arrival of the F.4 that really saw the Meteor in its ascendency in RAF service as more and more squadrons converted to the type, largely driven by the onset of the Cold War, followed a few short years later by the start of the conflict in Korea, both of which created a rapidly increasing demand not only for aeroplanes, but also for pilots to fly them (in 1950 alone the target annual intake of new pilots was raised from 300 to 3,000). This created an issue which Glosters appear to have been the first to recognise. They realised that the practice of only putting experienced pilots into the Meteor could only go on for so long and that newly trained pilots would have to be taken on by the squadrons as the numbers required continued to escalate. The issue here was the lack of a two-seat trainer, so chief designer Richard Walker and his team set to and produced a prototype, modified from an F.4, as a private venture which first flew in March 1948. The Air Ministry had already taken up the idea and at the end of that same year the first T.7s were issued to the service; eventually 641 were accepted by the RAF and the Royal Navy.

The concerns about training proved to be fully justified and even with the advent of the T.7, the Meteor accident rate rose to astonishingly high levels in the first two to three years of the 1950s. In 1952 alone, no fewer than 153 were written off in accidents for the loss of 94 pilots plus two people on the ground. By comparison, in the same year the Vampire suffered 82 accidents and 40 fatalities. Of the Meteor accidents and fatalities, the overwhelming majority occurred on training units, not helped by the fact that in addition to the T.7, the schools were all equipped with F.3s and F.4s (discarded by squadrons re-equipping with later models), none of which were fitted with ejection seats. Many factors can be considered to account for this appalling loss rate, not least the challenges of asymmetric flight especially in the circuit during training. The so-called 'Phantom Dive' was another factor, where pilots were failing to retract the air brakes before lowering the undercarriage, a set-up known to make the aircraft highly susceptible to a loss of control. In addition, many pilots who were trained on the Meteor at that time have criticised the standard of training, with instructors who had spent their careers on very different piston-engined types and had only limited experience on any jets, let alone the Meteor. To balance this however, without exception, every pilot interviewed for this book has expressed his liking for the Meteor, with many describing it as a "lovely aeroplane".

Equipping several advanced flying schools (AFS) – later renamed flying training schools (FTS) – from 1952 onwards the T.7 shared the flying training task with the Vampire T.11. One interesting factor concerning which type a student pilot trained on was the identification of a problem of ejection from a T.11 by a pilot with upper legs over a certain length which, due to the confines of the cockpit, could result in him leaving his legs behind! Happily, this was not the case in a Meteor T.7 as the cockpit was somewhat roomier. In addition to the training schools, most fighter squadrons, regardless of which type they flew, had one or two Meteor T.7s on their strength to enable such things as instrument ratings to be carried out and for general communications tasks. This was primarily because of the lack of two-seat versions of such types as the Venom and Hunter (in the early days), and restricted availability of Vampire T.11s for squadron use. The T.7 also served in considerable numbers with various station flights and group communications flights; even the RAF's flagship Transport Command squadron, 216 at Lyneham, initially supplemented its shiny new Comets with a handful of T.7s to help incoming crews become acclimatised to jets.

Almost forgotten now is the use of the T.7 by the Royal Navy, who received 43 of them for their training schools at locations including Culdrose, Ford and Lossiemouth from 1948 onwards until they were supplanted by the Sea Vampire T.22 (a simple renaming of the T.11). The remaining Meteors then followed a similar pattern to the RAF's being used for continuation and refresher training and general 'hack' duties in the UK and Malta. They were also used by the civilian-run (by Airwork) fleet requirements units at St. Davids and finally Hurn from where the last one was retired in 1970.

The Meteor that was, in the view of almost every pilot who has flown the type, the finest of them all, was the definitive F.8 day fighter. This was produced in very large numbers, with no fewer than 1,090 going to the UK military alone and it proved to be a major step forward in almost every respect. While primarily produced to address the fact that the F.4 was quickly being outclassed by later types, the opportunity was taken to introduce cabin pressurisation and for the first time, an ejection seat. Some of the stability problems of the F.4 were tackled by the adoption of an enlarged fin and rudder (which appeared to have eliminated the Phantom Dive risk from this variant), while visibility was considerably enhanced with a one-piece cockpit canopy. Later models introduced spring tab ailerons for less taxying manoeuvrability for the pilot and so-called 'deep breathers' – enlarged air intakes for improved engine performance.

The F.8 first entered service in 1950 and re-equipped large numbers of both regular and auxiliary squadrons, but already their improved performance was proving less than adequate and the advent of the renowned Hawker Hunter in 1954 spelt the end for the Meteor as a first-line day fighter. Despite this, the F.8 achieved arguably the Meteor's finest hour flying with the Royal Australian Air Force (RAAF) in Korea, where it became renowned for its capability in the ground-attack role, armed with both rocket projectiles and bombs. It was even able to achieve three air-to-air victories against the far superior MiG 15, engaging them at lower levels where the performance difference was less marked.

Despite rapidly approaching obsolescence, the Royal Auxiliary Air Force (RAuxAF) squadrons hung on to their F.8s until all the units were disbanded on mass at the beginning of 1957, after it had been decided that part-time weekend flyers would not be able to cope if their Meteors and Vampires were replaced by more advanced aircraft like the Hunter. In effect this was merely a prelude to the now notorious 1957 defence review by the Conservative Defence Secretary Duncan Sandys, who said there would be no further need for manned fighter aircraft after the then not-yet-in-service Lightning. At a stroke, the RAF fighter force started a severe pruning from which it never recovered.

For those who flew the F.8 on front-line squadrons, these were heady days indeed. They all speak with great fondness of the *esprit de corps* on large squadrons with lots of flying to be had and a considerable freedom of action with little or no interference from higher authority. Every year brought detachments for air-to-air firing practise, multiple air defence exercises and *ad hoc* air combat encounters with anyone else who happened to be about in their part of the sky. Possibly without exception, every squadron (and every FTS) had its own aerobatic team of typically three or four aircraft. When asked to sum up how it was, everyone says the same thing: "great fun".

As with earlier Meteors, the F.8 still found itself in demand once its squadron days were over. Quite a few senior officers had already managed to appropriate an F.8 as their personal run-about, usually looked after for them by the local station flight or group communications flight. Many other F.8s retired from the front line were put to use as target tugs and referred to as the F(TT).8. Unlike the later target-towing conversions of night fighters, these were not equipped with a winch, but required the long-suffering ground crew to hook-up the end of the towing cable, which had been laid out at the end of the runway with its target banner attached, immediately before take-off and subsequently released back over the airfield after the air-to-air firing session had been completed.

In parallel with the F.8, a fighter-reconnaissance variant known as the FR.9 was produced, with 126 being completed for use in the low level tactical reconnaissance role and retaining the four-cannon armament. The airframe was identical to the F.8 except for the extreme nose which housed an F24 camera which could take photographs either straight ahead or obliquely on either side, controlled by the pilot. The FR.9 served with two squadrons in Germany and in the Middle East, where low level often meant operating down to as little as 50 feet at 400 knots! A second reconnaissance version was the unarmed PR.10 intended for high altitude work, for which it reverted to the long-span wing used on the F.3 and the original smaller tail assembly; it had a service ceiling of 47,000 feet – despite the pilot having no navigation aids other than maps, a compass and a wrist watch. In addition to the nose-mounted F24 camera, it had two F52 vertical cameras in the rear fuselage. Together with the F.8 and FR.9, this was the only other version of the Meteor to be fitted with an ejection seat and just 59 were built, serving with three squadrons, one each in Germany, the Middle East and Singapore. In 1961 there was great rivalry at Tengah between 60 Sqn with their NF.14s and 81 Sqn with the PR.10 to see who would be able to claim the title of the last operational Meteor unit, with 81 finally losing out by less than six weeks, making their last two flights on 7 July while the last two NF.14 flights were on 17 August.

The most radical change to the Meteor came with the decision to produce a night fighter version to replace the Mosquito. This entailed a significant fuselage

Fg Off Philip Murton of 92 Squadron in his personal F.3 'Letitia III' during a 1947 detachment to Lübeck. [Philip Murton]

stretch to make room for a navigator sitting in tandem with the pilot in a pressurised cockpit, plus an air interception (AI) radar equipment in the extreme nose. To make room for this, the armament was moved to the outboard wings which saw a return to the earlier long span, albeit considerably strengthened. Two 28-volt engine-driven generators were required to cope with the increased electrical demand not only from the AI radar but also from the GEE navigational aid and an AYF radio altimeter. Armstrong Whitworth built them all and delivered the first of 318 AI Mk.10-equipped NF.11s in October 1950, with peak production reaching no less than 32 aircraft a month. Next to follow in 1953 were 40 examples of the NF.13, a tropicalised NF.11 for service with two squadrons in the Middle East. Modifications including cold-air intakes on the fuselage, new equipment in the form of distance measuring equipment (DME), a radio compass and on some aircraft, an increased flap area to compensate for the additional 450 lbs weight. Then came the NF.12, basically similar to the NF.11 but with a further extension to the nose to house an improved AI Mk.21 radar.

The final variant was the NF.14 which arrived in 1954 and had yet another length extension and, much to the delight of the crews, a one-piece blown cockpit canopy, electrically operated to replace the old manually operated, greenhouse-style one which had been inherited from the T.7. Production of the 12 and 14 totalled 100 of each and both were fitted with the Derwent 9 and across the Meteor range the available engine thrust had increased from a modest 1,700 lbs on the Welland to a far more punchy 3,800 lbs. The night fighters were comparatively short-lived in service, having all gone by 1959 with the single exception of 60 Sqn in Singapore as already mentioned. Aircrew views on its effectiveness vary from "good" to "useless"!

Having been replaced by the Javelin, a modest number of NF.14s, with radar removed, soldiered on in the navigator training role until October 1965, but were outlasted in service by the TT.20. This was a target-towing conversion of the NF.11 which had all armament and radar removed and a wind-driven winch fitted to the upper surface of the starboard inner wing, operated by the rear seat occupant to wind out towed targets from a housing under the rear fuselage. It served with both RAF and Fleet Air Arm units before finally fading away in 1970.

The final Meteor variants to consider are the unmanned target drones flown from Llanbedr in West Wales to serve the missile ranges over Cardigan Bay (with a few others being flown by the Fleet Air Arm from Hal Far in Malta between 1959 and 1961). The first of these was the U.15 – a converted F.4, with the work on this and all other Meteor drones being carried out by Flight Refuelling Ltd at Tarrant Rushton in Dorset. Conversion included the removal of all armament and fitting radio link equipment, an automatic pilot, infra-red homing flares (to attract the missiles!) and wing-tip camera pods which could be jettisoned. The aircraft could still be flown manned and were often done so to act as shepherd aircraft for other drone types such as the Jindivik, before being scheduled to be shot down on a one-way trip over the bay. The first one was flown in 1955 and in all 92 were produced, with some going out to Australia for use on the ranges at Woomera. As with its role as a day fighter, the F.4 was soon showing its performance limitations, so the availability of large numbers of surplus F.8s led that mark to take over on the drone conversion programme and emerge as the U.16 (later renamed D.16), with in excess of 100 being produced. Subtle differences in those shipped out to Woomera resulted in yet another designation change to U.21. The designations U.17, U.18 and U.19 were reserved for drone conversions of the NF.11/TT.20, NF.12 and NF.14 respectively, none of which progressed beyond the design stage.

By the 1980s only two or three D.16s remained in service at Llanbedr and on 11 October 2004 the final sortie was flown by WK800, a very significant aeroplane that as an F.8 had served with the RAAF's 77 Sqn in Korea. Thankfully, common sense prevailed and the aircraft was flown to Boscombe Down for storage before being passed for preservation in the museum there, which has since moved to Old Sarum near Salisbury.

However, that did not mark the end of the Meteor. Amazingly, even in 2016, some 73 years after it first flew, it soldiers on still earning its keep as two aircraft fly for Martin-Baker testing ejection seats for 21st century combat aircraft. The company has flown Meteors from its test airfield at Chalgrove in Oxfordshire since November 1945, an astonishing record, and the two T.7s currently in use have been with them since the 1960s. There remain three other airworthy Meteors as cherished air show performers, a T.7 and NF.11 in the United Kingdom (although up for sale at the time of writing) and an F.8 in Australia with the Temora Aviation Museum in New South Wales – long may their sight and sound continue.

When Meteor production ended in 1954 a total of 3,194 had been delivered to the RAF and Royal Navy, while a further 728 had gone to overseas customers (including 330 assembled by Fokker at Schipol, Netherlands). Destinations included the air forces of Argentina, Australia, Belgium, Brazil, Denmark, Egypt, France, Israel, the Netherlands, New Zealand (a single F.3) and Syria, with many former RAF machines joining them; an impressive total that underlines the importance and appeal of Britain's first jet fighter. Although there is no record of Egyptian and Israeli Meteors meeting each other in anger it is interesting to record that Israeli aircraft had a number of air-to-air successes against Egyptian Vampires.

This book would not have been possible without the tremendous help and encouragement from so many Meteor Boys who have enthusiastically invited me into their homes, suffered lengthy telephone calls, answered interminable questions and opened up their log books and private photograph collections to scrutiny! Gentlemen, I thank and salute you all.

The late Wg Cdr Brian Ashley, Sgt Alec Audley, Flt Lt John Batty, AVM George Black CB OBE AFC, Flt Lt Peter Bogue, Flt Lt Rupert Butler, Sqn Ldr Robin Chandler, Gp Capt Chris Christie, Air Cdre Alan Clements, Sqn Ldr Alan Colman, Darren 'Buster' Crabb, Chf Tech David Curnock, Robert Dalton, Flt Lt Derek 'Moose' Davies, Sqn Ldr Rod Dean, Don Emerick, Fg Off Bill George, Flt Lt Bill Gill, Malcolm Glenister, Cpl Norman Haffenden, Flt Lt Sir Paul Holden BT, Sqn Ldr David Jackson, Flt Lt John James, Sqn Ldr Mike Kemp, Wg Cdr George Lee, Plt Off Derek Lowther, Flt Lt Peter Macintosh, Flt Lt Eric Marsh, Wg Cdr Alan McDonald, Sqn Ldr Bruce McDonald, Flt Lt Les Millgate, Flt Lt Derek Morter, Fg Off Philip Murton, Gp Capt Kel 'Johnny' Palmer, Flt Lt Desmond Penrose BSc, CEng, FRAeS, Brian Phillips, Gp Capt Derek Rake OBE AFC and bar, Flt Lt Mike Read, Sqn Ldr Tony Robinson, Gp Capt Peter Rogers, Rob Rooker, Peter Sawyer, Sqn Ldr Mike Sayer, Sqn Ldr Dave Southwood, Wg Cdr Chris Strong, Al Taylor, Fg Off The Lord Tebbit, Sgt Peter Verney, Sqn Ldr Gordon Webb, Sqn Ldr Colin Wilcock, SAC Alun Williams and

WO Sid Woodacre.

In addition, I must also say a big "thank you" to many others who have helped along the way. Richard Andrews, Peter Arnold, Air Marshal Sir Roger Austin KCB AFC FRAeS, Adrian Balch, Martin Fenner, Michael Fopp, Keith Hawes, Tony Hawes, Neil Meadows Naval 8 / 208 Sqn Association, John Mounce, Jeff Peck, and Stephen Phillips. If I have forgotten anybody please accept my humble apology. Finally, I must also single out Grub Street's John Davies for his continuing faith in my writing over a good few years and my daughters and faithful proof-readers, Elizabeth and Rebecca.

Steve Bond
Milton Keynes
2016

THE TIGERS – 74 SQUADRON

THE BOYS

Sqn Ldr Alan Colman

National Service, joined in 1949. Trained on Meteors at 205 AFS, first tour on 74 Sqn, CFS, 211 FTS instructor, Ferry Training Unit, subsequently 216 and 51 Sqns Comet. Left the air force in 1976 to fly Comets for Dan Air.

Flt Lt Sir Paul Holden

Enlisted in 1942, trained in the US, 287 Sqn Hurricane, Spitfire and Tempest, 74 Sqn Meteor, demobbed 1946, later joined RAFVR and flew Harvard, Spitfire, Vampire, Chipmunk and Tiger Moth.

Flt Lt Derek Morter

Joined in 1948 as a wireless fitter, pilot's course 1949. Trained on Meteors at 205 AFS, first tour on 74 Sqn, instrument rating examiner, 79 and 541 Sqns Meteor, OC Station Flt Oldenburg/Ahlhorn, 229 OCU Chivenor, 14 and 20 Sqns Hunter, HQ MEAF, retired 1968.

Gp Capt Derek Rake

41 Sqn Spitfire 1945, 20 Sqn Spitfire and Tempest 1946, 74 Sqn Meteor 1946, CFS, followed by tours on Hunter, Lightning, OC 192 Sqn (later 51 Sqn) Comet/ Canberra 1958-1960, as OC Wyton flew 58 Sqn Canberras and 543 Sqn Victors, retired 1976.

EARLY DAYS

Following the Meteor's successful introduction to service with 616 Sqn, it is somewhat curious that the unit was disbanded by renumbering as 263 Sqn in August 1945. Nonetheless the Meteor force had started to grow and Colerne near Bath in Wiltshire was chosen to be the RAF's first major Meteor station. By late 1945, it was home to 74 and 504 Sqns (which was quickly renumbered 245 Sqn) and for a brief period, 1335 Conversion Unit which soon moved out to the former USAAF station at Molesworth in Huntingdonshire. All three units were equipped with the F.3.

Of these new units, arguably the most famous was 74 Sqn, which had converted to Meteors just as the European war was ending and it would become the squadron to fly the Meteor in its original day fighter role longer than anyone else, just over 11 years in fact. Their motto is 'I fear no man' but they were – and indeed still are – better known simply as the Tigers from the animal's head on their original badge dating back to World War One.

For pilots posted to fly Meteors in those early years a major challenge was the fact that there was as yet no two-seater in which to give them instruction. Having just completed a tour flying Spitfires and Tempests with 287 Sqn, **Paul Holden** was posted to Colerne where, in December 1945 he had four sessions in a Link Trainer to prepare him for the Meteor – and for 74 Sqn.

Cadet Paul Holden 1 BFTS Terrell Texas 1943. [Paul Holden]

"I started on the Meteor at 1335 Conversion Unit at Molesworth in February 1946. The conversion course was less than a week. It consisted of one hour in an Oxford doing simulated wheeler landings and asymmetric flying, some lectures on jet-engine handling, and then it was four flights in a Meteor. Two were sort of air experience flights, one was a high altitude flight and one low level exercise with a single-engine approach. We didn't do any circuits and bumps or anything. One of my fellow pilots on the conversion course got carried away by the thrill of flying at low level. He consumed far too much fuel and arrived back at the airfield with his cockpit aglow with red (low fuel warning) lights! He made a quick and dirty dart at the first runway he came to and was in such a hurry to get it down that he flew right into the ground without levelling off first, thereby collapsing the nose wheel and skidding down the runway on his nose. Fortunately he was unhurt, but it didn't do the aircraft any good at all. I can't remember what happened to him after that but, after my three exciting Meteor flights at Molesworth, I reported to my new squadron at Colerne as a qualified jet pilot – I don't think! I really learned how to fly it after that.

"We didn't do any gunnery in my time; there was some problem with that. We did a lot of demonstration flights, squadron formations over air shows and that sort of thing and for some reason unknown to me, we specialised in landing, with 46 feet wingspan aeroplanes, in vics of three on a 150 feet wide runway! It was quite a tight exercise, but we took it in our stride. We did a lot of aerobatics, a lot of formation flying and the occasional low level sortie. I remember one flying over North Devon (I was a very keen amateur cine photographer) and I had my clockwork-driven 9.5-mm black and white movie camera taped to the gunsight. I filmed flying at low level along the railway line towards Barnstaple flat out at about 200 feet.

"The Meteor was fantastic. All my flying until then had been on single-engine aeroplanes sitting behind a ruddy great engine when you couldn't

A pair of 74 Squadron F.3s getting airborne from Colerne in 1946 in a screenshot taken from a cine film. [Paul Holden]

see out of the front, until you got your tail up. Suddenly, you get into a Meteor and you drive it along looking out the front and you can see where you're going. You get on the runway, open up the taps, let the brakes go and it pushed you in the back and roared off. First time off, I was at about 2,000 feet doing 250 knots and halfway into the next county before I got my breath back and the wheels up! It was tremendous, a wonderful aeroplane.

"Funnily enough, after hundreds of hours flying single-engine aircraft, I'd never had any engine failure at all, never a cough. The only engine failure I ever had was in a Meteor, which was surprising because basically jet engines are more reliable than piston engines. It was a problem with the barostat; when you're up at high level, it controls the amount of fuel going into the engine so that it uses a lot less fuel at high level than at low level. Apparently the barostat stuck, so that when I came down I got a flame-out in the starboard engine and couldn't light it again. I'd been at about 30,000 feet and was over 8/8ths cloud, so I made a 'PAN' call (declaring a problem) on the distress frequency and asked for a homing to base, which they gave me. The next thing that happened was that all the power failed, because the only generator was on the starboard engine. Unknown to anybody the battery was no good. When the engine was running you didn't need it and when the engine failed, shortly afterwards, so did the battery. All the electrics went out, R/T went off, no contact, no lights, no anything. After the one 'PAN' they tried to give me further calls and there was no reply, so there was a certain amount of panic and concern on the ground obviously. Everybody on both squadrons was alerted to the fact that there was a major problem.

"Fortunately, on the way home following the original homing bearing, there was a hole in the cloud. I managed to get down underneath it and map-read my way back to Colerne. I flew over the runway at about 1,500 feet waggling my wings as a request for an emergency landing. All the stops had been pulled out and fire engines were racing up and down the runway and everybody on both squadrons had turned out to watch. The particular concern was that a week before one of the chaps on the other squadron, doing simulated single-engine landings, had undershot and opened up the engines too quickly. The engine that was live opened up to full power, the engine that was idling grumbled and sort of stalled and didn't build up, so he turned over and went in on his back from low level on final approach. He was quite seriously injured, so there was a certain amount of concern about me doing a single-engine landing for real. I came in with about 20 knots to spare and 100 feet extra in height and landed a bit fast – about half-way down the runway and used a lot of brakes to stop by the other end. Lots of cheering, but when I got to the end of the runway, I found it was absolutely impossible to taxi a Meteor on one engine, because there's no steering on the nose wheel and the engines are immediately over the brakes; so you could either go round in circles or stop! I therefore had to sort of park it against the hedge and wait to be rescued; so there was a certain amount of hilarity all round.

"Two incidents stand out in my memory from this period; the first through my own clottishness. It arose after a discussion in the crew room whether it was theoretically possible to fly a perfectly straight loop on the basic turn and bank indicator alone. This was before the days of fully aerobatic artificial horizons (which are the gyroscopically controlled instruments used in blind flying to show the pilot his attitude in relation to the real horizon, when it can't be seen because of cloud or darkness). In our time, you had to 'cage' the artificial horizon before performing aerobatics to prevent it toppling and damaging the sensitive bearings and gimbals on which it is mounted. So my next flight, when I had the opportunity, found me with my head in 'the office' concentrating on trying to keep the turn needle centred during a series of attempted perfectly straight loops. I should explain, in self-defence, that such manoeuvres in a jet at high altitude tend to mean that you wander all over about three counties; this is how I almost became an unexplained fatal accident statistic.

"Without noticing it, I suddenly found myself entering the top of a cumulonimbus (thunderstorm and very rough) cloud, upside down, and two thirds of the way round a loop. Try as I might, by use of this basic turn and bank indicator only, I could not get the aircraft back under control and into straight and level flight again. Instead, I fought my way up and down this wretched thundercloud, watching the altimeter needles spinning first clockwise and then anticlockwise and the airspeed winding alarmingly up and down the clock. In the end I just throttled back, more or less let go and waited, hoping that the aircraft would just right itself. Instead, it came screaming out of the base of the cloud at about 4,000 feet, pointing almost vertically towards the ground. On instinct, I pulled the stick back into my stomach about as hard as I dared and instantly blacked out under the high 'g' loading. When I released the stick enough to be able to see again, I was climbing steeply through about 1,500 feet, still fully throttled back and doing about 20 knots more than the maximum permitted airspeed for the aircraft. So, highly mortified by the experience, I nursed it gently back to base and gave my colleague in the tower a practice QGH whilst I got my breath back before landing. As there was no doubt that I had seriously over-stressed the aircraft, I reported it to the Flt Sgt in charge of maintenance on the squadron – but the aircraft looked all right – that afternoon. It was a different and very sorry sight the next morning, however. It seems that I had bent the main spars beyond their elastic limit and overnight, they gradually resumed their proper shape. As a result, the whole skin on the underside of the wings and fuselage was rippled (where it had been stretched and was now too big for its proper size) and rivets were popped out all over the place. It had to be flown carefully back to Glosters for a total rebuild."

In the autumn of 1946, both of the former Colerne Meteor squadrons were moved to Horsham St.Faith just outside Norwich, which is where **Derek Rake** joined the Tigers.

"When I came back from the Far East after the end of the war, they sent me to Horsham St.Faith. I was only there for a few months, joining 74 Sqn in September '46, we had Meteor F.3s and I flew a total of about 23 hours on them. There were three other squadrons on the base, 245 and 263 with Meteors and 695 with target-towing Martinets. Our aeroplanes seemed to be unserviceable a lot of the time, but I'm not sure why. We didn't have any dual jets of course, we were just given the Pilot's Notes, then we did a blindfold cockpit check and then they sent us airborne. We flew up to Acklington to do air-to-air firing and air-to-ground firing; it was the first time I'd flown a jet. This was very interesting because I'd been flying Spitfire 14s, Tempest 2s and 5s out in the Far East and the Meteor F.3s were about 100 miles an hour faster when we were attacking the target drogue. So we were always worried that we were going to shoot down the aeroplane that was towing it – we'd frequently shoot the drogue off! The shells would hit the wire that held the drogue; it was quite fun. My average score for air-to-air firing was 7.2% and that was considered above average, while my air-to-ground average was 14.5% and that was considered below average.

"We did a lot of formation flying, single-engine flying and stuff like that – we didn't have any problem with the aeroplane. We did flypasts occasionally, but I'm not sure where. It was exciting at the time because it was the first jet that we flew. It was lovely, a very easy aeroplane to fly after the Spitfire 14, which had so much torque. That Spitfire mark had virtually the same airframe as the Spit 5s but you had the Griffon engine with just about twice as much power in the airframe as you had with the earlier Spits. The torque on take-off or any time you opened the throttle was terrific, and it had to be counteracted obviously. So, we found the Meteors very easy to fly, as they just went. Before my first trip, they told me what to do and the squadron commander Jim Cooksey* told me what it was like, but it did surprise me when I took off. It accelerated so fast compared with a piston-engined fighter that you had to tuck the undercarriage up before you exceeded the undercarriage speed, and then you were really going very fast. You cut the power back and all the noise disappeared; in fact I thought I'd had a double engine failure and by this time I was over the centre of Norwich. It was just after the war of course so we used to fight the other squadrons and do air-to-air combat against them with cine guns. I enjoyed the air-to-air and air-to-ground firing with the Meteors, and the formation flying, but it was all a bit of a bore after the war was over."

"I was posted away to the central instructor's school at Little Rissington in December '46. I was quite pleased to go on to Central Flying School (CFS) where one learned to be an instructor all over again, then taught the up and coming generation as it were. Mind you, I was only about 25 in 1947 when I started at CFS, but we thought of the youngsters coming through as the younger generation. Quite a few of us went from the Horsham St.Faith wing to CFS – about half a dozen I think."

* Sqn Ldr Jim Cooksey joined Glosters as chief production test pilot in 1947 and on 9 April 1954 he delivered the last production aircraft to the RAF – F.8 WL191.

F.8 THE ULTIMATE METEOR FIGHTER

The F.3s did not last very long in the front line, being replaced by the improved F.4 during 1947/48, but that variant was also destined to have a short operational life. The F.8 was the ultimate day fighter version of the Meteor and began arriving on the squadrons in 1950, heralding a rapid build-up, culminating in it being the equipment of no fewer than 20 home-based regular squadrons, plus another 11 in the RAuxAF (see Chapter 3).

Having also pioneered the F.4 in service, once again 74 Sqn (still at Horsham St.Faith) was one of the early recipients of the F.8 getting theirs from October 1950. When **Alan Colman** joined the squadron they had had a couple of years to settle in.

"I was called up for National Service in June 1949 and first encountered the Meteor at 205 AFS Middleton St.George, which had the F.4 and T.7; that was January to May 1951. I then went to 226 Operational Conversion Unit (OCU) at Stradishall in Fighter Command, they too were still equipped with the F.4 – I didn't encounter the F.8 until over a year later when I got to 74 Sqn. I didn't go directly to a squadron at the end of my training because, due to the vagaries of National Service, the Ministry of Defence (MoD) contacted me at Stradishall and said 'Your National

Service term is complete, you must leave the Service immediately.' I was a Sgt Pilot then and I said 'Hang on, I've just been to the 12 Group HQ at RAF Newton and been interviewed by the air officer commanding (AOC) with a view to the granting of a short-service commission. I'm waiting for the results.' The reply was 'Sorry, we have no record of that, you will be demobilised at once.' Subsequently, about nine months later when I was by then a civilian, MoD wrote to me and said: 'If you would be prepared to re-join, you've been selected for a course at the Officer Cadet Training Unit (OCTU) at Spitalgate. If you pass the course, you will be granted a four-year short-service commission. If you fail, you may leave the Service again if you wish.' I passed the course.

"During the OCTU course, my father had died and my mother, living near Norwich, then suffered a nervous breakdown. So, at the end of the OCTU course in July '52, I was posted 'compassionately' straight to 74 Sqn at Horsham St. Faith. I was a brand new Plt Off and I arrived there not having flown any sort of a Meteor for over a year, let alone an F.8. Because of that, the exchange-tour USAF major who was the squadron CO was not pleased to see me! My life was saved because one of the flight commanders, Joe Maddison, had been a Meteor instructor at Middleton St. George, so we knew one another quite well. He told the 'boss': 'No problem, I'll sort him out' and he then gave me a quick 'refresher course' using the Station Flight Meteor T.7, renewed my instrument rating and then sent me off in a Mk 8 to familiarise myself with it. So I remained on the squadron – basically with his blessing. Compared with the F.4 and T.7, the F.8 was a much nicer aeroplane. I wouldn't say it was noticeably faster or more manoeuvrable, but some of the adverse trim changes and handling oddities at high Mach numbers affecting the F.4 (and the T.7 to a lesser extent) were not so pronounced. It also had the luxury of decent pressurisation, much more modern instrumentation and a bang seat. You felt that you'd moved up a cog by flying the F.8; I always said I could have taught my grandmother to fly it! Also, in place of the Derwent 5, it had the Derwent 8, which was a more responsive engine and less prone to compressor stall at height.

"While in training at Middleton St. George and Stradishall, we didn't ever practise night flying. However, on 74 Sqn there was a requirement for all of us to be capable of operating the aeroplane in the dark. On the face of it, the answer would have been for each pilot to have been checked out at night in the Station Flight T.7. However, the way we acquired the necessary skill was to be sent off at twilight to do duskers – a short 'sector recce' followed by continuous circuits and roller landings that started in failing daylight and continued until it was completely dark. This scheme worked perfectly – except that, occasionally, pilots returning to Horsham St. Faith in near darkness would be confused by the landing and approach

74 Squadron's T.7 WL380 with deep breather intakes at Horsham St. Faith. [Derek Morter]

lights at the adjacent night fighter base at Coltishall. I was lucky not to get caught, but there was an informal squadron trophy – a mounted hand on a plinth giving a single finger gesture – which was labelled 'The Night Landing at Coltishall Trophy'.

"There was a flamboyant young flying Officer on the squadron who had a show-stopping aerobatic speciality that, soon after my arrival on the station, I saw him perform in an F.8 at a Battle of Britain display at Horsham St. Faith in 1952. The speciality was a 'square loop' - a brutal manoeuvre that entailed arriving in front of the crowd at fairly high speed, hauling the aircraft into a vertical climb with full power applied, snapping into an inverted horizontal section, then falling into a brief vertical dive with airbrakes out and throttles closed – which ended in a sudden recovery to level flight at low altitude. The abrupt and spectacular changes in attitude at the beginning and end of the manoeuvre took the airframe into the high speed stall and this, coupled with the simultaneous application of full power, produced a truly thunderous noise. When he landed after performing this stunt, the OC Engineering Wing was called to inspect the aircraft. There were folds in the skin on the top of both centre-sections and matching creases in the fuselage skin over the wing. We were later told that the aircraft had been declared Cat 5 (scrap) and it was dismantled and taken away on a 'Queen Mary' having been grossly over-stressed.

74 Squadron Horsham St. Faith's F.8 aerobatic team circa 1956. Led by WL104 X. [Alan Colman]

"Due to the restrictions applied following a collision with a seawall that had killed one of the students on my Stradishall OCU course, we had passed out without having undertaken any air-to-air or air-to-ground firing practice. Consequently, my total inexperience in air gunnery and consequent poor initial results provided the 74 Sqn American CO with a rich excuse for complaint and ridicule. Later on, perhaps stung by his carping criticism, I became one of the highest gunnery scorers on the squadron and very proficient at formation flying and mock dogfighting.

"Air firing proficiency was an obsession on the squadron at that time and 74 had a very high reputation in Fighter Command as the 1952 winner of the annual trophy awarded to the highest-scoring squadron, then called the 'Dacre' trophy. Not surprisingly in the circumstances, the real highlight of the squadron year was the annual detachment to the Armament Practice Camp (APC) at Acklington in Northumberland. The entire squadron went on these detachments, aircraft, ground support, fuel bowsers – everything. In 1953 car ownership was still very rare amongst the squadron aircrew so, as by then I was the owner of a three-wheeled and motorcycle-engined Bond Minicar, I was detailed as OC the squadron motor transport (MT) convoy, which I led in this small and fundamentally unreliable contraption all the 300 miles from Norfolk to Northumberland! At these APCs, we had a chance to fire on our usual 'flag' targets and on glider targets towed by Hawker Tempests. The big difference was that the targets were towed at 20,000 feet instead of the 7,000 feet or so which was the upper limit on our local firing range off the Norfolk coast near Yarmouth. The extra altitude made a huge difference to the handling of the Meteor during the standard, very close-in and abbreviated, 'high quarter' type of attack we used. Experience had demonstrated that the highest scores were obtained by using very short bursts of gunfire (about one second) thus requiring a large number of firing passes to expend all of your ammunition. On one occasion, 100 feet from the target, my aircraft suddenly flick-rolled out of control just as I had started to fire. Helpless, I watched in terror as I hurtled inverted over the top of the 'flag', missing it by about six feet! Another time, I carefully emptied every round of 20 mm ammunition I carried into a glider target, only to see it fly on serenely and, apparently, undamaged. Determined to see if I had hit it at all I approached the glider intending to formate on it to have a look. Just as I was easing into position the glider fell apart before my eyes, leaving nothing behind the Tempest but the tow-rope. However, my biggest air-firing drama had nothing to do with gunnery skill or handling qualities. Having completed my initial turn in during a 'quarter attack' on another glider target, I was tracking the glider through my gunsight when, without any warning from the tug pilot (or the ground controlled interception [GCI] radar that was supposed to be watching us), a giant American ten-engined B-36 bomber suddenly filled my windscreen, passing straight through my line of fire. Half a second later and I would have either collided with the bomber or shot it down!

"In those days jets were still quite a novelty and so soon after the war, there was still a powerful 'gung-ho' attitude on fighter squadrons. 'Flying the aircraft to its limits' was a much more powerful motivation than flight safety, which was then a new and suspiciously un-military concept. The maintenance and display of the aggressive operating reputation of the squadron was paramount. The rules controlling our flying were, compared with those existing today, very flexible and 'cowboy' operation was tacitly encouraged if it produced the desired results. The citizens of Hellesdon, who lived under the flightpath of the then main Horsham St. Faith runway, became very hostile at what they saw as the irresponsible behaviour of the pilots of the Horsham Wing. Letters appeared in the press and we were confidentially advised not to be seen in the Hellesdon area in uniform. In fact, the cause of the problem was nothing to do with the pilot's attitude, but primarily the greatly increased noise footprint and speed of jet aircraft when compared to that of their piston-engined forerunners. This characteristic was exacerbated by the requirement to repeatedly practise squadron and wing take-offs, sometimes involving around 30 aircraft in pairs or fours rolling at five or ten-second intervals.

In formation take-offs, to avoid the slipstream of the aircraft immediately ahead, it was necessary for alternate pairs (or fours) to 'stay low' initially, thus increasing the noise and disturbance below. Attempts to offset this adverse local reaction were made and Fg Off Derek Morter and I, both local boys, were featured in the East Anglian press in an article entitled 'Men With Thunder Under Their Gloves'.

"Such was the aggressive attitude fostered on a fighter squadron that one was always expected to mock-attack fighter aircraft from another unit if they appeared within range during a sortie. Sometimes these dogfights were pre-arranged – such as the interception of the Day Fighter Leaders' School (DFLS) Meteors returning from training sweeps across the North Sea. On one such occasion I was in a Meteor F.8 four-ship formation led by one of the flight commanders who was determined to ensure that we would have a height and 'out of the sun' advantage on the DFLS formation. To achieve this, we took off before the air defence radar had even sighted the incoming Meteor formation. We struggled up to 48,000 feet and just hanging there, were vectored into a position where we could see the DFLS Meteors several thousand feet below, but they didn't spot us. Unfortunately, as we began a formation quarter attack, every one of us encountered compressibility, lost control completely, and hurtled straight through the DFLS formation that had finally seen us coming and started to 'break'. All four 74 Sqn aircraft returned to Horsham individually

F.8 WF695 RDY flown by Wg Cdr Robert Duncan Yule OC Flying HSF with 74 Squadron aircraft during a Coronation flypast rehearsal, 21 May 1953. [Derek Morter]

after regaining control at lower level. This was a classic example of the uselessness of the Meteor as a high altitude fighter aircraft. On the other hand, at around 20,000 feet, the Meteor was in its element. We had great hunting when the USAF brought their first F-86 Sabres over to the UK. If we saw them while in the air, it was virtually compulsory to try and 'mix it' with them. At 30,000 feet or above they had us cold; all they needed to do was roll over and dive away. If we attempted to follow the Meteor would hit its limiting Mach number (around M.82) and loss of control was almost immediate. The Sabres would then use their speed advantage to zoom way above us and come down in a quarter attack. Around 20,000 feet or below it was a different story. The Sabre was still faster, but if caught cruising slowly, or tempted into a turning match, its acceleration / deceleration and rate of climb couldn't match the Meteor, which could also out-turn them, especially if one of the Sabre's automatic leading-edge slats deployed and flicked the Sabre out of the turn. Huge fun!

"Apart from the annual visit to Acklington, there were other regular events which dominated squadron life. One of these was the rotating requirement to mount the immediate readiness flight; known in those days as 'Operation Fabulous'. It required a flight of four fully-armed aircraft with pilots to be on immediate standby from one hour before sunrise to

Miss Trinidad's visit to 74 Squadron at Horsham St. Faith, winter 1952. [Alan Colman]

one hour after sunset. The first and last hour required the pilots to be in their cockpits with their headsets plugged in and connected to the sector controller via 'telescramble'. Fabulous came round several times a year and tied up aircraft and crews for a week at a time. If there was no 'trade' (i.e.: no unidentified aircraft over the North Sea to be investigated), it was normal for the Fabulous aircraft to be periodically allowed 'off the hook' to fly for training. This flying was normally utilised for practice interceptions (PIs), but on special occasions, it was used for other purposes – such as 'bombing' the Coltishall station commander's married quarter with toilet rolls at dawn on Christmas Day! (The toilet rolls were transported by trapping them in the flaps and released by momentarily selecting 'flaps down').

"The squadron was tasked with performing a formation flight over some function in Manchester on 1 April 1953. In preparation for that event, the squadron de-camped to Hooton Park on the southern side of the Mersey on 27 March and on the same day, carried out a dummy run with (I believe) just four aeroplanes. I was 'in the box' (No.4) in that formation and as we crossed the Mersey at quite low level, a seagull hit my aircraft with one hell of a bang, covering the windscreen and most of the canopy with blood and feathers and completely obscuring all forward vision. I had to pull out of the formation and return to Hooton for a landing with the canopy open and me, with goggles on, trying to see where I was going by sticking my head out to the side. Obviously I managed because I am still here to talk about it and I flew in the subsequent flypast on the

Alan Colman's personal mount, F.8 VZ512 D-Dog, 74 Squadron Horsham St. Faith, winter 1952.
[Alan Colman]

1st, so the actual damage was minor. Inevitably, the airframe concerned was my own VZ512. Probably as a result of my initial unpopularity with the CO, this Meteor F.8 allocated as my 'personal' mount was a real old 'dog'. In fact it carried the identification letter D and was therefore always referred to as 'D-Dog'.

"Another regular annual event was the station inspection by the AOC 12 Group. At this time, the AOC was the famous and eccentric character, AVM 'Batchy' Atcherley. One of these inspections was in mid-winter and we had held the usual practice parades with our greatcoats on. However, on the day, we were told that officers were to parade in their No.1 uniforms but with no coats on – the reason given was that the AOC did not have one! It was a clear and frosty morning and we stood on parade shivering, waiting for the AOC to arrive by air. After about 15 minutes, a Meteor arrived in the Horsham circuit at high speed, made a spectacular break on to the downwind leg and lowered the undercarriage. At which point, a USAF F-84 Thunderjet appeared and 'bounced' the Meteor as it turned finals. The Meteor immediately broke off its approach, raised its undercarriage and proceeded to 'mix it' with the Thunderjet. Round and round the two aircraft twisted above our freezing heads until, at last, the American gave up and set off for his own base. The Meteor landed, out climbed a red-faced and perspiring AOC and the inspection proceeded as if nothing had happened.

"The annual summer exercise saw both the Horsham squadrons, 245 and 74, dispersed out to the extremities of the airfield with the ground staff and aircrew living in tents. It was always good fun and an excuse to demonstrate just how fast the squadron could scramble and how tenacious the pilots were in making a successful interception. For example, it provided an excuse for the station commander to demonstrate his prowess by taking off from the perimeter track and for me to jump into a Meteor that was in the middle of being serviced, only to be stopped by an airman shoving his head into the cockpit and shouting 'You've got no radio sir, did you know?' Targets varied from very high flying Canberras and B-47 Stratojets, through B-29s at medium level and down to very low flying Thunderjets and Venoms. Another favourite was the convoy patrol, which usually involved a vicious tangle with Fleet Air Arm Sea Furies low over the sea. On one of these 'convoy' sorties, I was leading a formation scrambled to attack a convoy passing up the Norfolk coast off Cromer. As usual, we found the convoy defended by Fleet Air Arm Sea Furies and immediately engaged them, becoming involved in very low-level dogfights over the sea and in amongst the ships. During one of these dogfights, my No.2 saved my life by yelling 'Red leader, pull up, too low'. He later explained that he could clearly see my jet-wake on the surface of the sea as I attempted to get good camera-gun footage of the Sea Fury I was following. The Meteor was in its element at such low levels, but far from its best at high altitude, where most of the attempts to intercept really high flying raiders such as the Canberra or B-47 were doomed to failure because, although you could often see your target, you just did not have a sufficient performance margin to both climb up to its level and catch it before getting low on fuel *and* having to return to base.

"One of the senior pilots on the squadron was Flt Lt Bertie Beard. As a new pilot, I vividly remember flying as his No.2 as he led the squadron on my first summer exercise scramble, which also involved the whole Horsham Wing. The target turned out to be a stream of B-29s coming in over Yarmouth at 15,000 feet. By the time we saw them, we were already at 20,000 feet and Bertie calmly announced that we would attack them vertically from above. I had never seen or heard of this type of attack before and I didn't know quite what to expect. He rolled his Meteor upside down and fell away below. In order to keep him in sight I was forced to do the same thing and soon found myself diving absolutely vertically, struggling to keep him in sight, whilst also observing the rapidly-approaching top plan view of a B-29. It appeared that Bertie was determined to fly straight through his chosen target and I hung on to him grimly, fully throttled back and with airbrakes out, as we flashed by, feet behind the tail of his chosen target and then pulled hard out of the dive and zoom-climbed back to height to immediately do the same thing again, working our way along

74 Squadron F.8s on 'tactical dispersal' to the far side of Horsham St. Faith during Exercise Momentum, August 1953. [Alan Colman]

the bomber stream. This was again the Meteor in its element, operating against a target that was flying at a speed and height which gave this jet an enormous performance advantage. It was one of the most invigorating and thrilling sorties of my two years on 74 Sqn. Shortly afterwards, Bertie Beard was made an acting Sqn Ldr and left to become CO of 19 Sqn at Church Fenton.

"My Meteor VZ512 'D-Dog' was an early production model which lacked the improvements coming through on the newer aircraft, such as the larger engine intakes (always called 'deep breathers'), an all-clear canopy and spring-tab ailerons. In fact, the geared-tab ailerons on this aircraft were desperately heavy and much physical effort was required to manoeuvre it. Above 250 knots it became progressively right wing heavy such that both hands and a knee were required to hold the wing up at 350 knots – you can imagine the effort that was required to control that frightful aeroplane when formation flying. It was this aircraft that gave me one of my biggest frights in a lifetime of flying, when the canopy disintegrated with a huge bang at 27,000 feet in the middle of a cross-over turn in battle formation. I was blinded by cockpit dust disturbed by this explosive decompression and had to scratch the ice off the airspeed indicator, compass and altimeter in order to find my way back to base – luckily the weather was good. Apart from these inconveniences, wearing only a flying suit over my underwear, I was frozen with cold and soon realised that a bigger worry was that the ejection seat firing blind was flapping wildly in the airflow, partially deployed out of its housing on top of the seat. If it really caught the slipstream the seat would fire and the Meteor and I would part company! Needless to say, I flew back to Horsham very slowly and it was a blue-with-cold, but much relieved pilot who brought his aircraft to a stop out on the runway, while an airman climbed up and inserted the ejection seat safety pin. Eventually 'D-Dog' was subjected to a routine major inspection, during which it was found that the main spar was cracked. That almost certainly explained its weird handling characteristics and it never returned to the squadron.

"Looking back, I count myself lucky to be alive considering the structural condition of the aircraft on which I was destined to do much of my early squadron flying. However, in 1953, I was briefed to deliver a Meteor F.8 from West Raynham to Odiham where it (and I) was to go on static display for the Queen's Review of the Royal Air Force. Imagine my joy when, inspecting the Form 700 before signing for this gleaming freshly-painted fighter aircraft, I observed the bold annotation 'Straight and Level and Gentle Manoeuvres Only – Maximum Indicated Air Speed (IAS) 250 knots'. At that time, West Raynham was home to the Central Fighter Establishment (CFE). The Meteor was (as we used to say) 'built out of railway lines' so CFE must have done something pretty dire to that one.

Interesting, because I didn't have to do anything with that aeroplane after I delivered it (apart from stand in front of it in my No. 1s on THE DAY), so where it went after Odiham, I have no idea. At Acklington, it would have been used as a target tug, so wouldn't have suffered the dire 'to the limits' treatment we used to give those aeroplanes.

"At the time that I was coming up to the end of my two-year squadron tour, RAF fighter squadrons were being re-equipped with the Hunter and the Swift. No.74 Sqn was earmarked to be the second squadron to receive the Swift. As a result, I was sent on an Avon 100 course at Rolls-Royce Derby and told to expect at least a six-month tour extension, as only the most experienced squadron pilots would convert onto the Swift. No.56 at Wattisham was the first squadron to get them, but they soon discovered that the high altitude handling characteristics were so dire that the upgrading of further squadrons to the Swift was immediately cancelled. As a result and as I was already 'tour-ex', I was asked where I'd like to go – and given very little choice – either a ground tour, or CFS, so off I went to CFS. At the end of the CFS course in January 1955, because I'd already flown a full tour on the Meteor, I was posted to 211 FTS Worksop as a Meteor QFI.

"In the mid 50s, it was standard practice for Meteor QFIs who had originally come from Meteor fighter squadrons, to return to their squadrons once a year on 'reinforcement'. This enabled us to keep fully up to date with things like air-to-air firing and battle formation that did not feature in the normal Jet FTS schedule. Thus, I found myself detached back to my old squadron – 74 – in the spring of 1956. The ethos on 74 had changed little since I left and there was still a priority given to aggressive and 'to the limits' operation. So, on around 5 May, I found myself briefed to undertake a 'high altitude dogfight' sortie as No.2 to one of the established squadron pilots. My aircraft was Meteor F.8 WL163. We climbed up over Norfolk in battle formation to around 35,000 feet and the leader then announced that I was to drop back into line astern and that he would start a tail chase. I loved this and hung on grimly in the thin air as the manoeuvres became progressively more extreme. Eventually the leader pulled up vertically and I saw the altitude pass through 40,000 feet as I followed him until, running out of airspeed, he executed a sort of stall turn, narrowly missing my helpless aircraft as he fell past me. To ensure I didn't hit him, I had pushed forward on my controls so that I could keep him in view, but by this time, I had no airspeed whatsoever and the push forward developed into a violent hammer-stall, followed by the most vicious spin I had ever encountered. The rate of rotation was unbelievable and to my horror, the normal and instinctive spin recovery action – close the throttles plus opposite rudder and stick forward – only appeared to make the rotation even faster. After a few seconds I decided that I would centre the controls and try normal recovery once more before I ejected. Bingo! As soon as I put the controls back into the middle the rotation stopped abruptly and left me in a slightly inverted dive with a rapidly increasing airspeed and Mach number. With airbrakes out, I recovered to level flight at 15,000 feet. There was no sign of the formation leader, so I returned to base. End of story – but I thought hard about that experience. I concluded that I must have been (for the first time in my flying life) in an inverted spin. That was something that was not taught in training in those days. On reflection, I realised that had it not been a cloudless day, I could well have found myself spinning or diving out of control in cloud and I would probably have died. Now, I wonder if I had accidentally discovered a high altitude characteristic of the Meteor that might explain why so many of them ended up in smoking holes?

"The existence of the Phantom Dive characteristic was hotly disputed by many pilots with considerable experience on the aeroplane – as was the final conclusion that it was a feature unique to the extended-fuselage versions, like the T.7. I did have a fright though when, following a formation break in an F.8, it suddenly fell out of the sky sideways on the downwind leg and I had to level the wings and apply power in a hurry to avoid the topography! When you dropped the gear on a Meteor, the left leg always came down first, causing a sudden yaw. In a tight break onto the downwind leg the airbrakes would be already out, the throttles closed, the speed around 140 knots and there would be nearly 90 degrees of bank applied as you banged the gear down. Asking for trouble maybe, but that sudden sideslip only caught me out once."

One of Alan's fellow pilots on 74 Sqn at this time was **Derek Morter**, who had a remarkably lucky escape while exercising with the army in Norfolk.

"In August 1953, a Welsh territorial infantry brigade was on exercise in the Thetford training area. Early one morning, I was detailed to lead four 74 Sqn Meteors to strike the troops and equipment there, with simulated strafing, rocket and bombing attacks. After several attacks, I saw a group of men sheltering underneath a tree, who were making rude or brave gestures towards us, so I picked them as my next target determined to teach them a lesson. There was a reasonably long flat stretch to the tree, so I was able to run in at quite a low level at above 450 knots. Unfortunately, I left my pull up a little too late and hard and mushed noisily through the top half of the tree! I saw that the leading edges of the wings were badly damaged and assumed that I had probably damaged the ventral tank beneath the belly and lost its contents, but the aircraft was handling fine, the pitot head was still there and both engines were running perfectly. The ground liaison officer (GLO) assured me nobody was hurt.

"I returned to and orbited base, did a slow speed check, checked that the services (i.e. undercarriage and flaps) worked properly and without causing handling problems. Watching the number of cars rushing towards air traffic control, I became more worried about my suddenly very dubious RAF career. Down to landing weight, I crossed the threshold 15 knots faster than normal because of the damaged leading edges but landed, pulled up and taxied in as normal.

"Damage was severe to the leading edges, ventral tank and elsewhere, much more so than I imagined and was assessed as Cat 4 (repairable at depot). The engines, having ingested so many leaves were completely green, as if much paint had been thrown in. An inquiry was convened. Meanwhile, the Welsh territorials invited me and the other three pilots to attend a dinner with the intention of 'court martialling' me. The prosecution produced, as evidence, a few very much alive officers, a lot of tree branches and soiled underpants. The punishment was liquid, lots of liquid! From the RAF, I earned an AOC's reproof and a lesson never to be forgotten; also my undying gratitude to the strength of the Meteor and Rolls-Royce's engines."

In March 1957, time was called on 74 Sqn's halcyon days with the Meteor F.8 and it re-equipped with the Hunter F.4 followed soon afterwards by the F.6 and a move to nearby Coltishall. In 1960, it became the first squadron to fly the Lightning and later went on to the Phantom before leaving the fighter world in October 1992.

DAY FIGHTER ZENITH

THE BOYS

AVM George Black
Joined as National Serviceman. Trained in 1952 on Meteors at 203 AFS and 226 OCU, first tour on 263 Sqn later converted to Hunter, 802 Sqn Royal Navy flying Sea Hawks during Suez campaign, CFS, 74 Sqn Lightning, FCCS Meteor, OC 111 Sqn Lightning, CFI 226 OCU, OC 5 Sqn Lightning. Retired 1987.

Flt Lt Les Millgate
Joined in 1950. Flying training in Rhodesia. Trained on Meteors at 207 AFS and 226 OCU, first tour on 64 Sqn F.8 Duxford, then converted to NF.12 and NF.14 on the same unit. Retired 1958 and flew for BOAC.

Gp Capt Peter Rogers
Joined as National Serviceman in 1951. Trained on Meteors at 205 AFS and 226 OCU, first tour on 64 Sqn in both day fighter and night fighter phases, launch control officer on Thor missiles, 14 Sqn Canberra, 208 Sqn Buccaneer. Retired 1986.

Wg Cdr Chris Strong
Joined in 1951. Flying training in Rhodesia. Trained on Meteors at 206 AFS and 226 OCU, first tour on 72 Sqn F.8, moved to 19 Sqn, later flew Venom with 11 Sqn, Hunter with 3, 26, 111, 92 Sqns, 229 OCU, 20 Sqn Hunter, Singapore AF Hunter, MoD Jaguar team, OC Flying Lossiemouth RAFG, command flight safety officer, Biggin Hill Aircrew Selection. Retired 1987.

THE RAF FIGHTER FORCE IN THE 1950s
The advent of the Meteor F.8 coincided with the build-up in RAF pilot training as a result of the onset of what became known in 1947-48 as the Cold War and just two years later on 25 June 1950, the Korean War began when North Korea invaded the South. Two months later on 2 August 1950, the F.8 entered service with the delivery of VZ440 to 43 Sqn at Tangmere, moving shortly thereafter to Leuchars.

Before the year was out, several more squadrons had started re-equipping and by the end of 1951 the force build-up was more or less complete. Initially, the fighter stations which included regular F.8 squadrons were Biggin Hill, Church Fenton, Duxford, Horsham St.Faith, Leuchars, Linton-on-Ouse, Odiham, Tangmere, Waterbeach and Wattisham, later joined by North Weald and Stradishall. At various times (including after the regulars had re-equipped with Hunters) RAuxAF units added Finningley, Hooton Park, West Malling and Worksop to the list – it was quite

222 Squadron F.8 line-up at Leuchars. [Jack Frost via Peter Arnold]

F.8s VZ495 ZD-D and VZ515 222 Squadron Leuchars. [Jack Frost via Peter Arnold]

some force, reaching its peak strength in 1953/54. To this can also be added the Meteor night fighter force (see Chapter Four).

By this time, the pilot training system was in full swing (see Chapter Seven). Newly qualified pilots coming out of the AFSs and any others destined for a Meteor squadron were all sent first to 226 OCU at Stradishall in Suffolk, which had re-formed on 1 September 1949 to provide operational training. George Black, Les Millgate and Chris Strong followed this route to their operational units at Wattisham, Duxford and Church Fenton.

CHURCH FENTON – 19 and 72 SQNS

Meteor F.8s arrived at Church Fenton in April 1951 to equip 19 Sqn, followed two months later by 609 (West Riding) Sqn – whose very fighter-like motto was 'Tally Ho'. Then in May 1953, they were joined by 72 Sqn when it moved up from North Weald and **Chris Strong** eventually found himself serving on two of these units, starting with 72 Sqn. However before that he had to cope with a couple of startling experiences while he was learning to fly and fight in the Meteor.

"I joined up on 15 October 1951 and went to the Aircrew Transit Unit at Driffield shortly afterwards. An interesting way to get used to RAF life was that we all went on parade on the Monday morning and a number of us were selected to do a funeral drill for someone who'd crashed the previous Thursday. We had the funeral on the next Thursday and by then, somebody else had killed themselves in a Meteor, so there was a funeral the following Monday, by which time there was another fatality and we had another funeral drill the following Thursday. So in the first fortnight of my air force career I did three funerals. It was quite an effective selection process because there were those that then suddenly decided they didn't want to fly and went off to do National Service instead. Quite recently I found an old flight comment that summarised the accidents in 1952, stating total losses then of 515 aircraft, and 308 aircrew. It noted that Winston Churchill was concerned about these losses and asked the service minister about them. The service minister said that the figures were not abnormal and that there was no cause for alarm! Presumably true in ministerial circles.

"I then went to Initial Training at Cosford and was then posted to Heany in Rhodesia flying Chipmunks and Harvards. I passed out at the end of '53 and went to 3 FTS at Feltwell for a month's acclimatisation training on Harvards because we'd had so little cloud in Rhodesia. Then on to 206 AFS at Oakington from May to September on Meteor F.4s and T.7s.

"I really enjoyed the Meteor and it never let me down. The 10 to 15-second engine spool-up time had, I gather, led to problems for some pilots (converting to jets) who were more used to the instant response of a piston engine. Asymmetric practice in those days consisted in shutting an engine down rather than throttling it back which led to a number of accidents at low speed in the circuit. We mostly reduced the problem by entering the circuit at around 350 knots with a shut-down engine, throttling back the live engine as we turned downwind and landing, all with the live engine throttled back. Thus no asymmetric problem. Still, it was hard work doing a straight-in approach on one with one's leg at full stretch to counteract the live engine – something that some IF examiners seemed to want. Such practices were stopped much later on the Canberra for example when it was found that there more accidents during such practices then there were engine failures.

"Next I went to 226 OCU at Stradishall in October 1953 where, following a dual check, I was briefed to fly a sector recce. It was pouring with rain by then and there was a very low cloud base. I had been allocated OC Flying's Meteor F.8 (WK713), which had a bright red fin and looked very smart. As it was raining, I slid the canopy closed manually after start-up. I then had a problem as I had not locked it closed and I was about a quarter of the way down the runway when the canopy started opening. So I got airborne with my two hands trying to keep the canopy closed while my knees were flying the aeroplane. I entered cloud and managed to sort out the canopy lock and eased forward on the stick to get below the cloud base of around 400 feet. So I flew out to the coast, which seemed the safest place to be (albeit on a sector recce), and flew up and down it for 30 minutes before I decided I needed to come back to Stradishall and land.

"I called up for a steer and found myself overhead Stradishall, pretty pleased with myself considering there was no radar or anything like that. I set up downwind, or what I thought was the reciprocal to the runway, turned finals coming out of cloud at around 400 feet and the runway lights appeared at about 90 degrees to me. I banked quite steeply to get onto the runway heading, rolled out and landed. Unfortunately, the aircraft slid onto the grass leaving the three undercarriage legs behind. I got out and about ten minutes later a Land Rover appeared with OC Flying in it. He opened the window just enough to speak to me without getting wet and said, 'Strong, you have one hour to get off my airfield', closed the window and drove away. There was no sign of any fire engines or anything like that, so I walked in the direction he appeared to be going in (as it was quite foggy) and eventually got to the crew room where the flight commander asked me what had happened. I explained that I hadn't got time to talk as I'd only got five minutes left to get off the airfield. He came back after about three minutes and said 'It's all right; you don't have to leave until tomorrow morning'.

"So the following morning, I was standing in front of OC Flying who was having quite a go at me about his damaged Meteor. In the middle of this, the door opened and OC Admin poked his head through the door and said 'Is this the chap who crashed your Meteor yesterday?' 'Yes, it bloody well is', the OC Flying replied. OC Admin then said 'I remember the day you crashed three Spitfires in one day', to which OC Flying said 'Get out of my office Strong and never let me see you again' – I continued on the course. Bless the OC Admin. The course after us was halved in size because the Korean War had ended, so we considered ourselves quite lucky to have completed it.

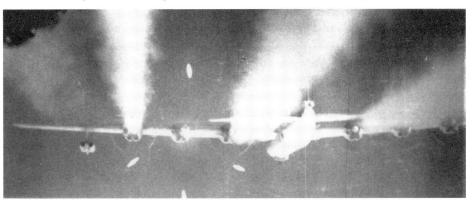

'Four burning, five turning' B-36 interception at 40,000 ft by Chris Strong flying F.8 WK714 G of 72 Squadron on 31 March 1955. [Chris Strong]

"I was then posted to 72 Sqn at Church Fenton. There was a big exercise on 31 March 1955 and I managed to get a close-in photo of my 'pipper' on the inboard engine of a B-36 Peacemaker, the one engine that wasn't trailing so I was quite pleased to take pictures – it was tempting to have shot the damn thing down. The squadron later changed over to NF.11s and I was sent on a night fighter course at North Luffenham where I did one trip in a T.7 and one in an F.8 before I found out that my physical geometry of leg length and thigh length was such that I couldn't actually use the rudder pedals in an NF.11, because they'd got a rad-alt on one side and something on the other side where my legs were meant to go. So I was sent on a pilot attack instructor (PAI) course at Leconfield with Meteors, Venoms and Vampires and then back to Church Fenton to join 19 Sqn – that was in February 1956.

"We did some low flying in Fighter Command but basically our routine was all PIs and day fighter combat. We had three squadrons there, 19, 72 and 609 (Auxiliary), so about once a month or maybe longer, the Wing would get airborne and join up with the Linton-on-Ouse Wing. Then we'd go down to Norfolk to take on the Norfolk Wings and theoretically take pictures of each other. So there would be up to a hundred aircraft making contrails all over the place until we returned to base – it was great fun.

"I stayed on 19 until November 1956 when I was posted to 11

Sqn at Wunstorf on Venoms where I was surrounded by all these little tiny people. The squadron commander was equally tiny and said 'What are you doing here?' and I said 'I've been posted here'. I had flown the Venom FB.1 at Leconfield, but not the FB.4 which had an ejector seat and if I'd ejected with my size and shape I would have left my knees on the instrument panel and gone around like a marionette for the rest of my life. Another aircraft I couldn't fly because of my height. So I was posted to 3 Sqn at Geilenkirchen in Germany on Hunters F.4s just before Christmas 1956. That was the end of my Meteor flying really except for occasionally flag towing.

"The Hunter was not really that big a change from the Meteor F.8. It went faster and it was a pleasure to fly, as had been the Meteor. Also, the Hunter was fully responsive up to about Mach 1– the Meteor went out of control at about Mach 0.84 when the elevators and ailerons became ineffective."

DUXFORD – 64 SQN

Les Millgate also had his hands full of a damaged Meteor while training at 226 OCU Stradishall. He too managed to survive the experience and went on to serve a full tour on 64 Sqn at Duxford (the second Meteor unit there being 65 Sqn – both squadrons had been early recipients of the F.8 in March and February 1951 respectively). Les was initially flying the F.8 before his squadron switched to a night fighter role at the same station in 1956.

"I went to Full Sutton to do the Meteor course on the F.4 and T.7. I had always wanted to be a fighter pilot, in fact if I go right back to when I was at primary school in Maidstone, we were out in the playground and it must have been a PT lesson. Running around like an aeroplane, I was running quite slowly and the teacher said 'No, no, aeroplanes are quite fast, look at that one above us now.' I said, 'No, that's slow' – 'That's because it's up high.' Bang! That was the spark, the fire was lit. I could only have been about five at the time I suppose.

"After that over to Stradishall for the Operational Conversion Unit. The course included learning to fly battle formation, finger four, which of course the air force learned from the Luftwaffe during the Battle of Britain, learning about and firing the guns, tactical flying generally. While I was there, some silly bugger collided with me; we were off on a snake climb, through cloud. That's where you take off – probably four aircraft, but it could be up to eight aircraft or more – in pairs at about ten-second intervals. To cut down the radio chatter, the leader just announces the heading they'll be flying, or you'll brief it beforehand, but then whenever he changes heading he says, 'Red leader turning, turning now'. So you then turn if you're leading a subsequent pair – and we were number three and four – you then turn ten seconds later on to the heading that he announces, so you're going up in a snake. We were climbing through cloud and I was sitting there on instruments fat, dumb and happy when there was a thump on the aircraft and the rudder bar kicked and jammed over to starboard. There I was on instruments in cloud with this very funny-flying aircraft. I said to Red Leader, 'Don't know what's happened, but there was a big thump on my rudder bar which is jammed over to the right' and before he could even reply to me, my number two (who was number four in the formation) said, 'Oh Red Leader this is Red Four, I think I collided with him'. He had lost me in cloud and the standard procedure was '10 for 30 or 30 for 10'; you either turned off 10 degrees for 30 seconds, or 30 degrees for 10 seconds and then turned back onto course. Instead of doing that, he'd just come back in to find me. Well he found me with his left wing and just jammed my right rudder over.

"Red Leader came back and looked at it. Fortunately, it was an F.8 so I could have banged out if necessary and I said I was happy flying it. It was flying sideways, so I had to fly with about 15 degrees of bank to maintain course; he led me back and that was fun flying in formation back to Stradishall where they realised that because my rudder was jammed fully starboard I'd only got right-hand braking. The braking on the Meteor was done by the position of the rudder bar, you squeezed on pressure and modulated it left and right. So they said: 'Right OK, wheels-up landing on the grass'. That's what I did and I ended up with a green endorsement, which did me no harm at all on my new squadron. The other aircraft had a hole in his port leading edge but fortunately not too deep, because the aileron control is a tube inside the leading edge. He was bollocked by the station commander.

F.8 WH460 B 64 Squadron Duxford. [Les Millgate]

"From there I was posted to Duxford and arrived in September 1952 on 64 Sqn flying the F.8. When I arrived, I got off the train at Whittlesford and rang up for transport. While I was waiting, I heard an aircraft flying, so I rushed outside to have a look and it was a Meteor F.8 doing a completely inverted display. Everything was inverted including bunts, finally putting his wheels UP downwind still doing the finals leg inverted and then at the last minute flipping over and landing. I was only just checked out on the Meteor, still somewhat in awe of the aircraft and my first thought was 'Bloody Hell fire! What have I let myself in for? Shall I get back on the train and go home?'

"The F.8 was a nicer aircraft but I don't think we had spring-ailerons by then; this was a later modification that came while I was on the squadron and made the aircraft a bit nicer to fly. But it was a lovely aircraft; I was very happy flying it. A lovely feeling knowing that if it all turns to worms, you could eject. I didn't have to but we had the odd occasion on the squadron when people had to bang out. We usually flew in pairs of course, but occasionally you were on your own and you went off looking for other aircraft to bounce or whatever. I bounced another 64 Sqn aircraft, and had absolutely no idea who it was. I didn't recognise the helmet and we started dogfighting. We were out in the Newmarket area I suppose, which was our usual area of operations, and we ended up really hard dogfighting and we got very low – we really were low. Then the other aircraft waggled his wings, the standard sign 'break off,' and got to go back for fuel. I joined him and we flew back as a pair and landed. After we had taxied in and shut down, I walked over to see who it was and it was the squadron commander. No bollocking or anything. I

'Gotcha!' a close view of a 64 Squadron F.8 from Peter Rogers' gun camera. [Peter Rogers]

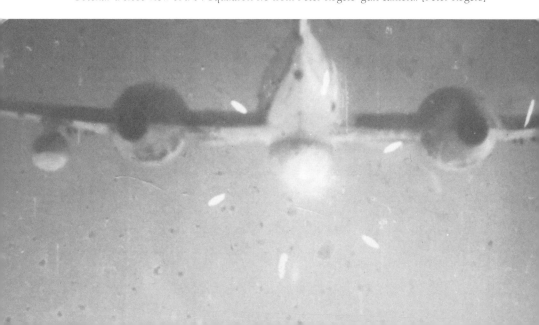

think because we'd had a bloody good work-out between us, he couldn't exactly bollock me for being a good fighter pilot. As we walked back into the office, I thought, 'Oh boy, I wouldn't have done that if I'd known it was the squadron commander'.

"On another occasion, we had just one aircraft with a piece of equipment, that I think they called Appendix and it was a VHF homer. They used this on jamming aircraft to jam the radar station frequency and the instruction from the radar station if there was a jamming aircraft – usually a Lincoln – was 'Open your tool shed' I think. I had a number two with me as well, so you followed the Appendix needles until you found the jamming aircraft. I looked out and I was directly overhead a Lincoln and they jammed by putting a microphone in the engine nacelle and just broadcast that on the frequency. Anyway, I was right over him, so I did what we called a C3; I just rolled horizontal and did a downward attack on him. As I broke away underneath him, there was a sort of flash and bang on the aircraft and I thought 'Christ, what's that?' Then the radar station came up and he said, 'Do not attack the aircraft, he's got a trailing aerial'. So I said: 'Not now he ain't!' My number two came back and he looked at me said, 'I can't see any damage on the aircraft'. We flew back to Duxford and landed; Wingco Flying came out and right down the nose of my Meteor, it was just as though someone had taken a hacksaw and sawn a vertical groove and stuck in it was a lead weight, just like the weight on a fishing line but bigger. That's what they had on the trailing aerial to keep it hanging vertically. The Wingco said: 'You had the line perfect Millgate'.

"One day the station barber rang me to ask if there was any chance of a flight. I had to do an air test on our T.7, and said, 'If you can get over here in 15 minutes you're in luck'. I found him a flying suit and a helmet and when he arrived he told me he had never flown before and would love to do aerobatics, so I provided him with a suitable receptacle and decided to take it easy with him. Off we went and he seemed quite happy so I tried a gentle barrel roll, 'That was lovely Sir, what was that called?' I told him and decided he was OK with gentle aeros so next I did a loop, pulling minimum g. Again he said, 'That was lovely Sir, what was that called?' Good, he was not feeling queasy and clearly enjoying it so I did a slow roll, then a four-point hesitation roll, each time getting the same delighted reaction from the back. I knew this aircraft well as I flew it often, and knew it was somehow bent and would not stall turn to the right, so I thought I would give it another try. So I accelerated in a shallow dive from 20,000 feet, pulled up into a vertical climb and as the speed dropped towards zero, put on hard right rudder, full left throttle, throttled back on the right, and waited – so did the aircraft.

"By now we were stationary, hanging vertically in the air, nose pointing slightly right and refusing to go any further. The aircraft then juddered and fell onto its back in to an inverted spin. My first thoughts were 'Goodness me!' or words to that effect. We had been told not to spin the Meteor at all and certainly not an inverted spin. I was working the controls hard to try and stop the spin and without really knowing what I did we came out of it by flipping over into an upright spin. The standard spin recovery, stick hard forward, full opposite rudder and we dived away to pull out at about 10,000 feet. I was about to ask my passenger how he was when he said, 'That was lovely Sir, what was that called? Can we do it again?' 'No!' I thought to myself, a cock-up was what it was called. We flew back to Duxford with me still sweating and my knees trembling. Back on the ground my passenger was profusely grateful for his first flight and went back to his hair-cutting; I had a strong coffee in the crew room!

"On 2 June 1953 we flew in the Coronation flypast, Duxford led it and 65 Sqn (our sister squadron), was in front; each squadron was in three boxes of four. It was a lousy day and the flypast was postponed. It was supposed to take place as the Queen got back from the abbey, but because the weather was so dreadful it was flown a couple of hours later.

65 Squadron team to lead the Coronation flypast on 2 June 1953 with Wg Cdr J. Wallace leading (in cap). [Les Millgate]

It bucketed down and was very bumpy. We flew the T.7 with a *Flight* magazine photographer in the back."

An unknown comedian at Duxford composed a mock message to the pilots involved in the Coronation flypast advising them that they must all wear No.1 Home Dress and carry their peaked caps in the aircraft. In addition, flight commanders were to wear ceremonial swords and belts. It went on to say that: "in the event of a forced landing in The Mall, the pilot will put on his peaked cap, step out of the aircraft, come smartly to attention and salute Buckingham Palace, and then turn left and march off with the Coronation procession." It was 'signed' by AVM G Malenkov, The Kremlin, Moscow. Les continues:

"We had detachments to Acklington for armament practice once a year, firing at towed flags which were about six feet wide and 30 feet long, towed by another Meteor F.8 usually. I flew as the tow pilot myself on occasion, because we did exactly the same sort of thing from Duxford and went out over the range off the east coast waiting to hear the sound of cannon fire and say 'break off, break off'. You were not supposed to fire at less than 15 degrees angle off the flag, but occasionally somebody would muck it up.

"One winter when there was lots of snow on the ground and no flying, someone had the bright idea to build a snowman on the pan, the model for which was our senior flight commander Flt Lt Tony Young who had been a qualified flying instructor (QFI) at Heany when I was there. He was a slightly portly gentleman and could be pompous and was a confirmed bachelor. The snowman was very lifelike, but overall I think Tony was not impressed.

"I was very happy on 64 Sqn, it was a very contented station. I was there from '52 to '55 and at the end of my tour the standard thing then was all fighter pilots went off to CFS Little Rissington

Senior flight commander of 64 Squadron Flt Lt Tony Young captured in snowman form on a non-flying day at Duxford. [Les Millgate]

to be interviewed to become an instructor. I was sent there and I made it fairly plain, but not too rudely, that I didn't want to go. Basically because on my course going through Heany we had one bloke who was about two or three years older than us and once he got his wings he went off to CFS and he said to me, 'Whatever you do, don't become a flying instructor!' So I said, 'Sorry Sir, I don't want to do this job'. The air commodore asked me: 'What do you think will happen to you now then?' I thought 'go back to the squadron, an ordinary posting'; three of us out of 100 at CFS said they didn't want to go there. A couple of months later a message came to all stations in Fighter Command saying that these three people were posted to Technical Training Command as course commanders. I went off to Halton for 15 months: a bloody miserable job. Taking the inventory of a barrack block and taking disciplinary hearings if the apprentices did anything wrong. But fortunately, while I was there, back at Duxford they were losing more and more pilots to ground jobs and they still had the same flying task but getting nobody posted in, so I was still going back to the squadron regularly to do some flying. I used to come back some weekends, but unfortunately a lot of the weekends were taken up at Halton with church parades and God knows what else. But I was in touch with Duxford and if there was a flying weekend, and I could get away, I used to take the place of another pilot so he could go off. There was also a requirement for people in ground jobs to keep current, so I did some additional official Meteor refresher flying back at Duxford.

"I found out when I got back to Duxford that once a month, the station commander wrote to the Air Ministry saying 'Give me back the pilots that you took away from me and put into ground jobs'. About 15 months after I left Duxford, he was posted as an air commodore in charge of aircrew postings. 64 had just changed its role as he got to the Air Ministry from day fighter to night fighter, so they were getting new aircraft (Meteor night fighters), but they were also short of reasonably experienced pilots, so I was posted back into Duxford, much to my relief."

Plt Off Peter Rogers, July 1953. [Peter Rogers]

Peter Rogers also had 64 Sqn as his first tour and, like Less Millgate, stayed with the unit when it converted to the night fighter role.

"In March 1954 I turned up at Duxford on 64 Sqn. When I arrived, two of us drove over from Stradishall on a Tuesday and found it was then almost entirely a bachelor squadron – I think one man was married. So the squadron induction party was that night in a pub at Great Chesterford. The Meteor F.8 was a lovely aircraft to fly; it was really simple (you didn't really want to fly the T.7 unless you had to). With regards to

the asymmetric handling, I never had any problem with the Derwent, a marvellous engine, although we abused it horribly. I did the instrument rating examiner's (IRE) course at West Raynham in 1955, flying both the Meteor and the Vampire, so of course I got stuck doing IRs on the T.7. It had no ejection seat, but it was the only way you could do the IR practice. One of the penalties of being an IRE was that any time there was a big formation, you invariably got the Meteor T.7. On a couple of occasions, we had a Wing Balbo when both squadrons flew together with the OC Ops leading, and I was sat right at the end in the T.7, with 24 aircraft lined up ahead of me, and almost airborne with the jet wash.

"It was great fun in the F.8, particularly when you got air-to-air firing. We did a certain amount of low level work – a 'Rat and Terrier'. You were given a low level target somewhere in East Anglia and somebody broadcast its co-ordinates. You had to recognise where you were and plot where it was going; we rarely got success, but when you did it was great fun.

"The great thing for 64 in those days was the aerobatic team, led by the squadron boss Harry Bennett. That was five aircraft, and it pioneered the downward bomb-burst which people like the Red Arrows got credit for later on. It was really rather a good outfit and I think one of the first days on the squadron, Harry Bennett took Stan Underwood (who was my friend from Stradishall) and myself up as a formation of three aircraft.

Fg Off Bob Deas and Flt Lt Pete Rogers in a staged scramble on 64 Squadron at Duxford, November 1954. [Les Millgate]

He hadn't briefed us and didn't mention anything when he did a barrel roll, which surprised Stan and I and we fell out of formation. This was obviously to test us for aerobatic potential and I don't think he ever spoke to me or even acknowledged my presence thereafter; he was obsessed with this aerobatic team. He moved on three or four months after that and later killed himself flying a Hunter, falling out of cloud in bad weather.

"Once, the aerobatic team was practising over the airfield as a three-ship with four and five in line astern; Johnny Heard was five. Coming down from a loop, when the boss called the break, he pulled, two and three pulled, but four and five had to rotate through 180 degrees and then pull. Bennett left it a bit late, so Johnny had to not only rotate through 180 but start pulling. We were watching this and he disappeared south westwards from Duxford below the trees, and the last we saw of him he was still quite low. Everyone said: 'That's tough on Johnny, that's the end' but he turned up later on. After pulling like crazy, he blacked out, hit the ground, bounced and recovered his vision at about 300 feet, with the runway at the disused airfield at Nuthampstead dead ahead. When he hit the ground, both engines were out; there was no noise, no nothing. He just put it down on its belly and got out, and they flew again with the team that afternoon.

"The only incident I had on a Meteor was when I lost a canopy. I was on a singleton air-to-air firing sortie on a banner out over the North Sea (at the Knock Deep range situated between two wartime ack-ack towers) and by the time I got there, the guy in front of me had shot the banner off. Standard operating procedure (SOP), I got rid of the rounds into the sea, flew back to Duxford full of the joys of spring and thought 'Ah, I'll do a loop'. I pulled up into a loop and at the top the canopy came off; it was no great problem, although a bit drafty.

"On the F.8s we didn't lose anybody but we lost a couple of aircraft. Two of them had a mid-air collision dogfighting over the Norfolk Broads, they ejected. We had an Australian exchange officer and he wrote off a Meteor taxying too fast. It was a scramble, and there was a very tight turn at the end of the runway at Duxford, and he slid off sideways and collapsed one leg of his undercarriage.

"We didn't get many detachments with the F.8s but I was very fortunate to get hooked up with a four-ship going to Laarbruch, the first time I had ever left British shores. It was a one-off jolly with the squadron commander, two flight commanders and me – a big deal and a very drunken weekend. The only detachments we did were up to Acklington for an APC, which was again a month's great fun, lots of air-to-air and in my time we won the Dacre Trophy for the best squadron for air-to-air. We tangled, or tried to, with anything that moved including F-84s – and we had a good relationship with the Wethersfield people. But we certainly

'Digger's Leap', F.8 WF713 U of 63 Squadron flown by an RAAF exchange pilot, which over-ran the runway at Acklington in 1955. [Peter Rogers]

met our match with F-86Ds; we quite often tangled with them, but of course lost hopelessly, and couldn't stay with them. If you could bring back cine on a different aircraft that was a few more points and we could predict where the B-45s were going into Sculthorpe. The Americans got very upset with this and through fighter command said, 'Keep your boys off our tails'. But anything that moved in the sky was fair game. I did almost two and a half years on the F.8 before the squadron switched to the NF.12 and NF.14 when it re-roled as a night fighter unit. We were given the option, stay with it and convert or take your luck – I stayed."

WATTISHAM – 263 SQN

Wattisham's F.8s arrived in October and November 1950 in the shape of 257 and 263 Sqns which moved down from Horsham St.Faith (via a short stint at Acklington in 263's case). On 30 June 1954 a third Meteor squadron 152 was reformed there to fly NF.12 and 14 night fighters. **George Black** started his long and illustrious career as a National Service pilot and had a similar test of confidence in his early Meteor flying before reaching a squadron.

Sqn Ldr George
Black, 263 Squadron,
Wattisham. [George
Black]

"One of the things you had to do as a National Service pilot was to commit to five years on an auxiliary squadron, in my case at my home town in Aberdeen, with 612 Squadron at Dyce. I was fortunate that I'd just checked in with them when I was there between courses, before I went to Driffield to do the Meteor conversion and the CO said, 'Would you like a trip in a Meteor?' I said, 'That would be great'. So he gave me a trip in the T.7 and it was most impressive compared with flying the Harvard and things of that kind. That was my first introduction to the Meteor.

"In 1952, I went to 203 AFS at Driffield and I was there for about four months doing the course; it was a pretty tough and exciting time. I arrived with 12 other students and by the time we had completed the course only five of us remained; three were killed. We were on funeral party quite regularly with an accident almost every week. The accident rate was horrendous. I attribute a lot of that to the poor standard of training. Reflecting back, many of the instructors were not well qualified on the Meteor, and it was an advanced aeroplane if you were an instructor who'd been on Shackletons or Lancasters or transport-type aeroplanes. The chap I had as my instructor initially was killed in a formation accident and the flight commander Stan Wandzilak, a Pole, took me on and I have him to thank for pointing me in the right direction. He was exceptionally good and I learned a tremendous amount from him. But 203 AFS was not the happiest of places because of the high accident rate during training.

"Many of the accidents were attributable to circumstances like: we don't just throttle back an engine to practise single-engine flying we flame the engine out. When you go downwind, make sure you've got the airbrakes in before you lower the undercarriage, otherwise you get this Phantom Dive and the aeroplane will roll: and never let your speed get too low on finals. There were a number of features on the Meteor that you really had to be on top of. The chap who took me for my night check out was a Canadian on exchange, who said: 'I want just one good night circuit and landing and then I'm out – it's all yours.' And that was it; he strapped up the back seat on the operational readiness platform (ORP), went into the caravan and left me to it. It was like that, but I survived; we did about 60-70 hours on the course and about half of that was on the single-seat F.4 Meteor. The Meteor F.4s were well used, having been in squadron service until replaced by F.8s, but they were good for flying solo. You had to wind the canopy – it was a pretty basic cockpit with 'steam driven' instruments.

"I went from there to the OCU at Stradishall, converted onto the

Meteor F.8 and where we also did air-to-air firing and all the operational training. It was great to get into an F.8, which was the latest mark and everything was that little bit better. The Meteor F.4s and T.7s at Driffield didn't have the spring tabs on the ailerons; they had the hard-edged ailerons, so you really were a bit of a strong-man to move them around. The F.8 with spring tabs was delightful, it just went where you pointed it. Then they put the larger engine nacelles on; they changed the canopy so you had much better all-round vision and there were a few other improvements that went into the F.8 to make it a much nicer aeroplane, it flew beautifully.

"When I'd finished at the OCU, I had four months remaining of my National Service and posted to 263 Sqn at Wattisham. Sqn Ldr George Strange – big handlebar moustache, great chap – was the squadron commander. The morning I arrived and checked in, a tragedy happened for the squadron when a pilot on A Flight crashed near Middleton St. George and was killed.* 'Oh well, I'm glad you've arrived because that'll fill the gap!' Anyway I had a great time for the four remaining months. The fact that I was National Service meant that there was a feeling there that he's not going to contribute much to the squadron, 'So we would like you to stay and then we'll feel a bit happier about you and your combat training.' However, for reasons which I have never fully understood in my own mind, on Guy Fawkes' night 1952, I set off from Wattisham and 263 Squadron and got the night train back up to Scotland. One of the less good decision I made!"

* The aircraft lost on 29 September 1952 nine miles south of Middleton St.George was WH472, which flew into a hill in cloud after take-off.

"Now my 263 CO, who I'd got quite friendly with, said when saying farewell: 'Now you've got to stay, we can't let you go'. He rang my father in Aberdeen and said 'Have a word with him. We've already spent a lot of time training him and we need to get the money back!' But I went home. Now for a 20-year-old, having had a great time for two years, having to go back and live with your parents? I missed the camaraderie, mess life, missed everything else and the auxiliary squadron really·wasn't for me. They didn't fly a lot and there was no great togetherness although they had two Meteors for instrument training in addition to the Vampire fleet. The few weeks that I was with them I flew the Meteor more than anyone else there; they didn't like it, they liked the Vampire. So I rang my 263 boss up and said, 'Sir, you were right. I've changed my mind, I'd like to return to Wattisham and join the squadron again.' He said, 'Right, there'll be a rail warrant in the post for you this afternoon. Get on the next bloody train and get back down here and re-join us'; as easy as that. Two days

George Black, 263 Squadron, Wattisham. [George Black]

later when I'd checked-in back at Wattisham, I was airborne in a Meteor again. I suppose I never looked back after that.

"My flight commander was Peter Latham, whom I worked for on three occasions subsequently. We also had a chap who was a large rugby type in every sense of the word; his head stuck out of the Meteor cockpit as he always had the seat right up so that he could see better! He opened up both throttles fully on the ORP and it sucked up one of the engine intake covers and broke the pitot head off en route to the engine intake. He was a good friend even after he left the squadron, but was clumsy in a fighter aeroplane. He didn't stay all that long after he had a mid-air collision with the flight commander who, at that time, was Geoff Hermitage. They were doing a snake climb behind each other and the poor chap was all over the place. Instead of being slightly out to one side during the climb, he got directly behind and lost contact with his leader because they went into cloud. Alas, he crashed into the flight commander and took the tail off his aircraft.* Geoff ejected but suffered serious back problems for quite a while afterwards. By brute force and 'ignorance', our rugby player brought his Meteor back and crash-landed on the airfield – only he could have done that. So his days on the squadron were numbered."

*The collision occurred on 19 August 1952. The Flt Cdr's aircraft was WA894, which came down at Gull Farm, Debenham, Suffolk. The aircraft recovered to Wattisham was WA779, which was repaired.

"There was no shortage of flying; we were doing 30 to 40 hours a month and two, three, maybe four trips a day. In early 1953, we went into three flights instead of two; we now had a C Flight. That was for more new people arriving, and the C Flight commander would keep an eye on them before they moved out to A and B Flights. We got additional Meteors to cope with the extra task so we were a large squadron with 27 or 28 Meteors on strength. We had two T.7s but they were all placed in a pool on Station Flight. So for all the instrument rating tests that had to be done you had to go to Station Flight, but the whole Wing used those T.7s. If you went on detachment they would allocate a T.7 to take with you. We had 257 Sqn with us at Wattisham, and then we got the new night fighters of 152 Sqn, first with the early Meteor marks and finally the NF.14. So it became a very busy flying station.

"The first deployment I did was to Fassberg in Germany, the whole

Wing went. Talk about a gaggle of fighters, how we never lost any aircraft to and from Germany I shall never know. The weather was awful and heavy drinking was the norm on the German bases – all duty free! We deployed for five days. When we took off to return, there were Meteors everywhere during the climb-out. I can see it to this day; I came out on top of cloud at about 30,000 feet and there were aircraft here, there and everywhere. Fortunately the weather wasn't too bad at Wattisham, so you just descended, 'Oh there's Felixstowe', 'there's Orfordness'…straight into Wattisham. There was great camaraderie but if you didn't show a bit of spark and individualism occasionally, you weren't part of the fighter force. It was expected and it was encouraged by your seniors.

"We went air firing at Acklington once a year. There was no air firing one day and we were all being allowed to do some general handling practice. I decided, in a hasty moment, that I would fly up to Aberdeen and return without refuelling! I got airborne, pulled the high pressure (HP) cock up and transferred the fuel. Then I navigated all the way up and round Aberdeen City, over my parents' house and then my girlfriend's, before turning to fly back over Edinburgh. I relit the engine I'd shut down to conserve fuel. Meanwhile, unbeknown to me, they'd started a search and rescue operation because they thought my overdue aircraft was missing – I hadn't answered the radio calls. My boss was waiting for me on landing back at Acklington and I got five days orderly officer for my sins. On my flight locker someone had chalked up 'Range and Endurance Specialist' – that's what life was like. Afterwards in the bar, the CO said you 'Silly b****r but yes, it was quite a challenging thing to do and full marks for that'.

"There were many incidents. We were given low level 'Rat and Terrier' exercises across Norfolk. One of the chaps on B Flight pulled up hard with a lot of 'g' and it broke the inner leading edge away between the engine nacelle and the fuselage – it came clean away. There was modification action taken and every leading edge had to be checked; there were some that needed strengthening. Some of the other incidents were people losing control in cloud. The early ejection seat wasn't great. A modified and upgraded ejection seat was fitted so you could get down to 90 knots and 100 feet and still parachute to safety. We had the occasional engine failure but not very much ever went wrong with the engine unless it ingested a foreign object. Only once did I have an engine problem on a T.7 when the RPM stagnated at about 11,000 but still produced enough power. I never had a total engine failure, or a fire. On the squadron, we each had our own aircraft and mine was WK802 D. My ground crewman LAC Webb, who looked after the aircraft on the line, made me a beautiful wooden model of my aircraft before we converted to the Hunter. I still have this model to this day – a treasure!

"We had an aerobatic team led by Peter Latham and I flew in that. He would fly upside down for as long as he could and we would join in formation and fly across the airfield, he upside down and the other two of us the right way up. Peter was a great boss. I remained on the squadron until 1955, but the last year we re-equipped with Hunters – the F.2 and then the F.5. They were the worst of all the marks of Hunter and had the Sapphire engine, unlike the Avon version, which was great. The Sapphire engine had serious vibration problems and with only a single engine, we were all going around with Silver C gliding badges following the number of total failures in the air.

"Compared with the Meteor, the Hunter was a big leap forward. You could climb to 40,000 feet in about half the time whereas in the Meteor 30,000 to 35,000 feet for the high-level interception role was a realistic operational limit. Until we got tasked into the Rat and Terrier low level exercises, it was all medium and high level operations. It was all done through the radar stations because we had no radar and they controlled and guided you towards the targets. At the end of the sortie, some air combat, then back for a ground controlled approach (GCA). We often did mock combat with American aircraft from Wethersfield, Bentwaters and Shepherds Grove; there was a lot of co-operation around East Anglian bases. They would invite us across for an evening and we would invite them back and if we wanted to get some air combat with different aircraft types we arranged it. As easy as that.

"Flypasts – Wattisham was a good location for such events as the Coronation flypast, Battle of Britain flypasts, 32 aircraft or even up to 200 in the early days. I was involved in the rehearsals and final for the Coronation Review flypast at Odiham in July '53. Formations had to join the stream at a designated gate and you'd have the different wings coming in from all over the country, auxiliary squadrons joining in who were not always that well practiced in formation procedures – there was always a lot of chatter on the radio!

"Meanwhile, there was the odd unusual accident that happened back at base like that with Hughie Edwards, our station commander and a famous wartime bomber VC.* He was flying a Meteor F.8 on the approach to the duty runway but instead of landing at the end of the runway, he landed into the approach lights with undercarriage and flaps selected down. He went through the lights, took the wings and engines off and everything else. He opened the canopy, walked away and was only a few feet from the end of the runway – but he didn't fly much. Red Bartlett was the Wg Cdr Flying and he was ex-Battle of Britain. They were great people to have served with."

* AVM Hughie Edwards VC KCMG CB DSO OBE DFC was an Australian who

flew his wartime operations with 105 and 460 Sqns. His accident happened when he was flying Meteor F.8 WL119 of 263 Sqn on 14 December 1953 during a night approach.

"I left in 1955 and many years later I was posted to Fighter Command as a staff officer. We still had a Meteor T.7 at Bovingdon which was used for communication flying. The Fighter Command Communications Squadron (FCCS) was a great asset for staying current, so I used to book the T.7 and do a staff visit to a station. It brought back memories of 263

Flt Lt Graham West-Jones of 222 Squadron prostrate at Leuchars. [Jack Frost via Peter Arnold]

Sqn days when you could take an F.8 Meteor away at weekends, fly up to Dyce, and return south again on the Monday morning. No problem, nobody asked any questions. Great times with many happy memories."

By 1954, the writing was on the wall for the F.8 in its original role. Many squadrons had started to re-equip, mainly with Hunters and a few with Sabres, although poor old 56 Sqn at Waterbeach suffered the indignity of wrestling for a while with the awful early Swifts. The Stradishall OCU had been disbanded on 1 June 1955 and the process accelerated during the period leading up to and immediately after the Sandys Defence Review. The last fighter squadron to cast off its Meteor F.8s was 245, also at Stradishall, in April 1957, by which time all the auxiliary squadrons had already packed up and switched off the lights.

CHAPTER THREE

WEEKEND FLYERS –
THE ROYAL AUXILIARY AIR FORCE

THE BOYS

Flt Lt Derek 'Moose' Davies

Joined in 1949 as an aircraft electrician at Finningley, then pilot training. 20 Sqn Vampire / Sabre Oldenburg, as 20's gunnery instructor flew Mosquito and Tempest at Sylt. CFS, instructor 8 FTS Swinderby also flying 616 Sqn Meteors. 1 ANS as unit QFI/IRE, Vampire T.10/ T.11, Valetta, Varsity, Marathon. Retired 1959.

Fg Off Norman Tebbit

Joined in 1949 and did basic flying training at South Cerney. Trained on Meteors at 205 AFS and 226 OCU. Flew Vampire and Meteor with 604 Sqn until shortly before it was disbanded in 1957. Later flew with BOAC before becoming a Member of Parliament.

THE NEED FOR MORE FIGHTER SQUADRONS

In order to bolster the United Kingdom's air defences during the increased tension in the early post-war years, on 2 June 1946, the Auxiliary Air Force was reformed. Originally intended to include day fighter, night fighter and light bomber squadrons, the plan was changed to 20 day fighter units. King George VI gave permission for it to be known as the Royal Auxiliary Air Force on 16 December 1947 and the fighter squadrons began to reform the following year, with main equipment initially comprising Spitfires (primarily the F.22). By 1951, all of them had changed to jet equipment, either Meteors or Vampires. Meteors were issued to the following squadrons: 500 West Malling, 501 Filton, 504 Wymeswold, 600 Biggin Hill, 601 North Weald, 604 North Weald, 609 Church Fenton, 610 Hooton Park, 611 Hooton Park, 615 Biggin Hill and 616 Finningley, later Worksop. A few of these had initially had Vampires before changing to Meteors.

In 1951, the RAuxAF squadrons, which made up approximately one third of the total strength of Fighter Command, were called up for three months continuous service in order to bring them up to an operational standard closer to that of the regulars. In times of lesser tension, however, they primarily flew at weekends apart from occasional exercises and their annual two-week summer camp when the entire squadron would de-camp to another RAF station, usually overseas. Typical of their set-up and operations were 604 Sqn at North Weald and 616 Sqn at Finningley.

604 SQN NORTH WEALD

Norman Tebbit, later perhaps better known as a Conservative cabinet minister, enlisted as a National Serviceman and, after pilot training, spent his RAF career with the Auxiliaries at North Weald in Essex.

"My flying career was all due to the Attlee Government, which came to office in 1945. Churchill's wife had suggested to him that losing the election was perhaps 'a blessing in disguise'. So it proved, because Attlee and Bevin were both great patriots who realised that Churchill was right about the Soviet menace and the 'iron curtain' descending across Europe. They also remembered that our victory in the Battle of Britain had been a very close thing as we almost ran out, not of 'planes, but of pilots. Indeed, but for the 145 experienced Polish pilots who escaped to fight with us, we would have probably lost. We were chucking in pilots with no experience many of whom lasted less than a week.

"So Attlee and Bevin took three decisions which, out of office, Labour would probably have opposed. One resulted in the creation of NATO, (which I heard Jim Callaghan later tell Helmut Schmidt, was to keep the Russians out, the Americans in and the Germans down!), the second was to acquire nuclear weapons and the third to rebuild our reserves particularly of trained pilots. They instituted National Service pilot training and I was in the first year's batch of 200. The scheme was to train us to squadron standard and then to be de-mobbed into the reserves, either the Volunteer Reserve (RAFVR) or the Auxiliaries (RAuxAF).

Line-up of 604 Squadron, Duxford, September 1953. [via Norman Tebbit]

"I was called up in 1949, gained my wings at 1 FTS South Cerney in 1949, completed conversion to Meteors at 205 AFS Middleton St. George and my operational training at 226 OCU at Stradishall. It was a very different world. The station commander at Middleton was the late, great Group Captain Coles, a rather wild character who, one memorable day, complained that the bar was almost empty at lunch time. Told that it was because 'the boys' were having lunch before flying he cried, 'Lunch? Give them beer and sandwiches'. I liked the Meteor straight away. It was a very early jet, enormously thirsty for fuel, particularly at low level where you could get through both belly and main tanks in about 20 minutes. It was viceless and indestructible in the air. People held that it was dangerous with one engine out, but so long as you kept above 150 knots, it was OK. On take-off there was a brief critical phase between getting airborne at 115 knots and reaching 150 or something like that. The critical speed was, I think, 130; for practical purposes, you needed 150 knots and, provided you kept that speed, it was a perfectly tractable aeroplane on one engine. In fact, to extend range at low level we would occasionally put one out, a recognised technique. If you were low on fuel at low level it was not worth climbing to extend the range; the best option was to close down one engine and run the other at a more efficient higher power setting.

"Its high Mach characteristics were very clear. As you approached the critical Mach, somewhere between Mach 0.78 and 0.79 on the F.4 it would shake, twitch and go no faster. If you pushed it downhill to increase speed, it would usually roll onto its back then as you got into thicker, warmer air the Mach number would go down, the airspeed up and you could regain control. From 35,000 or 40,000 feet you could even roll it onto its back, pull through to a vertical dive and it would hit critical Mach without anything falling off and it was not a problem to regain control. Of course it could be a bit tricky if you were instrument flight rules (IFR) but that was covered by the continuation and mutual training which we did in the two-seat T.7 trainer. The technique then was that the guy under training or being checked was in the back with his windows completely blanked out. The F.4 aircraft had an old fashioned topple-able air-driven gyro artificial horizon and the usual basic flying instruments just like a 1938 Hurricane or Spitfire. If you were the safety or check pilot in front, you placed the aircraft in a somewhat unusual attitude and said to the bloke behind, 'She's all yours mate'. So in the back you might find yourself inverted, steeply banked and approaching the stall, which tested you and the aeroplane to the limits. It was a great aeroplane but its downside was its poor instrumentation (although that was improved on the F.8 and later versions), its lack of navigational capability and its short endurance. That is where I think a lot of the losses arose, which gave rise to the suggestion that so many crashed in East Anglia that the farmers ploughed them in as top dressing.

"Having completed OCU at Stradishall, I was then released into the Volunteer Reserve (RAFVR) flying Chipmunks, but as soon as a vacancy arose, I applied to join 604 Sqn RAuxAF equipped with Vampires, at North Weald. There (and I use the words wisely), I was duly auditioned and permitted to join. The Auxiliary squadrons were bands of brothers, even tighter than the bands that bind together the pilots of the regular squadrons. Because we had no thoughts of postings, promotions or careers in the service, we were simply 'chums'. There were several wartime blokes on 604. Indeed shortly before I joined, the CO, Sqn Ldr Keith Lofts had been killed in an old-style 'round the pylons' low level air race for the Cooper Trophy (at Hatfield on 23 June 1951). Lofts pulled his Vampire too tightly in a turn round a pylon; it stalled and, as Vampires did, it flicked and went in inverted. He had been replaced by Tommy Turnbull, who was a Lloyd's underwriter and quite well off. He had been a PR pilot during the war and been shot down twice, by our own side, returning from long missions. Flying PR Spitfires as far as Berlin at over 50,000 feet you were away for a very time and forgotten by our air defences! Tommy was a great guy and Ian Ponsford, my flight commander, was an absolutely splendid leader. We had a squadron doctor, who was a leading consultant at Bart's, and the rest of us were a mixed bunch. One was Joe Hoare, who was a Hoare of Hoare's Bank. Joe was an eccentric character and had a weak bladder, which is not normally a problem in fighters, but on long hauls, as when we went down to Malta for our summer camp, it did constitute a problem for him. Nothing that could not be solved with a chamois level flying glove and an elastic band, although trying to maintain formation whilst having a pee in those circumstances had its difficulties.

"When I arrived on the squadron, I had to convert on to the Vampire, which was quite a hooley with there being no two-seat trainers. It was known as the 'kiddy car' as when you were sitting in the cockpit on the ground, you were eye to eye with the 'erk' standing outside with the trolley-acc starter. It was not very fast; it did not accelerate very quickly, but was very manoeuvrable, even to the flick stall in a tight turn which could be used to get away from someone on your tail – he would be unlikely to follow that. I had fun flying the Vampire and we had a Meteor T.7 on the squadron for instrument flying checks and things like that.

"I had joined in time for the squadron's first overseas summer camp, taking our Vampires down to Ta' Qali in Malta to reinforce the RAF contingent there for the annual defence of Malta exercise against the US 6th Fleet. Ian Ponsford reckoned that the Americans would not expect the defenders to be equipped with the extra wing drop tanks, which we had fitted for the trip from North Weald via Istres in southern France. Relying on the advantage of surprise, we went out in search of the American fleet, sighted it and dived on it in a simulated attack on their big carrier whose flight deck was full of aircraft fuelled and bombed up. Ponsford was right; they were not expecting us and as we came down, we passed their interceptors, Banshees mostly, on their way up. The most spectacular bit of cine film was from Ian as he flew the length of the aircraft carrier about 15 feet above the deck going underneath one of their large twin-rotor Piasecki helicopters as it took off. I understand that the Americans thought it was all a bit rough and reckless. We were visited in Malta by our AOC, the late, great Paddy Bandon, widely known as The Abandoned Earl, an extraordinary man who had led a Blenheim squadron (82 Sqn) in the Battle of France, surviving by the luck of the Irish.

"A couple of years later, having re-equipped with the Meteor F.8, more powerful, better aerodynamics and more powerful Derwent engines, we went to Wunstorf, a NATO 2nd Tactical Air Force (TAF) RAF base in Germany for our fortnight's summer camp. I remember it most for the Rudesheim Wine Festival on the Rhine, which coincided with our mid-weekend break. Somehow most of us pilots bogged off, taking the Helvetia Express, a great diesel engine train. The ticket collector, noticing that we were travelling on military tickets, asked about us. We told him who we were and what we were doing. 'Ah, you are air force,' he said, adding to my flight commander Ponsford, 'You flyers had an easy war', to which Ian observed, 'It didn't feel like that at the time'. 'Well,' responded the German, 'I was an infantryman on the Russian Front.' So we all agreed that he was right, before he added that the train driver had been a Luftwaffe pilot on Heinkel 111s and had bombed London, 'I'm sure he'd like to meet you. Come up to the front of the train.' So we arrived up at the driver's station, introduced ourselves and the driver confirmed that he had bombed London several times and before long, he and Ian were trying to remember dates to see whether they had indeed met before. Turning to the conductor, the driver said that as he finished his shift at the next station he could relax a bit: 'So bring up a crate of wine.' So we sat there, guys who had tried to kill each other, roaring across Europe on a railway train drinking together. We enjoyed a good time at the wine festival, as the Germans take such things very seriously. It was all very typical of the way the Auxiliaries operated, having fun while preparing to fight again if needs be.

"As fighter pilots we had to have great reliance on our leader or conversely, to look after your wingman or number two. I was leading a live air-firing detail with my number two off Foulness or Clacton one winter's day. The weather was poor and I should have cancelled the detail, so everything that went wrong was really my responsibility. We were between layers of cloud and the tug towing the target was in and out of cloud. I made a pass at the target which was too loose so I did not fire, but pulled away and repositioned for another run. My number two, Bingham Dore, then made a pass, but as he broke away we ran into thick cloud and, as he said in the accident report, he went on to instruments to stabilise. Having done so, he looked out to see if he could see me and in his words, saw the biggest f*****g Meteor he had ever seen in his life immediately in front of him. He made the right decision and tried to go underneath as he was closing quite rapidly and almost made it, but I felt the thump of a contact under my starboard wing. I looked out and saw the biggest f*****g Meteor I had ever seen in my life emerging from under my wing with the top of its fin and rudder still crumpling and folding up. I shouted to Bing over the radio, 'If you haven't got control, bale out now'. I thought for a moment that we were both going for a swim in the North Sea, but he was just playing it cool. In fact we both had pretty near full control and we turned westwards to come home. Mercifully, the weather improved as we crossed the coast and Bingham, the good number two called up saying, 'I have got you in sight. Shall I re-join formation?' To the great amusement of all the others on that radio frequency, I exploded: 'Don't ever come within a f*****g mile of me ever again!' We both got home OK, but Bing's rudder was jammed, so on the landing run he had no brake control and ran off the side of the runway. The gash under my wing had increased the stalling speed, so I just approached a bit faster than usual. That was that – great mirth all round and drinks in the bar. It was the way we operated. A band of brothers, pushing our luck, but it underlined the robustness of the Meteor.

"The weaknesses of the aircraft was its limited range, poor instrumentation, absence of navigation aids and limited radio equipment, which nearly landed me in trouble a while later. One of my chums from pilot training days, Bob Ewing, was a Scot who had emigrated to Canada, where he later became a considerable figure in the educational establishment. He had let me know that he was coming over to see his parents in Edinburgh and I had a couple of days spare at that time, so I naturally asked our squadron commander, Tommy Turnbull, if I could borrow an aircraft for an extended cross-country navigation exercise. 'Of course dear boy, no problem at all; take mine.' His aircraft was rather distinctive with a bright orange painted tail. A day or so later I headed off, clad of course in civvies under my flying overalls and with an overnight bag in the ammunition bay. Bumbling along quite happily at 35 grand along the east coast, about half way to Edinburgh, I thought I had better give them a shout at Turnhouse because the weather was a bit mucky. To my surprise, I found that the approach frequency there was blocked by a BBC Test Match commentary. I thought that was rather nice, drifting along at M.7 and 35 grand, though I might have spun in from the shock when an England batsman was out. Then came the thought, what if the channel remain blocked as I descended to Turnhouse? What if the weather was bad there, how much fuel would I have left to divert? Discretion being the better part of valour, I lobbed in to Acklington which was a master diversion airfield some 20 miles north of Newcastle on Tyne, all straightforward with a couple of radio bearings to let down over the sea and home straight back in. I parked the aircraft and said to the ground crew guys, 'I am on my way to Edinburgh, Turnhouse but the weather is a bit dodgy so I thought I'd better pick up some more fuel. Just fill it up, it will be about 500 gallons.' There I was, obviously in civvies with a fancy-painted aeroplane but nobody worried and I bogged off again at low level below the weather up the coast, up the estuary and into Turnhouse where another Auxiliary squadron looked after my aircraft for a couple of days. It was in that way that we operated, enormously informal.

"It did get serious at times. We were in the midst of the Cold War and we always played our part in the annual defence of Great Britain exercise. The North Weald Wing consisted of 601 and 604 Auxiliary Sqns and our regular colleagues on 111 (who had earlier replaced 72 Sqn). So normally we would muster 30 aircraft in the wing. We would be flung into the air as the Americans flying B-29s played the role of the Russians, who had B-29 copies, coming across the North Sea. We were marshalled to go out to intercept them and if it all worked as it should, the North Weald Wing would meet up with the Duxford and Waterbeach Wings and you would have three wings totalling almost 100 fighters. Manoeuvring 100 aeroplanes is no easy task for the fighter controllers or the formation leaders, particularly if you have to do much turning which required crossovers of aircraft within flights, flights within squadrons, squadrons within wings and wings within the whole Balbo. At the critical moment, half way through a turn you would be in a vertical stack of aircraft thousands of feet deep. The possibility of mishaps was enormous.

"But if it all went well, the first interception would be made head-on at a closing speed of 1,000 mph. That way, the B-29s could bring less guns to bear on you and your shells that hit the front of the enemy would go the length of the aircraft, continuing to do damage all the way. You would complete the head-on attack and then according to your fancy, pull over, or duck under the bomber. I usually went under because there was no tail fin to avoid, less guns to bear and less pictures of me on the American gunners' cine film. The scenes were quite remarkable. The second wave of fighters would be vectored about 3,000 to 5,000 feet above the bombers and would do rolling attacks, over on to their backs then pulling through into a vertical dive, again to limit the number of guns able to be brought to bear on them. I think the Americans found it all quite exciting, although somehow I think they were slightly more serious than we were. Once through the bomber formation, we fighter pilots were looking around. Is there anyone else in sight? Except my number two, if I am lucky. There were remarkably few incidents, although a Pole of my acquaintance lost the pitot head from the leading edge of his wing on a B-29 propeller blade, but by the time the following blade came round, his wing was past. Then, ultimately, everyone got home to have a few beers. Rather like the great cavalry battles of the past, nothing like these scenes will ever be seen again with such huge numbers of aircraft clashing in set-piece battles.

"I came memorably unstuck in one such exercise, code-named

Dividend in 1954. It was my own fault, although it was precipitated by the decision taken on high that, as in wartime, the defending fighters would be scrambled regardless of weather conditions. That weekend, the weather was foul. We were scrambled on Saturday afternoon, made our interception well out over the North Sea, but the weather was really thick with nowhere above limits. I was leading a pair and I managed to get some vectors from Waterbeach and descended over the Fens on the basis that there was nothing high enough to hit in most of Norfolk. We broke cloud at about 200 feet, pissing with rain and I suddenly saw a runway below me. I told my number two what I was doing, a procedure turn to find the runway again, by which time we were down to about 100 feet and had bugger all fuel, so we were not going to go anywhere else. A tight 180-degree turn got us lined up with the runway again, landed and skidded to a halt on it; both getting in with sod all fuel and a pretty high heart rate and that was that.

"We stayed there overnight and the next morning 18 July, Sunday, a bit before Holy Communion time, we were at readiness and were quite soon scrambled. Waterbeach had a hump towards the end of the runway, so you could not see the end of it. Off we went, everything was normal, bounding along with my number two tucked closely in on my starboard side. As we came over the hump there was very little runway left. My number two shouted, 'What goes on?' I pulled at the stick but my aircraft (WL132) showed a complete disinclination to get airborne. 'Pull up', I called back 'I'm ploughing in'. I raised the gear, bounced on the belly tank, which ruptured and caught fire, went across the main road, very fortunately early Sunday morning so no-one was coming and into the cornfield on the other side of the road, well on fire. No electrics so the power hood didn't open, pulled the emergency release handle and it still wouldn't open. One could eject, but the seat had a throw of only 60 feet, too little for the 'chute to open and the thought of coming down from that height was not immediately attractive. I tried again, but still the emergency release would not release. 'Try everything', I thought. I unstrapped myself, stood up and put my shoulders against the hood. It has happened to me once or twice in my life....when your life is in imminent danger, several things happen. All the normal restraints which are there to stop you damaging or rupturing yourself, are removed and everything seems to happen very slowly because all your functions including thought, are going very fast. I actually broke the hood rails and pushed it off, got out, staggered a few yards, giggling a bit and sat in that cornfield watching the aircraft burn unchecked. The station fire engines arrived and I asked one of the boys if I could hitch a lift back to sick quarters. I'd got my face pushed in and the stick thrashing around had bashed my legs about quite a bit. It was some years later when I discovered that I also had two compression fractured vertebrae. The station medical officer (MO) sort of tidied me up a bit and I was resting on the bed when a couple of the boys from the fire section came in to see me. They asked very politely if I thought that they would have got there in time to get me out; 'Yes,' I said, 'I think you probably would.' One then said, 'There is just one thing, sir. It would have been nice if you'd told us that you were carrying a full war load (of six hundred 20 mm shells) because they started going off as we were trying to put the fire out!' I hung my head in shame.

"Later, one of the boys from the squadron, Johnny Bishop, drove up from North Weald, picked me up and we drove back to North Weald by which it was time for lunch. The officers' mess at North Weald backs onto the road with a half-moon shape road around the front. Sometimes late at night, we had time trials to see who could drive fastest around the mess. We were highly responsible, closing the road to traffic with red lights borrowed from down the road, and I said, 'I think I could do with a drink'. I walked through the doors, a fairly awful apparition, stained with and smelling of blood and smoke to see there, standing at the bar, our new AOC (Paddy Bandon had been promoted away) and the boys were saying to him that they thought it was a bit f*****g much the way in which the exercise had been run. Fighter Command had lost six aeroplanes and four pilots that weekend. Of course that did not even merit a mention in the newspapers, let alone in Parliament in those days. I heard the AOC say, 'What you chaps have to understand is that fighter aircraft are expendable'. I tapped him on the shoulder and as he turned around and looked at this awful spectacle I said, 'May I quote you at my Court of Enquiry sir?' 'No,' he said 'but would you like a drink?' which I accepted.

"You simply cannot imagine such a conversation these days and not only because a Meteor cost about £30,000 and a modern fighter tens of millions. It was just hilariously different and it was (provided you survived) just enormously fun. It was not until many years later in 2013, when I was carried out of my home at 3.00 am on a stretcher, that I realised that the Waterbeach incident was probably the first of a number of incidents when I had briefly lost full consciousness, which had wrongly been attributed to fatigue but were in fact due to a heart defect. That has now been corrected with a pacemaker.

"I had left my job in publishing and joined BOAC to make a career in civil flying. They had a policy of re-training all their specialist navigators and training all newly recruited pilots to be navigators. I started by doing the written Flight Navigator's examinations, then my practical training, navigating old York freighters by astro and dead reckoning mostly across the Sahara to West Africa. Then on my days off, it would be Whoopee, out to North Weald and back to Meteors. Then one of my fellow 604 pilots had a girlfriend, a nurse at Westminster Hospital, who was giving a party for some of her chums and needed some more men folk to even up the numbers. We did not worry so much in those days about drinking and driving. There were far less cars on the roads and most not capable of more than 50 or 60 mph (except of course Tommy Turnbull's Aston Martin). However, I drew the short straw and was nominated as duty driver and not allowed to drink. One of the nurses arrived off shift a bit late and as almost everyone except we two were somewhat pissed and we were stone cold sober, we got talking and six months later, were married. Now, almost 60 years on, we still are.

"I decided that marriage, BOAC and the RAuxAF could not all co-exist and rather sadly, I resigned from the squadron. I flew with BOAC until 1970 when I was elected to Parliament, which was another of my errors of judgement. The master plan was that I should fight a Labour safe seat in 1970, doing well but not quite well enough to win, then find a safe Tory seat for the next election four or five years later. By then I would have built up a reasonable BOAC pension. So I took on Labour's 7,500 majority at Epping and won by 2,575. I remember waking next morning, my wife beside me, in a hotel bed in Epping and saying, 'Now what have I bloody well done?!' The first thing I had done was to take a 50% pay cut. That pretty well was the end of my flying career. I kept my licence going for a while with Eric Thurston's firm, Thurston Air Taxis, based at Stapleford Tawney. I sometimes used to fly with him and I wrote for a flying magazine a sort of 'Will it fit your garage?' series that got me flying light piston-engine singles and twins and jets from the HS.125 to, biggest of all, a DC-10 off the line at Burbank. A while after having become a minister, I realised I was not getting enough flying practise and recollecting that there is no fool like an old fool I packed flying in."

616 SQN FINNINGLEY AND WORKSOP

Having begun his RAF career as an engineer, **Derek Davies** (known to everyone as 'Moose') was soon able to transfer to flying training and, thereafter, began a lengthy career flying a number of jet fighter types.

"I was stationed at Finningley as an airman electrician and knew 616 Sqn RAuxAF which flew Meteors. Being accepted for aircrew training, I left Finningley to complete the aircrew course followed by the Advanced Flying Course. On finishing that, I was posted to 2nd TAF on 20 (Vampire) Sqn as day fighter/ground attack. On our squadron, we had a Meteor T.7 for training purposes and, on each leave, I visited 616 Sqn to keep in touch and have the odd flight in a Meteor F.8.

"After 2nd TAF, I had to become a flying instructor and was posted to 4 FTS at Swinderby as a Vampire instructor. Swinderby being only a short

616 Squadron pilots. From L to R: Flt Lt 'Moose' Davies, Fg Off Tony Marshall, Fg Off Geoff Holmes, Sqn Ldr George Bain, Hong Kong Auxiliary AF. [Moose Davies]

distance from Finningley, I was able to visit 616 again many times. I used to drive over on Thursday nights to night fly the Meteor F.8 and was there most weekends to achieve yet more flying. The CO and the other officers regarded me as an honorary member of 616. As such, I was issued with my own call sign '1.1'. In all the auxiliary squadrons the call signs were the same, the CO was '1.4', adjutant '1.5', flight commander '1.6' and so on down the line; why I got '1.1', I know not. On one occasion I diverted into Horsham St. Faith to pick up fuel. Apparently in ATC, they phoned the station commander and said, 'There's a 1.1 call sign coming in'. He drove to the airfield expecting at least an air commodore to appear. He was surprised when I got out, but fortunately he knew me and was amused.

"Being a regular attender at 616 and also an instructor, I was able to help their training officer by taking some training sorties. A visitor to the squadron over several weeks was a Sqn Ldr who was CO of the Hong Kong Auxiliary Air Force (who flew Spitfires); it was decided to convert him to Meteors. The training officer and I flew with him and eventually sent him solo. He then flew several sorties until a query from Group Headquarters asked who this civilian flying Meteors was, as apparently the Hong Kong branch had no official standing with the RAF. From then until he left some weeks later, I used to ride in the back seat of the T.7 so he could still fly a Meteor. I performed a few aerobatic displays for the squadron as the auxiliary pilots were not in such current practice. It was a marvellous period of flying, all unofficial and with an excellent bunch of chaps.

"The squadron was going on a fortnight's summer camp to Celle in 2nd TAF and I had organised my leave from Vampire instruction in order to attend. In the evening before departure came the usual briefing and as I entered the room an attempt was made to knock off my hat. I defended by putting up my hand, but the fellow officer assailant had large hands and virtually broke my second finger. I visited sick quarters and medics strapped fingers 1, 2 and 3 together. Back at briefing, the CO said, 'You can't fly like that, travel in the York transport'. I replied, 'I will be all right, the only difficulty being braking' (the brake lever in the Meteor is on the control column so to use it I would have to change hands). It was agreed.

"On the following day I am No.2 to the leader, while 3, 4, 5 and 6 are lined up behind. On lift-off the leader retracted his gear; I would have to wait until slightly later and higher to change hands in order to brake before selecting gear up. Unfortunately, the leader sank down again and in formation with him, I struck the runway with the wheels whilst he touched with his ventral tank. The tank immediately flamed and I could not see any fuselage or tailplane due to the mass of flames. I transmitted, 'Drop the ventral!' and I could hear those behind saying, 'Stop! Stop! Stop!' The leader's hood came off before the ventral dropped. One aircraft behind became airborne and the other three ran off into the bean field at the runway end, where pickers were working. When the ventral tank hit the ground a tremendous shockwave was visible. The leader had his hood off but headset on, so I said, 'Left turn, left turn'; he replied, 'I can see'. The other aircraft in the air called 'What shall I do?' The two of us could have gone to Celle but with the shambles on the ground, I felt we needed to regroup so I said, 'Land after the leader', which he did. The leader had placed his hat alongside his ejector seat. Having taxied in, shut down and got out of the aircraft, we were now walking up and down the airfield looking for his hat. Later I said, 'This is a waste of time, let's go to the crew room'. Passing his parked aircraft I saw his hat was still alongside the ejector seat! From that time he was known as Torch. For the rest of the day we were flying to and from Wymeswold to borrow aircraft from our sister squadron 504 and on the following day we flew to Celle. The three aircraft in the bean field were recovered; all still had wheels down and were not damaged.

"Whilst at Celle, I flew to Oldenburg to visit my old squadron and managed a quick flight in a Sabre. Later I visited again, but on the return flight to Celle I had a fright as both engines flamed out at 35,000 feet due to turbulence and heavy rain in the top of a thunder cloud. They both restarted as the book says at 19,000 feet. Torch saved my life on one occasion when I was flying as No.4 in the section. We were high and I had dropped back and in trying to catch up, I zoomed past the formation. Torch said, 'What are you doing?' I replied, 'You're buggering me about'. Torch immediately lowered the formation and I was in their vicinity. When we were back on the ground it was found that my oxygen pipe had disconnected.

"On one late Sunday afternoon, we were in a six-aircraft formation and the leader took us back across The Wash at low level. The birds were flying south and we met them. I think we had a mainplane, tailplane and two nacelles requiring change. The engineering officer went berserk when we got back. On another flight doing aerobatics above Finningley the port throttle jammed at about ¾ power and to land, I needed to have the port engine shut down. It was found to be a 2BA nut jammed in the throttle slide. One day in 1955, I managed two excitements in one day. First the rudder jammed during an asymmetric approach. Later in the day, I diverted to Horsham St. Faith due to smoke in the cockpit, which was found to be an electrical short circuit under the seat.

"To practise gunnery we fired at a target flag, 30 feet long and six feet deep with a six-foot pole at the front which had a 30 lbs weight at the bottom. This was towed by a Meteor at maximum speed of 180 knots. Our tow was from Finningley or Worksop to the north-east coast. On returning to the airfield, the flag was dropped and the armourers would count the different-coloured holes to assign the scores. One Sunday, a young Plt Off was returning from a tow and as he approached Finningley, a voice said 'Drop'. He pulled the lever and the whole lot dropped through the local church roof. Nobody was injured and the source of the transmission was never established.

"The Meteor was involved in proving to me two things I had never believed. I was in the back of a T.7 over the Frisian Islands with a new squadron member checking his spin recovery. I said, 'Put it into a left-hand spin, do not recover until I say so'. After three turns I said, 'Recover', nothing happened. I again said, 'Recover'. He replied, 'Take your foot off the rudder', 'I am not pushing the rudder, recover'. We were wearing the leather helmets which had a large open horseshoe shape at the rear where the wires entered above this hole and it was possible to see a lot of the back of the head. Sitting in the back, still spinning, I saw his hair go stiff and stand out. I said, 'On the count of three, kick the rudder'. Magically it loosened up, we recovered and flew back to Oldenburg. The engineers discovered something wrong with the turnbuckles on the rudder control cables.

"The second non-belief happened thus: our T.7 kept having radio failure. This was not good in some of the weather we flew in, radio being our only means of recovering to the airfield in complete cloud cover. The radio mechanics kept trying but still it failed. I was adjutant at the time and through the interlinking office door, the boss shouted 'I am fed up with the T.7, we're going to lose the aircraft and perhaps one of the younger pilots if we're not careful. I want you to take it over until it's fixed.' The next day we flew to Sylt for three weeks armament practice. I flew the T.7 and true to form, the radio failed en route. I asked the Cpl radio mechanic to change as many components as possible and then it surely must be the wiring.

Moose Davies 616 Squadron. [Moose Davies]

"When it was done I took the Cpl in the rear seat for the air test. We took off on a glorious sunny day with broken cloud and flew east towards Shleswigland where there was complete cloud cover. Above this cloud we were not really expecting a failure due to the components change but after 20 minutes, we had a dead radio. I removed my mask and shouted, 'It's gone again, where do you think the airfield is?' I wanted him to appreciate the problem. We headed west back into sunshine and bumpy cloud. It was quite turbulent and the Cpl said he would be sick. Having landed back at Sylt and parked, the hood would only open two inches. I asked if he had anything jammed in the hood but no, the Cpl is quite sick and the smell is awful. Chiefy had appeared and I am saying, 'Get it open chief or I can jettison the hood'. (The hood jettison on the T.7 only tips it to 30 degrees, it is the airflow which takes it over the tail). Chiefy manages to partially elevate the hood so I can slide out. At this point I turned to look at the Cpl in the rear seat and his face was bright green! Before these two happenings I did not believe that hair stood on end or that somebody really could turn green.

"I had a good time flying Meteors on a course at the Central Gunnery School (CGS), Leconfield. We spent much time at altitude attacking a fellow Meteor using cine cameras. At times by way of a change we attacked a Lincoln bomber. Often, when returning from high altitude I would spin down, which was a fairly fast way of alternate descent. However the CGS staff found out and said I was disturbing the gunsights. I felt it was rubbish but returned to normal descents.

"The joy of Meteor flying ceased for me on 10 March 1957 when all Auxiliary squadrons were disbanded. The then government felt fighter aircraft were no longer needed, yet here we are in 2016 and fighter aircraft are still being used."

The axe fell on all the RAuxAF squadrons in January 1957, when it was announced that they would all disband forthwith, the formal date of closure being as Moose says 10 March, by which time they had ceased flying anyway, their aircraft all being ferried away for storage and for the most part, scrapping. The main reason given was that with the Meteor and Vampire fast approaching obsolescence, it was considered that part-time units would not be up to the job of operating more sophisticated types such as the Hunter. In parallel, the impending 1957 Defence White Paper forecasting the end of manned fighters in the near future, clearly had a part to play in the decision and the weekend flyers were required no more.

CHAPTER FOUR

'WE STALK BY NIGHT'* –
NOCTURNAL METEORS

THE BOYS

Flt Lt Peter Bogue
Joined in 1950. Trained on Meteors at 206 AFS, 228 OCU, 85 and 153 Sqns West Malling, Base Flight Seletar Meteor, Search and Rescue OTU and Leconfield Flt, Whirlwinds in Indonesian Confrontation, HQ Air Support Command. Retired 1968.

Sqn Ldr Mike Kemp
Four-year engagement from 1952. Trained in Canada. 46 Sqn 1954, left air force 1956. Re-joined 1964. 47 Sqn Beverley, 30 Sqn Hercules, Italian AF C-130, 24 Sqn Hercules, MoD, SHAPE. Retired 1992.

Gp Capt Kel 'Johnny' Palmer
228 OCU 1952, 96 Sqn Ahlhorn, NF.12 and 14, instructor 228 OCU, 23 Sqn Javelin, MoD, Air Staff Cyprus, director College of Air Warfare, MoD, SHAPE. Retired 1983.

Flt Lt Norman Spence
Joined in 1951. Nav/radar. 96 Sqn Ahlhorn 1952-55, 228 OCU, 238 OCU, Javelin Mobile Training Unit. Retired 1959.

Sgt Peter Verney
Volunteered in 1950, Nav/radar. 228 OCU, 39 Sqn Mosquito then NF.13, 152 Sqn NF.12 and 14, staff navigator 1 Air Electronics School. Retired 1958.

With further contribution from Peter Rogers (Chapter Two).

AN INTERIM SOLUTION
Recognising that with the rapid advancement of the jet age the Mosquito night fighter would soon become obsolete, Specification F.44/46 was issued for a replacement on 24 January 1947. However, none of the designs submitted in response was considered suitable and much further work was needed, meaning there would be an extended delay in procuring the desired all weather day and night fighter, which would ultimately emerge as the Gloster Javelin. To fill the gap Glosters were asked to produce an interim night fighter variant of the Meteor which emerged in

---

* The motto of 96 Sqn who flew Meteor night fighters from November 1952 to January 1959.

1950 as the NF.11, the work having been contracted to Armstrong Whitworth at Coventry who were to build all of them. These Meteors may well have been less than satisfactory, but they were at least something of an advance on the Mosquito.

The first NF.11 was delivered to 29 Sqn at Tangmere in July 1951 and eventually no fewer than 22 squadrons were equipped with the type. It served primarily in the UK and Germany, plus two squadrons in Egypt and one – No.60 – in Singapore which had the distinction of being the last unit to fly any Meteor in a front-line role.

EGYPT

Peter Verney flew in both the Mosquito NF.36 and the tropicalised Meteor NF.13 during his service with 39 Sqn in Egypt before going on to the NF.12 and 14 on his return to England.

Peter Verney about to climb into his NF.13 39 Squadron, Kabrit. The protective rubber mats didn't last. [Peter Verney]

"I volunteered for aircrew in 1950 when I was 18. You did about four or five days at Hornchurch doing all sorts of IQ tests and they said, 'Your results said that you will be a navigator', end of story. I signed on for eight years, you had to then if you wanted to fly. After training on Mosquitos at OCU, I was posted out to Egypt, which p****d me off enormously because all the squadrons in England were being re-equipped with the Meteor; I wanted to fly these fancy jets. There were two squadrons – which hadn't long been formed – still with the Mosquito, so we had them at Kabrit on 39 Sqn. I was very disappointed about it, but I'm now very proud that I had a year or so on them. We went out there in February '52 and in March '53 we changed over to the Meteor NF.13. With the Mosquitos we used to do these exercises when they would put us up as bombers during the day. There were three or four Vampire squadrons in the Canal Zone as day fighter defence and they would be put up to intercept us.

"I am very proud that my squadron commander Sqn Ldr Cogill* and I were, I believe, the very last squadron crew to fly a Mosquito night fighter. We brought NF.36 RL141 home from the Middle East to Benson, arriving on 25 July 1953. They had about four or five Mossies left over in the MUs being repaired and the ferry pilots would bring out a Meteor and pick up a Mosquito. Crews were given a chance to have a leave at home by taking one back to the UK, so he took this last one and took me with him."

* Sqn Ldr John Cogill was awarded the DSO and DFC flying Mosquitos on 142 and 192 Sqns.

"My pilot Joe Halkiew, was a first class pilot who was first on the squadron to obtain his master green instrument rating on the Mosquito. When we were upgraded to the Meteor we got the occasional trip in the T.7 which had been sent out for the pilots to train on. Joe Halkiew was an excellent aerobatic pilot and vainly tried to teach me to do a neat barrel roll. He also let me take it round the landing circuit, but took over when I was lined up for touchdown. Dick Grant was our gunnery officer on the squadron, a Plt Off who I guess had been an NCO and was a good lad; I used to help him. The Mosquito had a fixed ring sight and you did

39 Squadron change over from Mosquito NF.36 to Meteor NF.13, Kabrit, March 1953, WM313 newly arrived. [Peter Verney]

a lot of cine practice firing and those films had to be assessed frame by bloody frame. I used to do a lot of that for him and was quite friendly with him, so he gave me a trip in the Meatbox.

"We were to be re-equipped at the start of 1953 with the tropicalised

NF.13 but there was some delay in producing them. The Mosquito had a glue joint inspection at set intervals and if an aircraft failed to meet the required tolerance, it was scrapped. So eventually we ran short of Mosquitos and in late 1952, 219 Sqn was temporarily re-equipped with the Meteor NF.11, a technical conference was held and the glue joint tolerance was increased to allow us to continue with the Mosquito. In due course we ran short again and another technical conference decided that perhaps this glue joint problem was not important and could be ignored until the Meteors arrived!

"I think I'm one of the very few navs who have flown all four marks of the night fighter. We were the last people flying these Mosquitos, which were falling to pieces at quite a rate of knots by then and the other squadron out there, 219, had re-equipped with NF.11s (the NF.13s weren't yet ready). So they sent out a batch of NF.11s and we were given a couple at odd times to play with.

"We were periodically sent off on a navigation exercise, generally either to Luqa in Malta or Habbaniyah in Iraq. These made us work as it was necessary to land and refuel along the way, going to Habbaniyah meant Mafra in northern Jordan, while to Luqa meant El Adem in Libya – if there was a strong headwind then Benina in Libya in addition. The first time we landed at Benina was the first time I went on one of these jollies. We were part of a flight of three NF.13s, which we had only had for about a fortnight. When we came to leave Benina, one engine would not start so the other two went on without us and we had to wait for a servicing party to come by road about 200 miles from El Adem to fix it. As a result, we were there for four days and missed out on Malta. Flt Lt Ted Carlisle had a major electrical failure prior to take-off with the rest of us to fly home; we needed to get back to Kabrit. He said, 'I can't use my electrics and all the rest of it, so I want to formate on you on the way back', which he did, no radio or anything.

"The Mossie was vibration – noise. Three or four hours in a Mossie and your head was solid, whereas I wouldn't say the Meteor was silent but it was a lot quieter, a lot smoother. Of course it went a couple of hundred miles an hour quicker and about 10,000 feet higher. I liked the Meteor and I've heard it described as a gentleman's aeroplane – it was a good solid aeroplane. It was very difficult for pilots to convert from a single seater to having some idiot in the back telling them what to do – a lot of pilots couldn't trust the navs. If you imagine, on a black night, the idiot in the back is saying, 'We're at 600 feet, turn port hard', it must have been quite difficult for some of them to accept that they'd got to do what they were told. I stuck one into a few pilots I can tell you, including one Sqn Ldr!

"We were doing a formation of four take-off, one in the box and a vic. Joe Preston was leading with the T.7, which in retrospect was a

39 Squadron T.7 WL431 after failed formation take-off with NF.13s, Kabrit, 13 May 1953. [Peter Verney]

stupid thing to have done with three NF.13s. I was quite a keen photographer and wanted to take a picture of it getting airborne. Of course he raced away from us, being a lot lighter and I suddenly realised that we were then closing on him, so I took a picture. As I took the camera away from my eyes, I could see he was going back relative to us and as I lost sight of him, his belly tank was touching the runway. He'd realised he'd run away from us, throttled back, realised then that we were getting to him and opened

39 Squadron T.7 WL431 taking off in a failed formation attempt with NF.13, Kabrit, 13 May 1953. [Peter Verney]

up. On the Derwent, the throttle lag was tremendous and it just didn't happen and he went sailing a couple of hundred yards off the end of the runway on his belly tank.* That was hilarious!"

*This happened on 13 May 1953 and despite only suffering minimal damage, T.7 WL431 was not repaired.

Ad hoc 39 Squadron formation including WM310 and WM315 F. [Peter Verney]

"The first attempt by the Egyptians to remove us, was inspired by King Farouk in a desperate attempt to gain some popularity; he was deposed by General Neguib in July '52. Neguib was replaced by Colonel Nasser in mid '53, which led to yet another stand-off. Each time we would sit in the crew room with the aircraft armed up waiting for orders to carry out our part in a grand plan, which would see Britain attack and sort out the Egyptian military once and for all.

"There was considerable attention paid to gunnery, especially air to ground and we had a range at Shallufa some 15 miles from Kabrit. Here we would regularly go firing both by day and at night. The night air to ground was very interesting and navigators had to read off the altimeter to persuade the pilots to break off at a briefed 400 feet. The targets, ten-foot canvas squares, were marked at night by three gooseneck flares, one each side and one at such a distance to the rear as to be invisible if the dive angle was less than the briefed 30 degrees. My pilot was a press-on type and would go a bit closer, but he normally managed a good score. It was necessary after firing to pull up and turn sharply to avoid ricochets from the rocky desert and 219's CO had a very unnerving experience. He had closed the throttles to reduce speed to get a good steady run at the target, but on breaking away he opened up abruptly while turning port and the aircraft promptly rolled on its back. He had the presence of mind to hold the stick over and complete the roll, but at well below 400 feet at night, his nav was not best pleased. During day firing, it was normal to see local women and children running about underneath the aircraft, picking up the spent 20-mm brass cases as they fell.

"Most of our time was spent on practice interceptions under GCI control, doing the odd cross-country, much cine-gun work and single-engine practice. The pilots were required to do one single-engine landing and two single-engine overshoots per month so that they could cope when the real emergency arose, luckily for Joe and I, it never did. These were fun at night, when a decision to land had to be made while at 800 feet on one engine."

WATTISHAM

"I finished my two and a half year tour with Joe and then we were posted home. We came to RAF 'What-a-shame' on 152 Sqn, which had only been formed about three or four months prior with NF.12 and 14. They had the APS 21 radar, which was and wasn't better than the Mk.10 – both were American radars. The display was poor compared to the Mk.10 but the range was much better; that was a 3-cm radar and the Mk.10 was a 10-cm radar. The Mk.21 had a wedge-shaped screen and it meant that even if somebody did an evasive manoeuvre at close range, you were lost because his image was just squeezed up in a corner of the screen and you couldn't really detect the lateral movement. That was a serious flaw in my mind, plus the fact that when we joined the squadron, those already there had had a session with a Brigand trainer and the navs had been trained on it, but when we came along a few months later, we didn't get any instruction at all. Luckily there was a Flt Sgt nav there who I'd met at Leeming when he was an instructor and he took me out to one of the aircraft. I sat in the cockpit, he hung over the side and he told me how to switch the thing on and what the controls did. That was all the

152 Squadron NF.14 line-up at Wattisham headed by WS754 D. [152 Squadron Association]

instruction I got on it – typical air force; it was a shambles! The radars weren't very reliable, four or five trips and something would go wrong. Both Wattisham squadrons were short of navigators, so I was flying with all sorts of different pilots. They tried to boost up the numbers of navigators but they never seemed to really catch up.

"There was an annual big NATO exercise when you'd get scrambled after different odds and sods playing silly whatsits. We were being used as day fighters and were on one of these, Exercise Vigilant, when the hood opened at 38,000 feet, which was a very entertaining experience; that was on my last trip with that pilot and he'd never had the hood properly locked in the first place. The night before, we'd done a trip and I'd made a mess of intercepting a Valiant. The target was too fast and we hit his slipstream very badly which just about turned us over; I was partly at fault and so was the pilot. It was always the case on those sort of things that you'd be scrambled too late, you'd still be climbing when you started your interception. It used to annoy me, they'd burble away saying, 'We've got a target for you, range…' what height, speed and track it was doing and so on, but they wouldn't scramble us. They'd keep us waiting and waiting and then say 'Scramble' when someone had worked out that when we got to the top of our climb we'd be in position to intercept. We were climbing like mad at very slow speed and I'd not made a sufficient adjustment on the radar to pick him up, I don't think I'd lowered the scan properly. So I never saw him until quite close range, shouted a turn, then the pilot saw him, started to turn and we went straight into the slipstream very close behind him – I think we were lucky not to hit it. The pilot lost control virtually and although we got back behind this target, it was going away from us as we still hadn't got speed up and we had to abandon it.

"The Meteor was outclassed by this time. We did exercises against Canberras, but they had to be told not to go above 40,000 feet or so because they could just sail away from us. I went after a B-45 once when they'd put us out to just over the North Sea as this thing was heading inland. We came in late and were still climbing when we got the turn onto the target. Then it was a matter of dive to get up speed, pull up to get to his height, dive again to get the speed back, about four switchbacks like that before we caught the thing. On practice intercepts, the Americans used to join in and bounce us in their F-84Fs from Shepherds Grove. When we turned into them and they tried to tighten their turn, they couldn't and fell out of the turn into a spin. I remember a couple of times looking below us to see an F-84F spiralling down until I lost him.

"Once we were on Operation Fabulous and we used to have to go to Waterbeach every so often to be on standby. The briefing was that they were afraid that the Russians might sneak an atom bomb in and we were there to intercept any unidentified aircraft. You'd got the guns loaded, it was all for real, except that the terms of engagement were absolutely stupid. You had to approach this aircraft, recognise it, tell the controllers what it was and you'd get further instructions what to do. You'd then got to fly up alongside it and attract the pilot's attention – at night at 40,000 feet. You'd got to try and contact him by radio and failing that you'd then got to fly across in front of him and direct him to land. If he didn't take any notice, you'd then got to draw up alongside him and lower your undercarriage to indicate he'd got to land. With a Meteor, the drag would just have knocked you out of the sky. Of course it never happened; all we ever intercepted were American B-45s.

"One of our better pilots decided one day to do a practice single-engine overshoot. He slightly misjudged the speed and we crabbed across the airfield while he struggled to get climbing speed. I vividly remember looking down on a hangar roof as we were just starting to climb. By then, I'd been put off the squadron because I'd more or less done my time. My pilot was posted away before I finished on the squadron, so I was flying with gash pilots all the time.

"At the end of my time, they'd abandoned Meteor nav training; the Javelin was coming in and they didn't need half the crews because they were cutting the air force down in a big way. We were told we'd done two tours and when you'd done that, you had to have a rest tour, you couldn't do another flying tour. Another rumour was that NCO aircrew would not get onto a front-line squadron again. My last trip on the squadron was on 27 May 1957 and I left the air force the following year."

Plt Off Pete Bogue, Flt Sgt Jock
Armour instructor, and another pilot
name unknown, 228 OCU Leeming.
[Peter Bogue]

WEST MALLING

Having learned to fly the Meteor at Oakington and to operate it as a night fighter at Leeming, **Peter Bogue** was posted to 85 Sqn at West Malling in Kent, later moving over to 153 Sqn on the same station.

"I finished at Oakington on 28 November 1952 and then I went to the night fighter OCU at Leeming where I picked up Alan Meredith, my navigator and the pair of us went off to get our first solo on type in an NF.11 on 16 January 1953. The course lasted until 10 March and then we started at 85 Sqn West Malling on 8 April. They still had NF.11s then, there were one or two NF.12s but they got rid of them in the end and we solely had NF.14s. We had APS Mk.10 radar in the NF.11, which had a nominal range of five miles – you could usually reckon to get two – then we had the APS Mk.21 in the NF.14, which was actually about a 21-mile range; we didn't always get that. The layout in the cockpit was much nicer than the earlier Meteors; you didn't have a spade grip, you had a sort of little pistol grip with buttons all over it. It was a nicer aeroplane to fly and of course, the NF.14 had this lovely blown canopy. The engines gradually got uprated, we ended up with the Derwent 9 but they weren't that much more powerful. As an aeroplane, first of all, it was not very well balanced; it was heavy in roll, it was OK in pitch and you never used the rudders unless you lost an engine – or you didn't appear to. It did tend to yaw and they were all fitted with yaw dampers eventually. But as a night fighter, it was very good.

"I think we were all very good at what we did and we would intercept targets in cloud and terrible weather at night, by day, whatever. There was only one slight snag, because if we'd taken on Mr Bulganin (Russian defence minister), we would have had to send a message and say, 'Please can you slow your aircraft down and not fly so high?' because we couldn't catch them. I would have said a fighting ceiling was 30,000 feet but we could go up quite comfortably to 40,000 feet. Bearing in mind that we weren't going to dogfight, we were going to get behind a target and shoot it down from behind, it was all right. A lot of our sorties were practice interceptions, the RAF had Washingtons and Lincolns and we chased those. We chased Canberras but I don't think we could actually catch one unless they co-operated – they could fly higher than we could anyway. Alan and I tried to get up to 50,000 feet; we got to, I think it was 47,600 feet and we were so bored, we gave up!

"From time to time, the powers-that-be put on an exercise and Momentum was one where we were deployed to Thornaby. They were doing an intensive trial to see if we could do three or four trips a night; I must say, we were fairly well knackered by the end of it. We did quite a few of those and Alan and I chased a Canberra all the way from the east coast and we came down short of fuel at Hooton Park.

"We transferred across to 153 Sqn on the same station; it was in the days when the RAF was very large and the number of fighter squadrons was incredible. The Meteor F.8s were going out and we had one on the squadron as a target tug. I was a pilot attack instructor, so I used to

Plt Off Pete Bogue and his navigator Alan Meredith lead the gang of 85 Squadron crews in a posed shot at West Malling. [Peter Bogue]

sometimes tow the banners or the glider. I was supposed to make more holes in the target than anyone else, but I don't know if I ever did. In fact one of the problems was (they wouldn't let me do it), I wanted to spot harmonise the guns because they were on the wings and they were a spread harmonisation. They did say that if you were doing a quarter attack the wings would flex and where the gunsight was aiming was not were the guns were aiming. Whether this was actually true or not, I don't know, but the proof of the pudding was, we didn't hit the target. If you were flying a Meteor F.8, you had the guns in the nose and they were more or less spot harmonised and you could get 20 or 30 holes in the target if you were lucky. The F.8 was fun.

"On 85 Sqn, we had our own aircraft and mine was WS737. You did not always fly your own aircraft but usually did. We helped to clean the thing on Saturday mornings and got to know the ground crew thereby. Alan and I 'bagged' a whole 5-gallon drum of Sinec Perspex polish and our 'crew' polished the whole aircraft with it. It shone and we swore it was quicker! The 100-gallon drop tanks we carried on the NF.11/12/14 frequently imploded during a fast descent. Apparently the water trap in the system froze and air could not enter the tanks – they fitted the component upside-down and all was well. Another peculiarity of the Meteor was the pressurisation system. The aircraft was pressurised to 25,000 feet at 40,000 feet, at least that was what we were told. On one occasion we started up, closed the canopy and got neat fuel out of the holes drilled in the pipes round the canopy, which were meant to deliver pressurised air. We also had an armoured glass windscreen which sometimes iced-up and defied all attempts to clear it.　However, we did have a clear vision panel on the left-hand side, which could be opened to allow a brief glimpse of the outside. We often got St Elmo's Fire in vertical streaks on the windscreen and, occasionally, horizontal lines as well. So very pretty – in spite of rumours to the contrary, Meatbox pilots did have some soul!

"They were good and carefree days at West Malling when the RAF was led by ex-wartime 'names' and still had some of the old spirit left. We got away with murder then."

GERMANY

A couple of years after Peter Verney had gone through the night fighter OCU at Leeming, **Kel 'Johnny' Palmer** did the course where he had some pretty hair-raising experiences. After finally graduating safely he left for his first tour to RAF Germany and 96 Sqn at Ahlhorn, which had a mixture of NF.12s and NF.14s.

"In 1952, I was selected to fly night fighters and started my conversion programme on the Mosquito at Leeming, knowing that I'd be finishing it on the then new Meteor NF.11. It was an exciting time, with the slight disappointment that we didn't get many hours on the wonderful old Mossie before the thrill of the new aircraft. Looking back, the course can rightly be described as mayhem. Out of a starting line-up of 11 crews, we lost over half to flying and motorbike accidents that either killed them or caused injuries that ended their flying days or retarded their training. We actually lost one pilot to an irate wife who literally walked into the crew room one night and dragged him out by the ear, never to be seen again!

"It may have been a coincidence, but the crew numbers we lost were replaced on the course by three French crews, who always flew as a French duo as their English was decidedly dicey. With three of our instructors being Polish, two hailing from deepest Ireland and one a Highlander, there were nights when the circuit at Leeming was like a madhouse with the excited babble of the French clashing with frequent Polish-accented cries of 'Do bloody something!' Order and calm reigned only when we were under air traffic control or fighter intercept control by the soft-voiced unflappable young WRAF officers. Not only was their pronunciation so good and their words so clear, but they took the trouble – not being aircrew themselves – to find out what it was like on a GCA at 300 feet on a dark and dirty Yorkshire night, or trying to find another Meteor at 20,000 feet with a duff radar and the navigator throwing up his night

A fine study of an 85 Squadron NF.14 WS723. [Adrian Balch collection]

flying supper in the back.

"One such night we were on our final check ride joining the circuit and being told by ATC that we were number three to land with one on finals and one downwind ahead. It was a pitch-dark night with rain lashing against the hood and the brightness of the runway lights on the port side, making sighting of another aircraft's navigation lights almost impossible. Neither of us could see the aircraft ahead and as we turned onto finals, a shrill French voice shouted hesitantly, 'Bellboy 20, downwind – at Leeming, Dishforth or Linton'. Apart from being somewhere in Yorkshire, he was lost and was actually in the Dishforth circuit some 12 miles south. Almost simultaneously, I heard the tower say, 'Bellboy 22, you are lined up on the Great North Road, overshoot and re-join downwind'. Even as the exclamation 'Bloody French' reached my lips, I sensed, rather than saw, a black shape loom out of the glare from the runway lights and pass so close over our canopy that I distinctly saw a spinning wheel extremely close to my right earhole. For a split second, I waited for the noise or feel that would herald the departure of our tailplane. This was the third of our French farces that had tried to land in the wrong direction and had mistaken the overshoot command to 22 as being for him. He had landed the wrong way and without the tower knowing where he was, I suspect he'd have been very surprised at our arrival straight down his throat. That could have spoiled the whole day for at least four more of us. It was a Friday night in early October; we had all landed from our second sorties that night at around midnight and after a quick debrief, shower and change of clothing, we dashed back to the mess for a traditional night flying supper of bacon, eggs, beans, tomatoes and fried bread. In the dining room sat the senior ATC controller whose only comment about the mayhem that had been his circuit 45 minutes ago was, 'If that daft sod (Bellboy 22 at Dishforth) doesn't get here soon, the kitchen will have packed up'. I wonder why we weren't all nervous wrecks! Had that happened in the Honington circuit in the '70s when I was the boss, I'd have hung up a few guys. If that happened today, the entire Air Force Board would sit on the Courts Martial.

"At 08:00 on Christmas Eve, we turned up at briefing to hear whether we'd each be able to fly our three remaining sorties and go home for Christmas as properly converted crews. 'Tell you what we'll bloody do', said our Polish instructor, 'if the weather improves and we have good diversions, we'll fly your final day sortie, followed by a dusk night flying test and do the final check ride tonight. Stay kitted up, don't leave the hangar and don't break the aeroplanes – we've only got five serviceable.' The weather became flyable at noon, so two pairs of aircraft plus the chase instructor, roared off into solid black clouds at 600 feet to emerge at 26,000 feet to complete our day interception techniques. We landed around 2 p.m. and took off again at dusk into a still 600 feet cloud base, emerging into a blue and orange twilight at 30,000 feet. We checked our radars for our 'finals' that night, then recovered via GCA close to our Meteor experience limits, to land at 6 p.m. Two down, big one to go.

"At 7 p.m., Met reckoned the cloud base had dropped to 500 feet – still just acceptable – and we should be able to get back OK if we landed by 9 p.m., or we'd be diverted to Norfolk or Scotland – not the ideal Christmas present. At 7.30, we took off in stormy pitch-blackness to emerge into star-filled heavens at 30,000 feet. My pair completed their final interceptions to become operational on the NF.11 and immediately started recovery to Leeming on instruments all the way. We broke the dicey cloud base at 400 feet and splashed down in visibility of 200 yards. The smokers had a quick nervous drag, showered and in 30 minutes were scoffing their night flying suppers in our ever-so comfortable officers' mess.

"Now that we had completed the course, we were going overseas brim full of enthusiasm; Dusty to 256 Sqn, the rest of us to 96 Sqn at Ahlhorn. When we arrived there in November 1952, we didn't have a single operational aircraft on base. RAF Germany was expanding rapidly to counter the growing Warsaw Pact threat and new squadrons were forming every month with Meteors, Sabres and Venoms distributed around the 12 northern airfields. The Meteors destined for Ahlhorn had been delivered to Wahn outside Cologne and the squadron commander gathered us all together to tell us that he would be delivering our first aircraft the next day. We sprogs were to gather at the runway caravan to observe how to land an NF.11 on an icy snow-covered runway. This, of course, was a splendid idea coming from an experienced pilot with many rare jet hours; a sort of mother hen teaching chick that had been flying jets for only four months and picking up some 80 hours, but none of them in runway conditions such as these.

"Early the next morning, Ahlhorn's entire aircrew population stood huddled by the caravan in driving snow as Joe Crowshaw's Meteor came screaming in out of the murk above the pine forest, touched down in a flurry of snow and proceeded to go off the far end of the runway still doing around 60 knots. As the RAF bus passed the end of the runway on our way back to the squadron, we saw what was left of our first aircraft strewn between the poles of the approach lights with the cockpit embedded in a thick hedge and surrounded by curious German cows. Fifteen minutes later we all sprang to our feet in the crew room as Joe stomped in, glowered at us as if defying anyone to say a word, and growled, 'I've just demonstrated how not to land a Meteor on snow; this afternoon I'll show you how it's really done', and he did – a most capable and professional pilot.

"I had another reason to think well of Joe after a night exercise involving four Meteors. It was unusual to put four aircraft in close proximity at night, even though we had AI radar. Two of us had only 60 hours on type, the others being Joe and another experienced pilot. We set up an intercept at 30,000 feet with two pairs head on, no lights, no moon, and pitch-black. I picked up the other pair at around 20 miles, manoeuvred to slide in behind them and either misjudged the final turn-in, or they turned towards us. Suddenly, the distinct 'blip' on my screen disintegrated, losing range and angle-off data. Levelling out abruptly and throttling back, a huge black mass filled the canopy as someone screamed abuse that was not in the training manual. Joe calmly transmitted 'Let's go home', leaving me sat in the dark aware of creating a situation that had put three aircraft in serious danger of collision. I taxied in to be met with, 'I've never seen another aircraft that close at night – you're for the high jump mate!' from my navigator; I was too worried to respond. Along came Joe saying, 'Get changed Johnny, grab a beer and we'll swap stories about the night we scratched the paint off four new Meteors'. We did just that, recommended adjustments to the radars, amended our procedures to make night flying safer and save my blushes into the bargain.

"Those were golden days; days to look back on fondly. More importantly, I think we all knew we were special at the time. We had so much going for us; 96 Sqn had 16 crews for 12 aircraft and with the exception of the CO and his two flight commanders (ages 27/28), the rest of us were first tourists ages 21-23. Few were married, so the mess was full of young men having the time of their lives, accentuated by having two identically equipped squadrons with intense but friendly rivalry. Being specialist night fighters, our daily routine was to fly a night-flying test of radar in the afternoon, followed by two night sorties each of around one hour 30 minutes, which usually saw us finished by 11 p.m. in the winter or 4 a.m. in the summer. We carried out armament practice camps for air-to-air firing and flew dozens of exercises to keep us in shape in case the Russian sabre rattling turned to all-out war. We flew hard, but we played hard too.

"On one major exercise, we were bound for a new RAF airfield at Brüggen that we were to occupy with other 2nd TAF Meteor, Sabre, Vampire and Venom squadrons. Our 'enemy' was the 4th TAF USAF based in Bavaria, plus RAF Bomber Command operating from the UK. 96 Sqn was selected (or perhaps fingered) to lead a multi-squadron, multi-type formation that left Ahlhorn and picked up en route the Sabre wing from Oldenburg, Vampires from Jever and Venoms from Fassberg, which meant that SATCO at Brüggen had to segregate, land and park around 100 short-endurance aircraft on his brand new base. Near Fassberg the turning radius of such a large formation led to us coming awfully close to infringing the border and just to complicate matters, our American 'enemy' decided to bounce the arriving formation. As a lowly Fg Off, I

Early morning at Sylt, 256 Squadron NF.11s from Ahlhorn led by WD776 T-U. [Brian Phillips]

saw only the funny side in such a melee, but there must have been senior officers who died a thousand deaths at the potential for disaster.

"It was a sunny and warm Exercise Day 2 as we night fighter crews lazed on the grass aircraft-watching, our favourite custom. Our sister squadron, 256, had a pair airborne on night-flying tests and as they broke downwind they were intercepted by two USAF Sabres. The lead Meteor was committed to land, but No.2 cleaned up, accelerated and climbed to swat the offending enemy. We watched them twisting and diving in the bright sunshine, the Meteor outclassed and outnumbered but not letting the Sabres get on his tail. Then one Sabre got too fast, too close and without any noise or explosion, the two aircraft met and simply broke into pieces. The Meteor went into a shallow dive and one parachute emerged, but didn't open and disappeared behind trees. The Sabre fell at first, like a falling leaf with bits separating and then, urged no doubt by the prayers and soundless advice from dozens of watching aviators, recovered into a fast switchback approach to crash alongside the runway. Spontaneous cheers were muted as he suddenly veered off to slide between two refuelling bowsers, before flipping over onto his back and coming to rest in a cloud of dust and debris. We waited for the probable smoke and flickers of flame, but it didn't happen and there was nothing we watchers could do as the crash crews headed to the impact points. I didn't know what to do or feel.

"It seemed the Meteor pilot had transmitted before impact that he couldn't bale out even though his navigator had ejected their canopy. The navigator had left the aircraft only to be decapitated by the tailplane. The Sabre pilot escaped the collision without a scratch, but during rescue from his upturned cockpit had been struck by a fireman's axe and received serious head injuries; however he was to make a full recovery. Two other witnesses of the accident never flew again and became air traffic control officers. My reaction, as with later flying accidents, was a vacancy of feeling that I have never been able to express.

"After three wonderful years in Germany, I became an instructor on the night fighter OCU at North Luffenham. In flying terms, it was my least interesting tour in that we were simply a sausage machine for turning out night/all-weather fighter crews for the then dozens of squadrons in the UK and overseas.

"We each live in our own bubbles and I'm frequently amazed when looking back and hearing of someone's history, just how differently I saw them from the way another saw them. Our first station commander at Ahlhorn was Piers Kelly*, a guy I knew well and liked and respected enormously. I flew with him a few times on exercises when I was a young cocky so-and-so and thought of him as out of touch and a bit senile at the controls. At night, he was particularly uncertain but of course, I was not really aware that he had very few jet hours. I looked at his war record and felt ashamed of my feelings back then as a young man and not knowing he was a true Battle of Britain veteran with decorations to match." **

* Gp Capt Piers Kelly DFC flew Spitfires with 74 Sqn during the battle and downed a Bf 109. He later served with 604, 93 and 235 Sqns and claimed a Ju 88 in 1942.
** 'A Roving Commission' by Kel Palmer, iUniverse 2007, with his own additions.

OUT OF FUEL AND NOWHERE TO LAND

Norman Spence was a navigator on 96 Sqn at the same time as Kel Palmer. He and his pilot had a very lucky escape when bad weather, fuel exhaustion and low altitude all combined to leave them with no option but to stay with their aircraft and put it down anywhere they could.

"On 23 January 1953, my normal pilot Pete Driscoll and I took off in WM149 to carry out multiple practice interceptions with our playmate, Val Harder and his navigator, Don Busby. Several other pairs, including aircraft from 256 Sqn, took off ahead of us and Pete and I were last to get airborne.

"Apart from the squadron commanders, flight commanders and a few experienced pilots who had master green cards, the others had only white cards and could not fly if the cloud base was below 1,000 feet.

Weather conditions were poor but within limits, however, something obviously went wrong with the Met forecast, because within moments of getting airborne, ATC aborted all the sorties and instructed us to divert to Oldenburg because the cloud base had fallen to 700 feet. Not only was the weather 'Harry Clampers' but we also experienced the most horrendous icing I have ever seen, with the ice on the leading edges growing at a rate of knots.

"We were diverted to Oldenburg because they had GCA, which had not yet been installed at Ahlhorn. We all came under control of ATC Oldenburg and formed a queue, with Val and Don next to last and Pete and I behind. There was a problem with the aircraft flown by Kiwi

96 Squadron NF.11 line-up at Ahlhorn.
[Norman Spence]

Graves and his navigator, Ron Lawrence, from 256. Oldenburg thought that Kiwi's compass was u/s and gave him priority. By the time it was our turn, Oldenburg didn't seem to know where we were, although we were identified as being over Osnabruck at one point. The penny hadn't dropped with Oldenburg that it wasn't Kiwi Graves' compass that was u/s – it was ours. Eventually, they lost us completely and by then we were over Holland.

"ATC at the Dutch air force base at Twente took over, but they too experienced difficulties, lost us, and control was handed to Leeuwarden. Shortly after Leeuwarden took over we ran out of fuel and the engines went quiet. Pete sent out a Mayday and we started our way down. The last thing we heard on the R/T was a slanging match between the controllers at Twente and Leeuwarden, each blaming the other for our predicament! We continued our descent. By now there was no cloud below us and visibility was perfect – that being so, I thought there was little excuse for Pete to shortly demolish twelve of the few trees that grew in Holland! We followed the usual procedures, but instead of releasing my parachute harness, in my cack-handed way, I unfastened my safety harness!! I yelled to Pete to 'Hang on!' Well, there wasn't a lot he could do, was there? – I

How not to land an NF.11, 96 Squadron Ahlhorn. [Norman Spence]

moved with a certain amount of alacrity, and re-fastened it.

"We jettisoned the drop tanks and canopy, passed under some power lines, clobbered the aforementioned trees and then I looked ahead. To port a house was coming up, to starboard another. I could not see directly in front because the view was blocked by the radar, but ahead was an embankment about 100 feet high – and for all I knew, more houses between us and it. As Pete put the aircraft down, I braced myself and on initial impact chipped my left kneecap on the Mk.10 tilt switch. We stopped short of the houses and before the aeroplane came to a complete halt, we leapt out. Unfortunately, we both leapt at exactly the same time, with Pete veering to the left, and me to the right. Consequently, we collided and sent each other flying. Picking ourselves up, we continued our dive for a nearby ditch. We thought that there might be some residual fuel in the tanks, or that there might be fumes which could ignite. This was reinforced when we heard a hissing from the aircraft. Gingerly poking our heads above the top of the ditch to look, we felt complete idiots when we realised that the hissing was from the oxygen supply, which was still switched on.

"Pete went to a house to phone for help while I stood guard over the aeroplane. At the first house someone answered the door, took one look at him and promptly shut it in his face! He had better luck at the next house and the chief of police from Zwolle, accompanied by a number of his officers arrived, followed swiftly by a large number of Dutch army personnel. We were driven to Leeuwarden where we were kitted out in

Dutch uniforms before being taken to the bar. The loan of the uniforms was necessary because of the way we were dressed under our flying suits – the heating system in the NF.11 was activated automatically when the pressurisation system was switched on, with no means of controlling the temperature and it was normally too hot. Consequently, Pete had no shirt under his flying suit and I had neither shirt nor trousers. Once in the bar, we were joined by a large number of pilots from the base, who promptly started to fill us with Bols Gin and meatballs."

ODIHAM

Like Norman Spence in Holland, **Mike Kemp** and his navigator also fell victim to foul weather and a rapidly depleting supply of fuel. However, in their case they had just enough remaining to gain the height they needed to bale out – a tricky exercise without ejection seats – abandoning their NF.14 over the heavily-populated Home Counties.

"I was on 46 Sqn at Odiham and the night-flying programme for 25 January 1955 had me down to fly one of a pair of Meteors on two sorties of PIs. The weather was appalling and the forecast was for the prevailing fog to thicken quite quickly. Resigned to flying being cancelled, we were surprised to be told to get airborne; the first sortie was completed and by the time we landed, the fog had thickened considerably and we did not expect a second launch – we were wrong and departed again.

"We completed the departure procedure and climbed to our allotted flight level, being handed over to Sopley Radar for control. No sooner had we levelled out than we were instructed to return to base because of worsening weather and then, still in the turn, a further instruction came to divert to Lyneham. My navigator passed me a heading and we set off, calling Lyneham on the frequency given by Sopley Radar – there was no reply.

"There were two radio boxes in the aircraft with ten frequencies in each. After calling Lyneham several times without success, I called them on the emergency frequency of 121.5 – still no reply so I made an 'All Stations' call on that frequency but met only silence. I then transmitted on every frequency in turn but there was no response and it became apparent that we had suffered radio failure. The problem was where to go, for the weather briefing forecast poor conditions over a wide area and approaching an unfamiliar airfield at night in such conditions, without radio, was not appealing. Playing for time to think, I shut down one engine for endurance and decided to head back to Odiham, transmitting on all frequencies, planning to do a procedural approach in the hope of picking out the approach lights for a landing.

"As we began the approach, contact was re-established on the local frequency which was then, as if by magic, set up for a precision radar approach. Fuel gauges indicated a near zero level but, as I looked up, I saw a very faint glint of light that must have been the runway lead-in lighting and I thought we'd made it. This was immediately dashed as the controller told us that the other aircraft of the pair had crash-landed, completely blocking the runway.* I immediately overshot – there was only one action open to us now, to gain height and abandon the aircraft. I climbed to 1,500 feet, levelled out, noting that the fuel gauges showed empty, and told the navigator to prepare to abandon the aircraft."

*The second aircraft was NF.14 WS670 and the accident report says the pilot was dazzled by the runway lights, making a heavy landing which broke off the undercarriage.

"The NF.14 canopy moved fore and aft; in emergency it was designed to lift a few inches at the front and the slipstream would jettison it. I activated the jettison lever, the canopy lifted the requisite few inches and there it stayed. To cater for this, a small lever resembling a bicycle tyre lever had been provided; I took hold of that, bending it double with my effort, but the canopy didn't budge. Loosening my harness, I slid down until my back was on the seat, placed my feet on the canopy and pushed with all my might, to see it disappear. Regaining my position I extended the airbrakes to slow down and told the navigator to jump. He disconnected his radio lead but almost immediately re-connected, to tell me I'd forgotten to retract the airbrakes, which I did immediately and he departed. I made a final radio transmission, 'Navigator gone, I'm going now, goodbye'.

"Tumbling through the blackness I counted to ten, pulled the rip-cord and, after the crack of the parachute opening, found myself suspended in a silent world. Convinced that I was over the sea, I removed my leather flying helmet, held it at arm's length ready to drop it – so that the lead would not cause any entanglement in the water – when I saw lights below me. Replacing my helmet, I prepared for a hard landing, but it went well. I could just make out that I had landed about ten feet from the edge of a quarry and that there were houses behind me, one of which had lights on. Rolling up the parachute as best I could, I walked towards the house and knocked on the door, which was opened by a little old lady in a dressing gown. I explained what had happened and requested the use of her telephone. I made a call and the operator quickly had me talking to the ATC controller at Odiham. A vehicle came to collect me and returned me to the mess bar, where my navigator joined us. His landing had been cushioned by a large heap of farmyard manure and one of his flying boots was hung in the bar until, much later, it finally disintegrated.

"A medical once-over the following morning revealed no damage other than a strap mark probably caused, the doc said, by the harness when my parachute opened. The aircraft had crashed in the grounds of a retirement home (near Kingsley Green, some 25 miles south east of Odiham), fortunately causing no damage; there was no sign of fire for there was no fuel to burn. I later sought the person who had packed my parachute and found a lovely young lady in the packing hall. Sadly, the only spare money I had in the world at that time was a grubby one-pound note and I was embarrassed as I handed her such a paltry reward for saving my life, but she seemed well pleased."

DUXFORD

In Chapter Two, **Peter Rogers** recounted his experiences flying the F.8 with 64 Sqn at Duxford. Given the option, he elected to stay with the unit when it switched roles to night fighting.

"We all went up to North Luffenham for about six weeks to convert; really it was about getting used to flying with a navigator and the navigators getting used to flying with GEE Mk.3. As far as the aircraft was concerned, it was really no problem at all; no great move from the F.8. Its performance

Peter Rogers on 64 Squadron's NF.14 line at Duxford. [Peter Rogers]

wasn't that much different, time to height was comparable, max height, max speed. There was no real handling difference between the NF.12 and NF.14 either, but we preferred the 14 with much clearer vision.

"We crewed up with navigators at North Luffenham and mine was a chap called Harry Marshall.* He was an extraordinary individual, unique at the time for having a post-war DFC as a navigator. He'd spent his first tour flying Valettas supply dropping in Malaya, which is where he earned his DFC. It was a nasty shock for him to come and fly in the back seat of a Meteor! We had a good tour together. We both played rugby and matches were on a Wednesday afternoon and our boss was Wg Cdr Bill Sise, a New Zealander, who disliked sportsmen of any sort. So after playing rugby we could guarantee being put on the night-flying programme instead of having a beer with the rest of the team. Nonetheless, one big advantage of flying with Harry, was that he was bar officer, so when we landed at two o'clock in the morning he'd get out his key and open the bar.

*Sqn Ldr Harry Marshall OBE DFC later commanded 511 Britannia Sqn.

"Night fighter flying was a little bit dull; lots of practice interceptions and we quite often did two sorties at night, one hour 20 minutes each. But on one very nice clear night when we'd come back after the second sortie the boss said, 'Well let's do a third shall we?' Everybody groaned, I got airborne all right and did the same thing again, but one of the other crews leapt into their aircraft, roared up into the climb and only then checked his fuel – which was getting very close to zero. He managed to turn back and land and I think one engine flamed out while taxying back. It was seen as a result of both the aircrew and ground crew being overstretched on the three night sorties, so we never ever did that again.

"In 1957, I did the PAI course at the Fighter Weapons School, Leconfield. At the time, there was the thought that the NF.12 and 14 with the wing guns were nowhere near as accurate as the F.8s in the forward nose and this was certainly borne out by the results on 64 Sqn. Even the best of us were not terribly good; if you got 10 or 12%, you were doing quite well. A chap called Fred Lundy on his first air-to-air mission on the course got something like 62%, an extraordinary score and he carried on getting that sort of score, which really dispelled this thought about the 12 and 14. I think I had a course average of about 27%, which was certainly a lot higher than I had ever achieved on the squadron; my poor navigator Harry Marshall had to sit through everything including the final exam. A young Pakistani pilot on the same course Fg Off Jamal Khan, was extremely good. He was not only flying the Meteor but the Venom as well; got some extraordinary scores and many years later, the Pakistani Air Force put up a looping formation of 25 Sabres led by him. The next I

Above: 222 Squadron pilots at Leuchars. From L-R: Graham West-Jones, Nappy Carroll, Smythe, unknown, Duncan Simpson, unknown, Bunny Warren, unknown, with F.8 VZ554. [Jack Frost via Peter Arnold]

Below: F.8 VZ523 ZD-Q 222 Squadron being refuelled at Leuchars. [Jack Frost via Peter Arnold]

Opposite page, top to bottom, left to right: The second production F.1 EE211-G. [via Peter Arnold]; 56 Squadron's 1954 Christmas card, Capt Bodie USAF on the wing tip. [Steve Bond collection]; From L-R: Meteor F.8s WK742 F and WK722 of 601 Squadron, WH359 K and VZ551 B of 611 Squadron. Coronation review, Odiham 1953. [Jack Frost via Peter Arnold]; FR.9 WL263 O of 208 Squadron, Salalah, December 1957. [Adrian Balch collection]

Top and left: Waterbeach-based 25 Squadron NF.12 WS665 seen at Coltishall in September 1958. [Adrian Balch collection]; Brian Ashley at Seletar after flying the last Meteor sortie on 81 Squadron in PR.10 WB154 on 7 July 1961. [Brian Ashley]
Below: WS810 F in formation with two more 60 Squadron NF.14s up from Tengah in 1961. [Steve Bond collection]

NF.11 WD597 on a pre-delivery test flight in Ap[...] 1951. It later served wit[...] 29 Squadron. [Adrian B[...] collection]

NF.13 WM310 of 39 Squadron, Nicosia. [Dav[...] Bryce via Wally Civitico[...]]

NF.14 WS788 Z of 152 Squadron off Great Yarmouth, late 1954. [Pe[...] Verney]

above: PR.10 WB153 of 81
Squadron in Singapore. [via
Brian Ashley]

Right, top to bottom: Ground
crews preparing aircraft for
flight at Worksop. T.7 WL416
63, F.8 VZ519 19, T.7 WF784
or WF794 65 being refuelled.
[RAF Worksop, Danny
Bonwitt], F.8 WL181 G from
5FTS Strubby 1964-65, flown
by Plt Off Tim Smith. [Colin
Wilcock]

Above: RAFFC Strubby sent their 'Evergreens' aerobatic team to Abingdon's display in September 1961, including F.8 WL166. [Adrian Balch collection]

Below: T.7 WA602 W of the School of Refresher Flying Strubby, being ferried to Kemble for storage 2 April 1965, taken from T.7 WA593. [David Jackson]

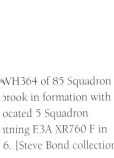

VZ508 of the
...perature and Humidity
...UM] Flight at Woodvale,
...e Rissington, 11
...cember 1971. [Adrian
...h]

WH364 of 85 Squadron
...brook in formation with
...ocated 5 Squadron
...htning F.3A XR760 F in
...6. [Steve Bond collection]

WL111 F of 41 Squadron
...ing at Biggin Hill in
...4. [Tony Hawes]

Above: F[TT].8 WE876 of 1574 Flight gets airborne from Changi in 1971. [Steve Bond collection]

Below: F[TT].8 R of TTS taxying out at Sylt 1957. [Peter Sawyer]

heard of him, he was an air marshal commanding the Pakistani Air Force.

"One night, Harry Marshall and I chased one of those strange radar blips under control. We followed instructions and letting down, I think we found ourselves almost down the main street of this little Belgian town; we never actually saw what the blip was. On 27 January 1958, towards the end of our tour, we actually got a Valiant at 46,000 feet. It was one of those extraordinary days when it was intensely cold at height and we were vectored onto a Valiant, which we could see at 50-odd miles due to the contrails. I turned in well ahead of it and managed to take some cine of it with the gun camera before I flopped out of the sky. I was astonished to find we were at 46,000 feet, which was way above the theoretical maximum altitude of the Meteor and it was more by luck than good judgement, that I got the offset and turn in right.

"The station commander was Gp Capt McDonald and I did his instrument rating one year. I flew five or six trips with him during the week and signed his master green rating card. He was then promoted to air commodore (Air Cdre) and went to the Air Ministry as the director of postings (air). He came back about six months or so, after I'd rated him, for a refresher. I flew him around again on five or six sorties. He was a very nice chap and during the debriefing after every sortie, we would chat about this, that and the other. He asked, 'Peter, when are you tour ex?' I said, 'Oh I forget the date' and he said, 'Where do you want to go next?' I thought, 'Great, here's the bloke who's doing the postings. Fill your boots, Rogers!' I think I said, 'Hunters in Hong Kong or Singapore, or failing those, I'd be happy with Hunters in Germany' – a lovely warm, fuzzy feeling. He came back another six months later after the Duncan Sandys White Paper and he said, 'Peter, you want to get into missiles – that's the career of the future'. A few months later, I was on the *Queen Mary* sailing for New York to undergo training as a launch control officer on the Thor missile."

An idea of the scale of the Meteor night fighter force can be gauged by considering all the stations which hosted squadrons. In the UK that included Church Fenton, Coltishall, Duxford, Leeming, Leuchars, Linton-on-Ouse, Middleton St.George, Odiham, Stradishall, Tangmere, Waterbeach, Wattisham and West Malling, while the bases in Germany were Ahlhorn, Geilenkirchen, Laarbruch and Wahn. The Middle East Air Force squadrons operated from Kabrit and later Luqa, while 60 Sqn, the single Far East Air Force unit, flew from Tengah, finally relinquishing its last examples on 17 August 1961.

On that day, the CO Wg Cdr Peter Smith and his navigator Flt Lt J. H. Adams in WS785, were joined by B Flight commander Sqn Ldr Peter Middleton and navigator Flt Lt Fred Butcher in WS787 for a 30-minute pairs sector reconnaissance sortie, landing at 19:50 hours and thus ending the Meteor's operational career.

The following day WS785 was flown by Flt Lt D. B. Taylor from Tengah to Seletar for scrapping, the pilot then being ferried back to Tengah in the squadron's T.7 WH248. The other NF.14 in the final sortie, WS787 was retained as a gate guard at its home base. Although the Meteor night fighter had been completely supplanted in the role by the Javelin, it equipped a somewhat smaller number of squadrons, a reflection of the times.

CHAPTER FIVE

LOW AND FAST –
FIGHTER RECONNAISSANCE

THE BOYS

Cpl Norman Haffenden
Joined in 1952. Armament fitter trained at Halton. Aircraft Servicing Flight Nicosia, Armament Practice Camp (Middle East) Ta' Qali.

Plt Off Derek Lowther
National Serviceman joined in 1952. Flying training 7 FTS, learned to fly Meteors at 215 AFS, 79 Sqn Germany, later flew with 607 Sqn RAuxAF Meteors and Vampires. Retired 1957.

Flt Lt Geoff Marlow
Joined on a short-service commission in 1950. Trained on Vampires. 2 Sqn Meteor and Swift, 2 Group HQ. Retired 1958.

Flt Lt Desmond Penrose
Learnt to fly Meteors at 207 AFS, 226 OCU, 208 Sqn Egypt, CFS, instructing at Cranwell, ETPS in 1958. Retired from the air force in 1961 and joined de Havilland as a test pilot. Long-time Shuttleworth Collection display pilot. Has flown in excess of 300 aircraft types.

REPLACING THE SPITFIRE
In the late 1940s, the RAF was still reliant on the Spitfire FR.18 for the armed fighter-reconnaissance role and this clearly needed replacing. Glosters responded with a relatively simple adaptation of the F.8 by the addition of a remotely-controlled camera in the extreme nose. First squadron deliveries were made in December 1950 and although 126 were built, they served in just four squadrons, initially 2 and 79 in Germany plus 208 in Egypt before relocating to Cyprus and later still to Malta. The only UK-based examples served with 226 OCU at Stradishall to train FR pilots.
 The mode of operation was typified by very low level tactical reconnaissance with the retention of the four 20-mm cannons to deal with any targets found. Both the Germany-based squadrons replaced their Meteors with the Swift FR.5 in 1956 (which was in turn supplanted by the Hunter FR.10 in 1960/61), while 208 Sqn soldiered on with the FR.9 until March 1958 when they took up a purely fighter role with the Hunter F.6. To retain the FR role in the region, a small number of their Meteors were passed on to the variant's fourth unit 8 Sqn at Khormaksar for a

further 18 months alongside its Venoms, before finally fading away in August 1959.

GERMANY

Derek Lowther's National Service was deferred while he was at college, but at his matriculation, the three Services attended trying to attract future recruits. He had no previous ambition to fly, but RAF aptitude tests found he was fit for flying training. After gaining his wings at Cottesmore he was off via the usual AFS and 226 OCU route to join 79 Sqn at Gütersloh.

Derek Lowther on arrival in Gibraltar having flown 607 Squadron's F.8 from Ouston via Tangmere and Istres, June 1955. [Derek Lowther]

"After gaining my wings on the Balliol at 7 FTS Cottesmore I next went to Finningley on an operational conversion course to fly jets, with my first flight there on 25 June 1953 in a Meteor T.7. Compared with the Balliol, where we had to zig-zag from side to side when we taxied around, it had a superb forward view, no prop in the way. It was not a pleasant aircraft, being uncomfortable with a very heavy hood. My instructor Flt Sgt Bradley DFM was a brilliant pilot and my first trip was unbelievable, great visibility and speed, everything happened so much faster. Unlike piston engines where after starting you had to wait for oil temperature and pressures to come up, you just start and go, no hassle; simplicity. Eventually I went solo in a T.7 on Exercise 6 on 29 June after asymmetric circuits and landings, about 40 minutes each trip totalling about four hours.

"My first trip in an F.4 was on 1 July and was such an exhilarating feeling, the very first time I had been in an aircraft with only one seat – you're on your own. I took off for local familiarisation, and turned north towards Newcastle to 'beat up' my girlfriend Kathleen's house. Her father was a colliery manager and they had a big house on high ground near Durham. On returning to Finningley with not much fuel left, they kept asking me where I'd been. 'In the circuit and local area', I told them. Aerobatics were terrific too and I only had one scary moment during a practice PAN call. I was descending rapidly towards Dishforth until they said to me, 'You may now descend to 2,000 feet'. I realised I was climbing to 2,000 feet, but my instructor never said a word. I finished the course on 10 September with an instrument flying revision sortie.

A pair of 79 Squadron FR.9s at typically low level. [Derek Lowther]

"Four of us were subsequently posted to Germany, turning up at Bad Eilsen, the headquarters of the 2nd TAF. My interview with Air Cdre Dudley Lewis was surprisingly brief, 'You play rugby?', 'Yes Sir', 'You play cricket?', 'Yes Sir', that was it. 'Report to Gütersloh tomorrow where you'll be met by Flt Lt McArthur.' With considerable trepidation, I was introduced to 79 Sqn who were gathered in the downstairs bar of the mess. The variety of drinks was quite remarkable. In my case it was orange juice which was clearly frowned upon. It was then that I became aware that the squadron was equipped with Meteor FR.9s. My first solo was on 13 October 1953.

"Gütersloh had been Goering's favourite station and was huge. For those interested in such things it also had a vomitorium (a place where diners who had overeaten could purge their stomachs so that they could return to the table for more), a facility frequently put to good use by Luftwaffe pilots as well as later generations. 541 Squadron were there too with Meteor PR.10s, but 2 Sqn at Wahn also had FR.9s and were the main competition as far as 79 was concerned. Overall they were a wonderful crowd of guys, in some ways almost elitist, and it was only later that I realised they were trying to persuade me to sign on. Later events proved this to be pointless.

"Having predominantly a low level role 79 Sqn had close links with

101

Ground crew set to on 79 Squadron's FR.9 WH557 T-P at Gütersloh prior to going to APC at Sylt, 1953. [Derek Lowther]

the army, taking them on familiarisation flights whilst we were given practical experience driving their tanks. A lot of our time was spent on the Nordhorn range for air-to-ground firing and I did two sorties in November 1953. On the first one, I was convinced the dive was vertical only to be told it was barely 45 degrees. The following attempt was more acceptable, apparently. The FR.9 was a different beast from the F.4 because it felt bigger, which it was and there was a special aura about it. You had to be the boss and with two powerful engines, asymmetric handling became a critical factor. 79 Sqn lost six pilots in the six months before I joined them, not entirely the aircraft's fault. Sadly, a Swedish exchange pilot, Capt Wolf Hjelm, was killed while I was there on 31 October trying to find a gap in the hills near Halle at low level. As a squadron, we were very well looked after and if anyone had too much to drink, which was not unusual, then the solution was to go on to pure oxygen the next day – it certainly seemed to work.

"Gütersloh had a top-class rugby XV and at that time we were successful against virtually all the teams we played. On 15 November I travelled to Berlin for a game against a leading army team, which we won, then returned to Hanover the following day to represent 2nd TAF against a German XV. Unfortunately, I suffered a serious shoulder injury, making me immediately unfit for flying with a medical category of A4 G4. This meant that I only experienced just over seven months on the Meteor FR.9 including formation and low level cross-country; we were also detached briefly to Bückeburg while the runway was being dealt with. It was a very impressive aircraft and when airborne made you feel you were lord of the manor. My last trip was on 9 November 1953, by which time I had been promoted to Fg Off. My recovery was a drawn out, painful affair and in due course it was decided I was not much use to 79 Sqn. As I became surplus to requirements the station sent me on a physical fitness course at St. Athan, which later qualified me to become the physical fitness officer at Gütersloh until I returned to the UK in August 1954.

"As my National Service came to its inevitable conclusion and I returned to university, the next phase involved being placed on the Reserve List. Luckily I was able to join 607 (County of Durham) Sqn RAuxAF based at Ouston. They had recently moved from Spitfires to Vampires but also had a Meteor T.7 and F.8. I went solo on both types and this continued until my last flight on 16 December 1956.

"Looking back what do I recall? A high speed run in a Meteor was almost surreal. Nose down, full power and if you got to Mach 0.84 you were doing well. There was slight vibration, then it would slowly drop a wing, out came the dive brakes, reduce power, recover and start again. It was great fun while it lasted and I consider myself fortunate to have been associated with so many remarkable events."

A contemporary of Derek's on the FR.9 force in Germany was **Geoff Marlow** who served a full tour on 2 Sqn and stayed with it when it converted to the Swift FR.5 in 1956. His most unnerving Meteor experience, however, came not when he was down low in an FR.9 but when he had an unexpectedly prolonged sortie in the unit's T.7. It served to reinforce both the issue of the type's short legs when it came to duration and the very different environment in the rather less than sophisticated cockpit of the two-seater.

"In 1953, I joined 2 Sqn at Wahn in Germany. The role was fighter reconnaissance flying the Meteor FR.9 and we flew at low level to the target area to do both a visual and a

Fg Off Geoff Marlow. [via David Jackson]

photographic reconnaissance. Our cruising speed was 360 knots. We had no navigational aids, just a map and a compass and had a secondary role as day fighters. One day in 1955, I helped to change the way forced landings were carried out in the RAF, as a result of what happened. Our training aeroplane, a T.7, was not being used and I obtained permission to take it up for a ride. I then asked one of our ground crew if he would like a joyride and he jumped at the opportunity. I gave my passenger the usual briefing on how to bale out if ordered to do so and told him of the importance of keeping his oxygen mask on all the time.

"When we took off and commenced climbing, it was a murky day with visibility down to two miles. There was broken cloud at about 1,000 feet and then solid cloud from 3,000 feet. I was unaware that this cloud was solid up to 37,000 feet. We continued climbing and at about 24,000 feet I saw that my airspeed indicator was failing, it dropped to zero. The pitot head heater was switched on though; this was a new experience for me and later it was learned that there were most exceptional freezing conditions in the cloud that day. I radioed my airfield to report the situation and suggested that I continue climbing to above the cloud top and that 83 Group Fighter Control send someone up to meet me. I would then formate on that aircraft and be led down and into a formation landing. This was agreed, and one of my friends who had heard my call volunteered to come up to meet me. This was 'Mac' Mackervoy, who had just commenced a low level cross-country flight.

"We both then switched over to the Fighter Control frequency. While Mac was being guided up to me, I continued my climb to the cloud top because there was no way we could meet in cloud. On top now at 37,000 feet, I circled waiting for Mac to appear but after a long wait, there was no sign of him. Later that day, the wreckage of his Meteor was found and Mac was dead; it was assumed that he had lost control of his aeroplane. After a while, I was instructed to descend, but I questioned the point of this as I still believed that Mac was on his way up. They did not tell me that he had disappeared from the radar screen. Still circling, I spoke to my passenger on the intercom but got no reply. On repeating myself, again no reply, so I turned round to see him, slumped in his seat, his face was blue and his oxygen mask was off. We were over 10,000 feet higher than that level at which a human being can survive without oxygen so I had to descend.

"Breaking the cloud base, then at about 2,000 feet, I found that I had severe icing on the windscreen and no forward visibility; my ASI was still not working. I couldn't land in that condition, so I flew around for a few minutes in the vicinity of the airfield at high speed trying to burn off the ice. If my passenger were still alive, he would be breathing normal air, so the delay would not harm him. This action did not cure the icing problems and as I was running very short of fuel by now I called the tower to ask if there was anyone near or in the circuit who could lead me in to land. I formated on an N.F.11 of 68 Sqn but unfortunately the pilot of this aircraft did a very wide circuit (probably thinking this was the best for me), and when we were on the crosswind leg my starboard engine stopped due to fuel starvation.

"Now I had to do some quick thinking. First of all, I feared that my other engine would quit any second, and I knew that the ground between us and the airfield was very rocky. I also knew the ground ahead of our present crosswind position was flat farmland stretching for several miles and far more suitable for a forced landing, even with no airspeed indicator or forward visibility, so I broke formation to go my own way. Now I had to make another quick decision. Ever since retractable wheels had been invented, a cardinal rule was that forced landings should be done with wheels up. This bothered me, and for two years I had given it a lot of thought. I believed that this rule came into being because aeroplanes traditionally had two main wheels and a tail wheel. If those main wheels were down, and were snagged by a ditch or other obstacle, or even soft mud, the aircraft would somersault with much greater chance of injury or death. I believed that, with a tricycle undercarriage, landing in open flat country, in the event of snagging, the nose wheel would absorb most of the shock and prevent a somersault even in the most violent impact on the ground.

"With my wheels already down for an airfield landing, I left them down and without the airspeed indicator, I decided to increase my rate of descent to maintain my forward speed to as low to the earth as possible and then level off and wait for the Meteor to slow down. When the controls felt sloppy, I would ease it on to the ground. My speed then would have been about 105 knots. At all costs, I could not risk a stall from 20 or 30 feet or more. It went as planned and we landed safely, with a short landing run. When I turned to look at my passenger he was still unconscious but appeared to be breathing, so I wrapped him in the silk of my parachute to keep him warm. The ambulance arrived in just two or three minutes and took him to hospital. When I had got down from the cockpit, I found the ground was quite soft and muddy. We were in a sugar beet field. Looking back to our touchdown point, I was horrified to see a row of high tension cables across our landing path some 200 yards beyond touchdown. With my shallow approach, I could not have done other than fly below them; the lower cable seemed a mere 15 or so feet above the ground so we must have been very low to pass under it. With ice on the windscreen, I had not seen this hazard.

"My CO told me that the pitot tube was still iced up three hours after landing, though it was quite mild at ground level. The aeroplane was towed, on its own wheels, back to the airfield. When there had been a thorough overhaul, which found no damage, I did an air test during which it flew beautifully – the Meteor was a tough bird. My passenger was none the worse for wear, suffering only inflammation of an ear, caused by his not being conscious to clear his ears during the descent. After about a week, he was telling his mates at work that he had enjoyed his flight!

"As an aircraft had run out of fuel and because someone had been taken to hospital, a Board of Enquiry had to be held. Its findings were that exceptional icing forcing the loss of the air speed indicator (ASI) was the primary cause of the incident, but that a secondary cause was my refusal to descend straight away when instructed to do so, thus leading to eventual exhaustion of fuel. I was asked then for my comments. My response was that at high level, fuel consumption was low, and that if someone had come up to lead me down to a landing, the incident would have been avoided. I said that I should have been told that no one was coming to meet me, as I had been led to believe earlier. Running out of fuel was caused primarily by the necessity for flying at high speed at low level with the object of clearing the ice on the windscreen and in the pitot tube to enable me to land. My views were not accepted, but a copy of the board's report, together with my theory on forced-landing procedures (which I had expounded at length), was sent to the Flight Safety branch at the Air Ministry. I was called to see the station commander, who pointed out to me amicably that he was obliged to administer a gentle slap on the wrist.

"A few weeks later, the rules for forced landings were changed and pilots were given the chance to choose wheels either up or down for emergency returns; after Air Ministry had examined a few more reports of forced landings, safely executed with wheels down, the rules were amended again and pilots were advised to adopt a wheels down procedure if over open and flat country."*

* Geoff Marlow by kind permission of Sqn Ldr David Jackson, Aircrew Association.

MIDDLE EAST AIR FORCE

Desmond Penrose found himself sent out to join 208 Sqn at Abu Sueir in Egypt's Canal Zone for his first RAF tour and clearly enjoyed his flying in the Meteor FR.9, in common with many other 'Boys' expressing quite a liking for it...

"I read engineering at Loughborough and after I qualified I did a university short course, six months, at Cottesmore on Harvards. I got my wings, then went to Full Sutton which was 207 AFS; one of my instructors was a Polish fellow, a Battle of Britain ace. From there to 226 OCU Stradishall, got an 'above average' and did the fighter-reconnaissance course, also at Stradishall, then joined 208 Sqn in November 1952. I was on the squadron until June '55, a two and a half year tour.

"We spent most of our time at ultra-low level and always around 400 knots, so you'd be at 50-80 feet dashing around doing fighter-reconnaissance sorties. It was a super place to be Abu Sueir, nice climate, never too hot. You had a little Khamsin wind occasionally, so you had sand everywhere. We had a good set of chaps on the squadron and I now look after the Meteor chapter on 208 Sqn Association and we're still in touch. Not only do we have our annual dinner, which is a formal affair every October at the RAF Club, but on the first Wednesday in May I organise for the Meteor chapter, that's both aircrew and ground crew,

Fg Off Desmond Penrose, 208 Squadron, Abu Sueir. [Desmond Penrose]

a lunch in Soho which is where the squadron had its first association meeting in October of 1919. Recognising the social strata then, I think it must have been one of the very first associations to have an all-ranks annual get-together.

"I liked the Meteor, because as far as I was concerned it was a tyro at

208 Squadron FR.9 VZ584 T airborne over Egypt with the early-style canopy and small air intakes. [Mike Bradley, Naval Eight/208 Squadron Association]

that time. I hadn't been to Test Pilots' School at that time so the Meteor was fine; it was only later that I realised just how heavy it was on the controls, but for the job that we did it was a very stable, docile, but slightly heavy aircraft. We thought of course, that it was a good fighter, but it was totally outclassed really by the opposition and by the Americans. There we were flying something that was World War Two vintage and other people had aircraft with powered controls and could go supersonic, whereas we got about Mach 0.84 and it just about shook your teeth out.

"We had one or two aircraft that shed their tails while manoeuvring but didn't kill anybody. I think it was round about 1953, when the Royal Air Force in Egypt was probably bigger than the present-day Royal Air Force. I'm not certain how many squadrons were out in Egypt, but I think it must have been getting on for about 12. There was an exercise called Sunbeam that involved a whole lot of Lincoln bombers coming in ostensibly from Cyprus to attack the Canal Zone. I don't know if it was this one, but there was this mass dogfight, mainly between Venoms and Meteors with the odd Vampire thrown in, and Pete Greensmith was being chased by a Venom; he pulled through and his tail came off. The Venom pilot reported seeing the tail and he said nobody ejected, so we just thought Pete had gone in. We sent out aerial reconnaissance, that was our job, and we couldn't find him; we didn't find the wreck or anything.*

*This accident was on 5 February 1953. The FR.9 VW368 was abandoned in a spin and crashed at Gebel el Ma'aza in the Sinai Desert.

"After about three days there was the standard Committee of Adjustment and all his kit was got together. Somebody bought his cap, somebody else bought his greatcoat and the money would obviously go to his relatives; the odd dirty postcard was quietly disposed of. Arrangements were made with the RAF Regiment that there would be a funeral for the relatives, they wouldn't know that we were burying sand. The Fg Off Regiment chap got hold of a gun carriage, rehearsed with a coffin on it and they looked very smart, it was going to be a good show, with photographs taken so that the relatives would know that Pete had a good farewell. On the day of the funeral, who turns up but Pete Greensmith! He'd ejected at low level and he thought that he was in a difficult situation, miles from anywhere and he said, 'But, a fly landed on me and because there was a fly there must be human habitation'. He was picked up by some Bedouins and he showed them his Gooley Chit and when they came to Abu Sueir they were duly given their money. One of the first people he met as he came in to the guardroom was this Fg Off Regiment chap, who said, 'You bastard! After all the work I've done, couldn't you have waited a day?!'

"Talking of flies, we had 205 Group HQ at Abu Sueir and there was an undeclared war between the squadron and 205 Group. Another chap and I made up a form, 'Number of Flies Killed in Airmen's Quarters, NCO's Quarters, Officers' Quarters'. We submitted this on a monthly basis and we varied the numbers, all laid out very carefully. We got one of the clerks in the orderly room to help us and sometimes the NCOs were better than the airmen, sometimes the officers came top. We kept on submitting this form and then we got bored – we stopped. What happened? We got a memo from 205 Group saying we hadn't submitted 'Flies, death of'. Either they had a sense of humour, or they were just form filling. We did no more.

"We had attached to us an army major as our ground liaison officer (GLO) and being a major, John Thraves was obviously 10-15 years older than the rest of us. He put up with an awful lot of ribbing about being a Brown Job, Pongo, various other derogatory names that we could think of; we used to sing at a dining-in night 'Thraves, John Thraves, solid ivory from the neck up Thraves'. One dining-in night, I don't know how the subject came round to parachuting, but I think Thraves had actually done a parachute course; anyway, it ended up with him challenging us to jump. It was that time of night, nobody minded, we weren't going anywhere. What we didn't realise, was that this chap had some influence and the following day the whole squadron exited a Valetta. Not the CO, but both flight commanders and everybody else went out as a stick. My log book informs me that we jumped from VW844 into the Bitter Lake on 18 May 1954. That was a challenge, he issued the challenge and we took it up. It's hard to imagine something like that happening today. At that time there was still a little of the ethos of wartime in the Royal Air Force, but it was gradually changing and people were thinking of their careers and promotion. They were watching their backs, which you didn't see until about 1953/54.

"We used to go across every year to Cyprus for air gunnery; very fortunately I was reasonably good so I got an 'exceptional' rating. We'd also take ourselves off on navigational exercises. When things started to get unpleasant with the Egyptians, from about 1954 onwards, they tried to put the squeeze on us by banning any import of alcohol and they tried to ban newspapers, but that didn't work either. To get round this, we'd take all the ammunition boxes out and we would then fly to Malta and I think you could get 96 bottles of gin or whiskey or brandy or whatever into the ammunition bay. We did start bringing champagne in, but we lost a few bottles at 37,000 feet when you heard 'pop'. But every time we came back we had to go through Egyptian customs and they particularly wanted to look into the ammunition bays. What we did was, we had one long runway at Abu Sueir and one shorter one which if you go down it, you disappear out of sight. So these two aircraft would land, taxi down the short runway and two aircraft would taxi in. I'd had two waiting there out of sight, the customs would examine them and of course there was nothing there. We did that very, very successfully. We than carried it a stage further, but we couldn't do it from Malta because we needed long-range tanks. We got new long-range tanks, each 100 gallons, washed them out and we'd fly over to Cyprus and fly back with 200 gallons of Keo brandy in each aircraft. We were supplying most of the messes. They were navigational exercises, maybe four or six aircraft – all that brandy.

"I was deputy flight commander of A Flight, and in September of '54, it was my first day in command. It was very, very misty and I was determined that A Flight would get airborne before B Flight. I was working on the principle that the sun would come along and burn all the mist away and I took off with just enough visibility and just after I left the ground,

FR.9 F.8 VZ588 C 208 Squadron crash-landing after losing starboard wheel on take-off, Abu Sueir 10 September 1954. The nose cone is red for A Flight. [Desmond Penrose]

there was a bit of a thump and my number two said 'Your right wheel's fallen off'. I was in the process then of just raising the undercarriage and it wouldn't come up, so I didn't use the over-ride because I worked on the principle, what if I couldn't get it down again? I flew around and burnt off fuel, came in and landed on one wheel on the right-hand side of the runway on the sand. I kept the wing up as long as I could and the only damage to the aircraft other than losing its wheel, was a gouge about six or seven inches long and about two inches wide, where the starboard nacelle impacted the ground. My CO was not very pleased with me, he'd told me to eject.

"When I finished on 208 I went, against my will, to CFS and then to Cranwell as an instructor on Vampires. I picked up the Clarkson Aerobatic Trophy at CFS and the first thing I did when I got to Cranwell was to form an aerobatic team. We'd had one on 208, we never gave ourselves a name, we just said that everybody should be able to do formation aerobatics.

FR.9 of 208 Squadron at Ta' Qali, 1956. [Steve Bond collection]

When I got to Cranwell we did our first display on my birthday on 1 May 1956. So I spent a lot of time, when not instructing, on the team, which was good fun.

"From there, in 1958 I went to the Empire Test Pilot's School (ETPS), then I was at Farnborough for four years. We had Meteors at Farnborough and there was one at Cranwell that I flew. We had them at ETPS and of course when I was in RAE itself, the Experimental Wing, we used them for a variety of purposes. I got head-hunted by de Havilland's and went there as a development test pilot in 1961. I flew the Comet, Trident, 125, a variety of de Havillands and was the project pilot on the Sea Vixen FAW.2. Whilst I was at Hatfield I looked after the Cirrus Moth there, G-EBLV. I used to fly with the Shuttleworth Collection and I displayed there for 42 years. I've been very fortunate, I've flown 300 plus types."

THE GROUND CREW

Every bit as important as the aircrew were the engineers beavering away to ensure the aircraft, comparatively simple as they were, remained serviceable and on the line as much as possible. **Norman 'Big Norm' Haffenden** was another Meteor Boy who was sent overseas as soon as he had finished his training, in his case a three-year apprenticeship at Halton. However, his first brush with the FR.9s of 208 Sqn made quite a mark!

"I am an ex Trenchard Brat. When I first went to RAF Halton for the final selection board I told them I wanted to be an armament fitter. I was most emphatic about that. So it was that I found myself on 3 Apprentice Wing at Halton on 9 September 1952 at the tender age of 15 years and nine months with a lot of other young lads who were to be collectively known as the 72nd Entry. Three years later, I passed out from Halton as a J/T and was posted to the Aircraft Servicing Flight (ASF) at Nicosia, Cyprus, in September 1955. Early in January 1956 26 APC, which operated Meteor F.8 target-towing aircraft together with a couple of Vampire T.11s was posted en bloc to Ta' Qali, Malta. They required an armament fitter, so I was posted onto 26 APC, later to be renamed APC (Middle East), and found myself at Ta' Qali, which was to be our base while we travelled around the Middle East airfields towing glider and banner targets for the fighter squadrons to carry out their annual air-to-air firing exercises. Towards the end of 1956, APC (Middle East) was disbanded and I was cross-posted to 208 Sqn as the NCO i/c Armament Section (I was a Cpl by then), who were also at Ta' Qali operating Meteor FR.9 fighter-reconnaissance aircraft.

"On a Monday morning, in late 1956, dressed in my best uniform, I reported to the 208 Sqn headquarters building and was shown into the squadron commander's office, where I was duly welcomed and briefed on the role of the squadron, what was expected of me etc., the usual stuff. On leaving the boss's office, I walked down the corridor of the HQ and on a table in an alcove were all the aircraft Form 700s (the servicing history of each individual aircraft). I picked up an F700 at random and proceeded to examine the records, especially those relating to the armament systems. I soon noticed that the ejection seat cartridges (ESCs) were out of date. In those days the Martin-Baker Mk. 2 ESCs were given a finite life of two years from the date of manufacture, or six months from the date of first fitment to an aircraft seat. They became unserviceable (u/s) at that time, whichever was the earlier of the two dates. Borrowing a red

A hangar full of 79 Squadron FR.9s, Gütersloh 1953. [Derek Lowther]

pen from the line chief, I made a red ink entry on the appropriate page of the F700, effectively grounding that aircraft until such time as the ESCs were replaced. Having checked that F700 and remembering that I had chosen it at random, I then decided that I should check all the others.

"To cut a long story short, within half an hour of first joining the squadron, I effectively grounded ten (maybe it was 12) of the aircraft leaving just two or three FR.9s serviceable to fly seat-wise and one Meteor T.7 which was not fitted with ejection seats. After frantic enquiries to the station armoury and the fort (the main explosive storage unit on Malta), I ascertained that there were no replacement seat cartridges on the island. As it turned out, it took almost a month before the replacement ESCs arrived; meanwhile, pilots were fighting each other to fly the remaining aircraft. I was the most unpopular man on the squadron and even the other ground crew members were referring to me as 'that bloody corporal'. My life on the squadron during that first month was not the most pleasant, to say the least.

"I got a lot of stick from all concerned. I could understand the pressures and frustration grounding all those aircraft caused, but the consequences of failing to do so do not bear thinking about. I pointed out that the station senior engineering officer could authorise flights with u/s ESCs, but of course he would not do so. When the new ones finally arrived, my workload was, to say the least, hectic. As I completed my final checks on the first aircraft on the line (it was before vital and independent checks were introduced) and left the cockpit, the F700 was thrust at me to sign, clearing the red line. The line chief then signed the 'fit to fly' entry, the pilot signed accepting the aircraft and, before I reached the next 'kite' on the line, the engines had been started and it was taxying out. And so it continued until all the aircraft were finally airborne. Whew! Certainly a day to remember.

The last FR.9 to serve in Aden, WH546 with Khormaksar's FR Flight in 1961. [Martin Fenner collection]

"Obviously, guns had to be serviced, release slips had to be checked etc., so when I asked to have access to an aircraft to carry out some routine servicing the cry went up 'that bloody corporal is at it again!'" *

* Norman Haffenden, Naval Eight / 208 Squadron Association.

Given the high accident rate suffered by Meteors in the early 1950s and the challenging nature of the FR.9 operation in squadron service, it is interesting to consider how they fared in their eight years of service. Of the 126 built, 38 were written off in accidents of which almost half (17) were lost by 208 Sqn, but there is little to suggest that the risk from low flying was considered to be an especially concerning factor. There were, however, four occasions when aircraft were lost by flying into obstacles or the terrain, one which suffered a bird-strike and two which flew into the ground during gunnery practice; all but one of these accidents being suffered by the squadrons in Germany. The one issue which does stand out from the statistics is that no fewer than 11 aircraft simply ran out of fuel, usually during bad weather.

ALONE ABOVE ALL* –
PHOTO RECONNAISSANCE

THE BOYS

Wg Cdr Brian Ashley
Joined in 1949. Trained 4 FTS Heany and Meteors at 205 AFS. 237 OCU. 1st tour 541 Sqn PR.10 Germany. 231 OCU. 81 Sqn PR.10 Singapore, later Canberra PR.7. CFS. Cyprus. Tornado Project Office. Retired May 1977.

Sgt Alec Audley
Joined in December 1958 as an air wireless mechanic and two years on 81 Sqn. Later served on Shackletons at Kinloss, then Khormaksar, Aden. Left the air force in 1969.

SAC Alun Williams
Joined in 1956 as an engine mechanic. 81 Sqn Seletar later Tengah 1957-58, 1 ANS Hullavington, Valetta 1959, Stoke Heath (Ternhill) Comms Flt. Left the air force in 1961.

STRATEGIC RECONNAISSANCE
At the same time that the FR.9 was being developed for the tactical-reconnaissance job, Glosters produced the PR.10 as an unarmed high-altitude aircraft for the strategic-reconnaissance role, which was still being fulfilled by the Spitfire PR.19 together with a similar number of Mosquito PR.34s. The airframe was a hybrid, combining a basic F.8 fuselage with the cannons deleted, coupled with the smaller T.7-type tail and re-introducing the long-span wings of the F.3 and early F.4. In addition to the same type of nose-mounted camera as carried by the FR.9, two additional cameras were installed in the rear fuselage for vertical photography.

PR.10 VS976 of 81 Squadron over Singapore. The camouflage scheme was later abandoned. [81 Squadron Association]

The prototype flew on 29 March 1950, just six days after the first FR.9 and the initial deliveries were made to 541 Sqn at Benson in December 1950, replacing Mosquito PR.34s. This was followed by 13 Sqn at Kabrit in Egypt a year later (again replacing Mosquitos) and finally by 81 Sqn at Seletar in Singapore in January 1954 where the PR.10 supplanted Spitfire PR.19s. There were no home-based operational units, but a small number of the 59 built did serve for training purposes at 237 OCU Bassingbourn (later merged into 231 OCU at the same station).

541 SQN

Just a month or so after receiving its first PR.10s at Benson, 541 Sqn moved to Bückeburg in Germany and for almost seven years it stayed out there, moving around various stations until it was disbanded on 7 September 1957. **Brian Ashley** was posted onto the squadron in 1954 after completing his type conversion and mastering the tricky art of photo reconnaissance on 237 OCU. After a short break on completion of his tour in Germany, he quickly resumed his acquaintance with the PR.10 in Singapore.

"In January 1954, I joined 237 PR OCU at Bassingbourn to begin my training as a single-seat PR pilot. Bassingbourn was busy training aircrews for the Canberra and 231 OCU was the main occupant of the station. Tucked away in half of the second hangar from the A14 road was 237 PR OCU. The only high level PR cover for the RAF overseas was provided by three squadrons of Meteor PR.10s, which were holding the fort until the Canberra PR.3/7 could take over. Because of the low number of Meteor pilots involved, the turnover of pilots was quite small and I was the only Meteor pilot on the course. The PR.10 was basically an F.8 but the long extended wingtips had been stolen from earlier F.3s to give more wing area and the T.7 tail unit was fitted. The aileron spring tabs that were fitted to other Meteors were removed to make the PR less sensitive in the rolling plane. The most surprising fact was that there were no navigation aids other than maps, a compass and our wrist watches. It had two VHF radio sets but as the pilots usually operated with minimum use of radio these were utilities rather than navigation aids. I was pleased to note that at last I would be able to fly with an ejection seat. No longer would I have to strap my parachute on before climbing up the side of the fuselage and down into the cockpit. The seat was an early model and could only be used above a height of 200 feet and a speed of 250 knots. After ejection, the pilot still had to separate himself from the seat before pulling the rip-cord to deploy the parachute but it was better than no ejector seat.

"My first PR.10 flight produced no surprises but I enjoyed the bigger single-piece canopy and the better view ahead through the gap where

* The motto of 541 Sqn who flew Meteor PR.10s from December 1950 to September 1957.

the gun sight normally sat. It had been removed and replaced by the smaller controller for the F52 cameras. I thought that the idea of using the water bottle in the survival pack as a seat cushion was a clever way of providing a soft incompressible seat; I soon discovered that on long high level flights it became a block of ice and froze your backside. The aircraft was very steady on the approach and it could be flown over the threshold as low as 95 knots, however at such a low speed, the bottom of the fin was very close to the runway and any twitching of the controls could result in it banging the deck.

"I had to start learning the art of taking photos. I did not find much difficulty with taking forward or side-facing low level photos but the high level tasks were another kettle of fish. Most peacetime high level survey tasks were standardised and taken from 30,000 feet which produced photos with a scale of 1:10,000. The photographic interpreters were well used to this scale and it made their difficult task a little easier. We had three main types of task. The first was a pinpoint target where only three overlapping photos were required to give a stereo image. The second task was a feature line which could extend for 20 miles or more. This required careful planning to be able to track along the required line without being able to see the ground underneath and without being blown off by strong winds. The third task was a small area cover which required two or more feature lines side by side. The basic requirement for all three tasks was for the pilot, who could not see underneath the aircraft, to be able to position it over a spot on the ground, heading in the correct direction at the correct speed and with his wings level, all at precisely 30,000 feet. That was the theory.

"Just north of Bassingbourn was a very easily visible crossroads known as Caxton Gibbet, which was an excellent target for beginners. The recommended approach to the target was to approach at 90 degrees to the photo run and bring the target close down the side of the fuselage. When you were almost alongside it, you turned hard left so that you had a good last look at the target and then tried to roll out on the required heading with the wings exactly level and then switch on the cameras. After my early efforts when my film had been developed, I often wondered where Caxton Gibbet had gone; slowly I managed to keep my photos within Cambridgeshire.

"We also had to brush up our navigation. This was one of the attractions of the job for me and low level navigation was fun. High level navigation was equally pleasing but in a completely different way and the solo navigation exercises were new to me. At last, I could reach out to a range of about 1,000 nautical miles without any navigational aids other than my maps, my compass and my eyes. The flights would have been splendid if only it had not been so cold. The engines could not push much warm air into the cabin at altitude and the temperature soon dropped well below freezing. We had no special clothing and could wear pullovers etc. but the biggest problem was cold hands and feet. I tried thick socks, up to three pairs of thin socks, silk socks and on one occasion no socks – all were equally cold.

"At the end of the course I was well pleased when I discovered that I was bound for 541 Sqn at Gütersloh. The first two days were a sample of the future: a sector recce with Peter Bridger in the Meteor T.7, a solo sortie in a PR.10, an instrument flying sortie with Gerry Mayer in the back seat and then a high level photo sortie over Hamburg. During this time, I was told I had been selected to go on the next squadron exchange to 13 Sqn at Kabrit in the Canal Zone of Egypt. This was one of the squadron's most sought-after tasks and I could hardly believe I had been selected to go after only three weeks on the squadron.

"I was allocated PR.10 WB156 for the journey and it required air testing after a thorough servicing. I had heard many tall stories about the maximum height reached in a PR.10 but as I was quite new on the type, I decided to find out for myself. I left the height climb part of the test until the end of the sortie when I had little fuel remaining. The climb was normal until I reached 45,000 feet but then the flying became very sensitive while seeking the best climbing speed. A variation of a few knots would result in reduced rate of climb or even descent. By milking every bit of climb, the aircraft eventually reached 49,700 feet but it was difficult to maintain and I let it sink to a sustainable height of 49,500 feet. After such a struggle I had to tell someone about it, so I called Gütersloh tower for a controlled let down. The controller on duty was Flt Lt Toby or 'Digger' Foxley who had been Micky Martin's rear gunner on the Möhne Dam raid. As expected he asked for my height and I proudly but breathlessly told him '49.5' whereupon he immediately came back with 'Roger Blue, make it 50.5. I already have one there!' I could think of no appropriate answer.

"After breakfast, we continued on our way towards Luqa, Malta. I was leading and was taking good care to keep a close check on possible diversion airfields because Met had forecast possible heavy thunder storms in the Central Mediterranean. All went well until we were about 200 miles from Malta and then my radio died. I was able to attract Ron's [surname unknown – ed] attention and by hand signals ask him to take over the lead. Fortunately he had been monitoring our navigation and he pressed on towards Malta. Soon afterwards we began to see evidence of cumulo-nimbus clouds building up along our track. As we approached Malta, the cloud rose above us and we were soon in thick cloud and I had to stay close to Ron as he was my only hope of a safe arrival at Luqa. My fate was in his hands. We entered rain and severe turbulence, which increased until we were having a very uncomfortable ride and keeping close formation required vigorous handling. By this time, we had insufficient fuel remaining to enable us to divert to an alternative airfield and all I could do was hang on to Ron like glue even though at times I could barely see him from a few yards. I was immensely relieved when I began to see glimpses of the ground as we descended through about 800 feet and when Ron eased on to the runway, I was right there alongside him. It had been the longest two hours and 10 minutes of my life. Even then, our problems were not over. As we taxied into the dispersal the rain was heaving it down in bucketfulls. If we opened our cockpit canopies, not only ourselves, but also the aircraft cockpits would be soaked in water and while our skins were waterproof, the cockpit was much more sensitive. Fortunately, the servicing crew had the good sense to leave us in our cockpits until the storm abated. Ron enjoyed his free beer all evening and I slept well all night.

"We were kept busy during the next two weeks by 13 Sqn. A long low level flight took me across barren desert to St Margaret's Monastery at the base of Mount Sinai. On the return flight, I came across an Arab with his camel plodding steadily in a westerly direction. My curiosity was aroused so I turned and set course in the direction he was following. Within about 20 miles, I flew over a small oasis and I am still amazed that

PR.10 VW376 A-C 541 Squadron taking off from Laarbruch in 1955. [Brian Ashley]

he could navigate so accurately. I frequently complained about having no navigation aids, but he did not even have a map and compass. When we left Kabrit on 28 April on our return journey to Germany we gave them the customary low flypast. As I passed the control tower I was pleasantly surprised to see that I was way below the wind sock.

"The mess at Gütersloh was shared with our sister 79 Sqn (with FR.9s), who claimed a small ante room on the left of the entrance and we occupied a similar one on the right plus the library. If someone was rash enough to venture into enemy territory the error was soon pointed out. While we operated singly and quietly at long distances from base, 79 Sqn normally flew in small formations at low level on tactical photo sorties for the army near the battlefield forward area. The character of the two squadrons could not have been more dissimilar. They were brash and noisy and had the highest flying accident record in RAF Germany, while we went about our tasks quietly and we hardly had an accident record. We fought tooth and nail in the mess but if strangers tried to intervene we would unite to see them off; rather like brothers.

"We had to produce a formation for the AOC's flypast and I was watching 79 Sqn landing as we taxied in to our dispersal. As a matter of pride they had to fly a curved approach all the way to the beginning of the runway. As Paul Worthington was approaching the threshold he must have flown into some jet wash from the aircraft in front and he made a beautiful three-point landing in the undershoot area, on his nose wheel, left wingtip and the left wing tank. He then bounced on to the runway, finished his landing run and returned to dispersal as if it was his normal method of arrival.

"The PR.10 seemed to have a personality of its own. It was very reliable and never let us down. It could fly much further than the others and although heavier on the controls because the aileron spring tabs had been removed, it was very manoeuvrable. All that was needed was a strong right arm. Occasionally I had the opportunity to fly an air test without wing tanks or cameras and it was great fun to fly a full range of aerobatics. It was very stable on radar approaches and it could be flown very accurately. The radar controllers could recognise the difference between a PR.10 sitting steadily on the glide path and an FR.9 of 79 Sqn yo-yoing its way home to roost. I became very fond of the PR.10 particularly VW376 A-C, Charlie, which I flew as often as possible. On a long flight when detailed maps were needed in the target area, a high degree of cockpit discipline was essential to avoid the cockpit becoming full of used maps. When the same maps were required in the reverse order for the return flight the pilot could easily get involved in a game of Hunt the Map.

"In June, Fg Off Denzil (Denny) Beard and Fg Off Lew Levitt departed on the next of the Sqn detachments to 13 Sqn at Kabrit. Just before they were due to return, we heard news that Denny's aircraft had last been seen spinning into the Mediterranean Sea without a tail unit. No parachute had been seen but the following day news came through that Denny had survived. He had been picked out of the sea after many hours by a French freighter and taken back to Tunis and was staying with the British Air Attaché's family, which included two attractive daughters. Immediately, the whole atmosphere changed and the bar was opened. When both Denny and Lew returned to base, we learned that on the flight from Tunis to Istres, Lew's aircraft had hit the tail of Denny's aircraft. The tail unit was knocked off and the aircraft fell into a spin. Denny immediately ejected and found himself on his parachute just below 30,000 feet. The temperature was extremely cold and the parachute began to swing. Soon he became air sick and continued to be so until he landed in the sea. After the collision, Lew's aircraft pitched up and went into a spin, from which he was finally able to recover at just above 20,000 feet.

"High level sorties were very demanding. We normally climbed to about 43,000 feet and then settled down at maximum continuous engine speed and allowed the aircraft to slowly climb as fuel was used. We often reached 47,000 feet towards the end of our sorties but our oxygen system was the same as the old Meteor fighters and was not cleared up to that height but we pressed on regardless. Although PR was a daytime activity, we still had to maintain our night-flying proficiency and one evening, after checking the weather forecast, the boss, who was a man of few words, declared, 'Everybody to Bristol and back!' As I was approaching the English east coast westbound at about 44,000 feet, I saw an aircraft coming directly towards me but about 2,000 above me. It was Derek Webb on his way home. Either the navigation was good or we were both lost.

"One of our pilots had been on a long sortie down to the Austrian border and on the return leg he was over full cloud cover. His let down point for Gütersloh was in the Frankfurt area, but he misread his navigation log and instead of setting the correct compass bearing, he set the number of miles to run. This took him in a heading just north of east. He broke through the cloud base at about 3,000 feet and was surprised to find he was in a strange area. A quick run around his map and he realised he was near to the River Elbe in East Germany. He immediately pulled up into cloud again and began heading west. A little later, he passed through a hole in the clouds and saw below him an airfield sprinkled with MiG fighters. He disappeared again into cloud with a much increased heart rate and continued tip-toeing home. Eventually he reached West Germany and scraped into Wunstorf with remarkably little fuel.

"On a low level cross-country flight, I was crossing a large lake known as Dümmer See and as I approached the far bank, I noticed a group of girls bathing. I immediately circled round with the intention of obtaining another entry for 'photo of the month'. When the girls saw the aircraft returning they climbed out of the water on to the bank. I had an F24 side-facing camera fitted, but to obtain a good close up we had to fly low and slow. As I approached to take it, I saw that the girls were all naked and realised this would make a much better picture. I was not satisfied with my first pass so I decided to go round for a better one. This time, I was lower and slower and to add value to the picture the girls were waving. As I took the photo, the aircraft began to shake and I realised it was on the point of stalling. I hit the throttles and by great good fortune, normal flight was regained. During my return to base, I pondered on how I would have explained to the boss that the aircraft came to be resting in water nearly up to the cockpit rails while flying a low level cross country.

"I was waiting one morning for one of our pilots to return. I heard the aircraft taxy into its dispersal, but the pilot took a long time to come into the operations room. I walked out to the dispersal and climbed the blast wall which protected it. Down below, the pilot was on his knees hammering part of his aircraft with a stone and beating it back into shape. I decided to retreat and wait until he came in to de-brief. I asked if he had completed his task and if the aircraft was serviceable and he assured me that he had got the target and the aircraft was OK. After he left, I collected our Flt Sgt and went to survey the scene. The pilot, while turning inside the pan, had scraped his wing tip along the revetment wall. He knew all aircraft were needed to meet our tasks, so he unscrewed the wing tip with a coin and then used a round cobble stone to beat it back into shape. Chiefy and I agreed he had done a good job and a coat of paint could wait till later. PR pilots were noted for their resourcefulness.

"In September came Exercise Beware when we acted as attackers against England to test the UK air defences. The Hunter was the newest fighter in the RAF and we found that we could avoid them. After a few days we were asked to limit our height to 45,000 feet to give them a more realistic target. This gave a boost to our confidence. During the exercise I flew an endurance test and logged a flight of three hours and 15 minutes which is the longest I know of in a standard Meteor aircraft.

"This period was one of the coldest periods of the Cold War and the political situation was very tense. This was brought home to me when the boss came alongside me while I was walking across the hangar and told me I was to go to a briefing in a couple of days' time and I was to talk about it to no-one. The briefing was given by two men in civilian clothes in a secure room and I was given a special target. I was left to prepare the flight myself without restriction. I chose my aeroplane, cameras, maximum fuel and time. Occasionally, the boss would quietly ask if everything was going well and I am sure he did not know my target. Before I departed on the sortie I had to authorise the flight myself and use a typical task number.

When I returned to base I was debriefed by one of the men in civilian clothes and a stranger. Normally all our films were processed, printed and plotted by our own photographic unit but this time, the films were taken away by the visitors and I never saw or heard of them again. I only realised much later that if anything had gone wrong the RAF could have denied all knowledge of the sortie. The only evidence was my signature in the authorisation book. Because of the secrecy, I do not know if any other pilots were involved in these missions but if so, it could only have been one of the other three officers who were able to authorise flights.

81 SQN

"After I left 541 in 1956, I went first to ETPS and then as flight commander on the PR Squadron Bassingbourn. Now the gods in their wisdom had sent me back to my old love, the PR.10, this time to 81 Sqn in Singapore. This was the RAF's last single-seat PR squadron and this was the only chance I would have to fly my favourite role again. Flying with 81 Sqn was very different from the Cold War confrontation in Germany and the squadron's main task was flying Operation Firedog operations over the Malayan jungle against the communist terrorists led by Chin Peng. The tasks were set by the army and usually consisted of rectangular areas of jungle which required three photo runs side by side from 30,000 feet to give a small area coverage. The flying had to be precise otherwise gaps were left in the coverage, but the really tricky part was finding the switch-on points in large areas of virgin jungle. We had no downward vision from the Meteor so the switch-on point, when found, was approached in a steep turn and the aircraft rolled out exactly over the switch-on point, on exactly the required heading and with wings level exactly at 30,000 feet. At least that was intended.

"A major problem with low level sorties from Tengah was the high cockpit temperatures. When the aircraft were standing on the tarmac any parts of the fuselage which were exposed to the sun became hot enough to burn a bare hand. Locally made sun shades were used but they had to be frequently moved to protect the cockpits. Taxying out to the take-off point was no great problem with the hood open but as soon as the hood was closed for take-off, the cockpit became a greenhouse and the temperature began to rise. The aircraft had no cooling air and the cockpit temperature control when selected to cold merely allowed warm, ambient air to enter the cockpit. We normally flew low level sorties clad in flying suits over socks and pants but our Mae West life jackets and parachute and seat harnesses prevented any air circulating. I don't know what temperature was reached after one and a half hours flying, but when we returned to dispersal both us and our flying kit were wet through. Our airmen were well aware of the problem and as they climbed the side to put in the

Three PR.10s of 81 Squadron in echelon port with Brian Ashley on the outside. [Brian Ashley]

ejection seat safety pins, the first thing that came over the cockpit side was an ice cold bottle of drink from the flight-line cooler. It normally disappeared in one quaff. The overall effect was to leave us very tired.

"Operating the Meteor PR.10 at maximum weight from the old runway at Tengah was dangerous. The runway was 2,000 yards long and when taking off in the middle of the day the high outside air temperature reduced the thrust from the engines. With 795 gallons of fuel and three cameras with full magazines, the aircraft was very heavy. The acceleration down the runway was slow and the nose wheel was still on the ground at 95 knots or more with the little wheel spinning around at speeds for which it had not been designed. Eventually the aircraft was hauled into the air at about 130 knots just before the end of the runway. It crossed the overshoot area very low and still accelerating slowly. At the south end of the runway, we had rocky ground quite unsuitable for a forced landing and at the north end, mangrove swamps, which were equally uninviting. At full weight, it was not possible to climb away on one engine until a speed of about 165 knots had been reached. If an engine failed before this speed, the aircraft was bound to crash land. Our ejection seats had a minimum ejection height of 200 feet at a minimum speed of 200 knots. Breathing was resumed when both these criteria were met! On one occasion, a PR.10 on take-off burst a main-wheel tyre just before lift-off.

The wing dropped and the wing tank hit the ground. A hole was filed in the bottom of the tank and 100 gallons of fuel flowed onto the runway and caught fire. The take-off was abandoned and the aircraft stopped in one piece. The blazing fuel had been left behind and did not reach the aircraft. We eventually discovered that we had been supplied with tyres which had been re-treaded three times. It did not happen again.

"One Saturday morning in October 1959, I was detailed to fly a low level task in the southern part of Thailand and because of the long range, I would have to fly at high level to the Thai border, descend to do my task and then refuel at Butterworth, the RAAF airfield just south of the Thai border. I filed a flight plan with air traffic control and set off on my task. All went well until after I had finished the task and came from behind Gong Kedah (a big hill just north of Butterworth) and called Butterworth for permission to join their circuit. I was disconcerted when they asked me who I was. I told them I had filed a flight plan to land there and they informed me the airfield was closed because a trench had been dug across the runway. I checked my remaining fuel and I had only 80 gallons per engine. The nearest diversion airfield was Ipoh which had a short runway, but was about 80 miles south of me. I did not have enough fuel to fly at low level. If I tried to fly at high level, I would run out of fuel on the climb so I chose the good old English compromise: I climbed as quickly as possible to 25,000 feet and then flew on one engine. Slowly, the valley in which Ipoh lay came into view but it was covered in low cloud. The airfield had no approach or landing aids and it was therefore no place to be. I had no alternative but to continue on towards Kuala Lumpur as long as my fuel lasted. After an agonisingly long time, the area of the airfield came into sight but the valley was full of haze and the sun prevented me from seeing the runway. I continued at height until eventually, I could see the runway and with the throttles closed I began my descent. Kuala Lumpur had been told about my problem and all was cleared for me but by this time, I had no idea how much fuel I had remaining. I spiralled down keeping well above a normal approach height. Unfortunately, the approaches were tricky. At the approach end I intended to use, there was a huge jam factory situated near the runway threshold but just off to the left side. At the far end of the runway was a railway embankment which would certainly stop me if I ran off the end. I began to breathe again when I safely arrived on the beginning of the runway. As I turned off the other end of the runway, my port engine stopped but as I only had one more left turn to make I could continue taxying. When I reached the dispersal area and started the left turn, the starboard engine came out on strike in sympathy and also stopped. While the aircraft was being prepared for the flight back to Tengah the ground crew brought up a 900-gallon fuel bowser and my aircraft gobbled up all the contents.

"On 16 December 1959, 81 Sqn flew its 10,000th Operation Firedog operation. Fg Off George Paul, who had flown very many of them, was given the honour of flying the task. I flew our Meteor T.7 with Cpl Court, one of our ground photographers and we took a series of photos as George departed from Tengah en route for the great occasion. In November, one of our Meteor PR.10s was found to have developed some dangerous behaviour and I was asked to investigate it. When a Meteor lost one engine at high thrust and low speed, it would rapidly roll towards the dead engine but WB165 rolled much faster to the left than to the right. The rate of roll was sufficient to be very dangerous. Problems of lateral and directional stability can be tricky to diagnose in older aircraft and during November and December I flew ten air tests until the fault was cleared. Several adjustments made minor improvements but the main problem was asymmetric friction in the rudder control circuit; a seemingly minor defect but a potential killer. The controls were refurbished and WB165 became a normal, well behaved PR.10 again.

"At this time, 60 Sqn was at Tengah equipped with Meteor NF.14 night fighters and I was asked to have a look at one of their aircraft WS805, which was throwing tantrums. Before flying the new type, I had a good look at the Pilot's Notes and the flying was no problem. I found the NF.14 a nice old lady and its handling was rather like driving a London bus. Later I discovered that the 60 Sqn navigators were not keen to fly with me again; they complained I flew it far too slowly on the approach. This surprised me as I was spot on the speeds recommended in the Pilot's Notes. I often wondered about the approach speeds used by their own pilots.

"On 1 August 1960, 81 Sqn was invited by the Malay government to participate in a large flypast of aircraft over Kuala Lumpur to mark a national celebration day. PR squadrons do not normally practise formation flying but relations with Malaya were very good and we were keen to take part. We managed to fit in some practice and produced a nine-ship Meteor formation. Only one full scale rehearsal was planned and then the great occasion was upon us. The flypast was led by the slowest aircraft and followed by successively faster flights. Our place in it was behind a flight of Beverleys and we were followed by an RN squadron of Sea Hawks from a visiting aircraft carrier (806 Sqn off HMS *Albion*). The timing of the previous flights was not good and as we approached Kuala Lumpur we could see the Beverleys ahead looming larger and larger and we reduced our speed and weaved from side to side to attempt to stay behind. Of course, this passed the problem on to the Sea Hawks behind us and as we approached the saluting base the Sea Hawks drifted slowly under us and won the race by a short head. Perhaps this is now recorded as another great naval victory.

"Soon afterwards, news circulated that we were about to re-equip with Canberra PR.7s. During the conversion period, I managed to get my share of Meteor operations so I had few complaints. We continued to operate both Meteors and Canberras and I flew my last two Operation Firedog operations on 30 June 1961; I refuelled at RAF Butterworth between sorties and then returned to Tengah. The end finally came on 7 July 1961, when Dickie Littlejohn and I delivered the RAF's last two Meteor PR.10s to the maintenance unit (MU) at RAF Seletar to be written off. I made sure I was the last one down! I taxied into the MU in WB154 expecting to be marshalled to a place of honour but instead a scruffy airman waved me off the taxiway and immediately stopped me and asked me to shut down. I could not believe the RAF's last Meteor PR.10 was being left cast aside and unloved. I remember standing in the cockpit feeling so disappointed that such a faithful old warrior was being dumped so shabbily and wondering what I could take as a souvenir. I decided to take the crowbar which was clipped into the left side of the cockpit to use if we had to break out of the cockpit in emergency. I think we may have been able to break the old two-piece cockpit cover but I doubt if we could have broken the later one-piece hood. The crowbar has served me just as well as the Meteor did for the last 50 years.

"I did not realise it at the time, but I had just become the last single-seat PR pilot in the RAF. Sidney Cotton had acquired his first Spitfire in about 1940 and by great single-minded drive had bullied or cajoled the RAF into forming small units and then expanding them into bigger units. RAF commanders were desperate for up-to-date information from inside Europe and Sidney Cotton's results were so impressive that in a short time the first PR units were established. The Spitfires were eventually joined by PR Mosquitos but they had navigators. Both continued to the end of the war. After the war money was so scarce that both types had to continue in service until jet aircraft could be introduced to replace them. The Meteor PR.10 took over the Spitfire role but by the late 1950s, they were replaced in Europe and the Middle East by the Canberra PR.3 and PR.7. No.81 PR Squadron was the last remaining Meteor PR unit but my flight with the last aircraft to RAF Seletar had brought the era of single-seat PR to an end. The whole period of the single-seat PR operations had only lasted a bare 20 years and I felt very proud to have closed the last chapter of the great contribution made by the unsung heroes of the PRUs. It had been my ideal role and I was happy that I had been the last of the cold and lonely pilots."

THE GROUND CREW

Working in the oppressive heat of Singapore was just as much of a trial for the ground crew as it was for the pilots. It was not without its compensations, however, as air wireless mechanic **Alec Audley** discovered when he was posted to 81 Sqn.

"I joined the air force in December 1958 and trained as an air wireless mechanic at Yatesbury. When I finished the course, I was put on a draft to Singapore which pleased me greatly; I didn't ask for it, that's where they sent me. I flew out in a BOAC Britannia which was fantastic, rather than a troopship. We got to Singapore on a Sunday, so on the Monday morning I reported to 81 Sqn after arriving and I was then issued with a toolkit by a Cpl Jones. I had to set to and paint it all a certain colour so if I left anything in an aircraft they would know it was mine. When I arrived there, I was the youngest person on the squadron and on the first night I was in the billet I think I was the only sober person there by the time the NAAFI closed. It was a very happy squadron and drinking was a big thing. Everybody retired to the NAAFI at one o'clock when we finished and if they had money – we only got paid once a fortnight – they would be up in the bar.

Alec Audley checking the VHF radios in an 81 Squadron PR.10 at Tengah. [Alec Audley]

"I started doing before flight, after flight, primary and primary star inspections on the Meteors. In terms of work, the PR.10 only had two 10-channel VHF sets, TR1985 and TR1987, so there was no other complicated equipment which we got later when we got Canberras. Because of that, my working load wasn't that great, so I was involved in doing starter crews, seeing the aircraft off, seeing them in, helping with wheel changes, cleaning them, all the normal extraneous duties you get on a squadron.

"It was all very straightforward, but the equipment we were supplied with to tune the VHF sets whenever they had their crystals changed for the operation they were going on, was what was known as a field strength meter. It was a little square box with an aerial on it which you stood on the ground because there was nowhere else to stand it. The two VHF sets were inside the back hatch and I had to stand in there facing forward and the sets were in front of me. How the hell you were supposed to tune those sets and look at the field strength meter...it was a physical impossibility, apart from the fact it was bloody dark in there anyway! So we had a bulb and an aerial connector, so you would take out the aerial from the top of the set, plug in your bulb and then tune it to maximum brightness. You thereby got the sets tuned perfectly. The VHF sets were easily located in the back hatch, nothing obstructed access to them and you could change them very quickly. They sat in their respective trays; there were two knurled nuts, on the front of each set, which you undid, pulled the set forward to slide out the two locating pins on the back of the set and you could then lift the whole thing out. We would occasionally have a Meteor come back and waggle its wings, as it flew low in front of the control tower, to say the radio had gone out, but not very often, they were quite reliable.

"We did get faults – particularly on the T.7; because it had two seats, you had to have an intercom between the front and rear. On the one we had, WA681, there was a mute switch on top of the rear control column whereby they could mute the receivers in the VHF – it also muted the intercom. It was supposed to be a spring-loaded switch so that you could press it, mute things and then when you released it, you were back on intercom. But I don't know who did it or if it was standard fit, but the one on our T.7 was not; it was just a switch. So if somebody inadvertently switched that switch over and you didn't know about it, nobody had any intercom and they would be screaming 'Radio, radio, radio'. I don't know if that was a design fault or if someone had fitted the wrong switch.

"I had a great time; it was a great formative period of my life. I was there for not quite two and a half years and was on the squadron when the Canberras started to arrive. From our point of view, it was really just a bigger version of the Meteor. We had a few more radio equipments, we had a radio compass and AYF radio altimeter I think, but it didn't create any problems. They were very happy days; it was the time before there was very heavy management. There was a Flt Sgt in charge of the ground crew – he was God. He sat in the office and looked after us all, doled out the work and got everything running. By the time I left, we had an engineering officer, lots of Flt Sgts and it was bureaucratic.

"One night, I came back from Singapore and as I was walking through the main gate and round the side of the guardroom, a voice shouted, 'Give us a cigarette'. I recognised the voice as one of the lads on the squadron, so I immediately took a cigarette out and threw it over the wall. He immediately threw it back to me and said, 'Light it you silly sod!' So I lit it and threw it back to him. Because it was about nine o'clock and quiet, they let him have a smoke and they let him out the next morning – he'd been drunk in the NAAFI or something.

"We had two billets and because we were a PR squadron, there were a lot of photographers and developers who ran the mobile photographic unit. They had one billet right down by the boundary fence, which still had bullet holes in it from the Japanese days. There was a gate in this fence and beyond that was a marsh full of mosquitoes and frogs that kept people awake (but not me); as soon as it got dark, the cacophony started. There was a path across this marsh and the Malayan air force had their billets on the far side of it; they used to come in through this wicker gate to go to the mess or whatever. Because we were right up against the fence, we were out of the way and above us were the Fire Section who we got to know very well, so much so that one Sunday morning, I got to drive all the fire engines. It was a different world in the Far East Air Force.

"We had our own hangar and because we had cameras in our aircraft, we had to put them in the hangar at night. We had a duty crew who started at half past six and I was a tractor driver, so I would go down to MT and book one out, then go down to the squadron and relieve the RAF policeman and his dog. Invariably, I would have to run them back to the bomb dump where they had the kennels with the dog sitting on the seat alongside me and the policeman sitting on the mudguard. There was one of each trade on the duty crew – airframes, engines, instruments, electrics, radio – so half a dozen of us would open the hangar and tow the aeroplanes out. Of course, if you do it by the book, you're supposed to have a person on the tail, one on each wingtip, one on the nose and somebody controlling operations. Two of us used to do it; one man in the cockpit and one on the tractor. We would tow them out onto the line then do the BFs. I would test both sets and call up, 'Tengah tower, Tengah tower, Meteor test broadcast, do you read?' and they'd reply, 'Read you strength five'. Later on, we had to stop using the word 'Meteor' and just say a number, so if anybody was listening, they wouldn't know what was going on.

"I came back to the UK in January 1961 to join my fitter's course at

Yatesbury again. Initially, I was posted to Kinloss for a month or so and then I was sent down to Yatesbury. There was a story attached to that. When I'd been on 81 Sqn for three months, Chiefy Atkinson – a very nice bloke, I couldn't have asked for a better Flt Sgt – came up to me and said, 'Audley, you're posted to 205/209 Sqn at Changi'. I said, 'I don't want to go, I've just settled in here; I feel part of the team.' Standing next to me was another air wireless mechanic called George Gatcombe and he said, 'I've worked on Shacks, I'll go', so Chiefy said, 'Right, you can go then'. But Innsworth didn't know that, so when it came to end my tour, as far as they were concerned I'd been working on Shackletons for the last two years so they posted me to Kinloss. I later went to Aden and finally left the air force in 1969 as a sergeant."

Alun Williams also served on 81 Sqn in Singapore. He was an engine mechanic and his description of the Meteor start and see-off procedure illustrates just how straightforward and basic an aeroplane it was in many ways.

"To get a PR.10 started, the trolley accumulator ('trolley-acc') was connected at the nose of the aircraft and the fire extinguisher was positioned at a point level with the wing tip and the nose. The parachute and ejection seats straps were pre-positioned over the side of the cockpit. As the pilot walked out, the pitot head cover was removed, rolled up inside its red warning flag and placed out of harm's way on the trolley acc.

"The pilot walked around the aircraft, carrying out his own checks, then climbed into the cockpit. First, you handed him the parachute straps, then the ejection seat straps. When he had buckled all these up, you plugged in the R/T connection, removed the ejection seat pin from the top handle and this was shown to the pilot. You said, 'R/T in, pin out Sir', then the pin was stored in a slot at the side of the ejection seat. You then got clear and, waiting with your mate by the fire extinguisher, signalled the pilot to start the first engine. The pilot pressed the start button, then you started counting slowly, one, two, three, four... If the engine had not ignited by the time you counted to twelve, you ran to the undercarriage bay and banged on the starter solenoid. Usually the engine would then ignite, sending a 50-foot jet of flame out of the exhaust tailpipe! The first few times were a bit frightening, but one soon got used to it.

"When both engines were running, the trolley acc was disconnected, the fire extinguisher removed and you awaited the pilot's instruction to remove the chocks. The second starter crew man, who assisted by manning the fire extinguisher, removed the chocks when signalled. You then marshalled the aircraft forward and signalled the pilot to turn towards the perimeter track when he was clear of the other aircraft in the dispersal line. You then signalled 'proceed to next marshaller', saluted the pilot and he returned the salute. No personal safety equipment, no ear protection, no fireproof clothing, but we're still here."

Of the three PR.10 squadrons, 13 was the first to relinquish them in favour of the Canberra PR.7. This was in August 1956, by which time the squadron had moved to Akrotiri in Cyprus. As has already been mentioned, 541 Sqn disbanded the following year which just left 81 Sqn in Singapore to continue flying the single-seat PR flag. Canberra PR.7s had already been on the squadron for well over a year when Brian Ashley made that final landing on 7 July 1961.

CHAPTER SEVEN
CHALLENGING TIMES –
PILOT TRAINING IN THE 1950s

THE BOYS

Fg Off Bill George
National Service, joined in 1952. Flying training at 2 ITS, 1 BFTS, 10 AFTS. Learnt to fly Meteors at 207 AFS. 288 Sqn Balliol Middle Wallop. Left the air force in 1954.

Flt Lt Bill Gill
Pilot training in RN 1945. Joined RAF in 1950, Meteors at 203 AFS, 1st tour 263 Sqn, CFS, instructing at 12 FTS Manby, 20 Sqn Hunter, instructed on Fouga Magister with German air force, JC&SS Bircham Newton, Syerston, Ternhill, 72 Sqn Wessex, 1310 Flt Whirlwind. Left RAF 1966. Joined RAAF, 9 Sqn Iroquois including a tour in Vietnam.

Wg Cdr Alan McDonald
National Service, joined in 1951. Flying training 4 FTS Heany, 6 FTS, trained on Meteors at 211 AFS, 203 AFS, 231 OCU and 76 Sqn Canberra, 138 and 214 Sqns Valiant, 27 Sqn Vulcan, CFS, 6 FTS, Canadian Forces CL-41 Tutor, OC Spadeadam, command flight safety officer. Retired 1984.

Flt Lt Mike Read
Meteor training in 1951 at 202 AFS, CFS, instructor at 210 AFS, 233 OCU Vampire, 34 Sqn Meteor then Hunter, 229 OCU, 224 Group Seletar, 229 OCU. Retired 1969.

Wg Cdr Gordon Webb
Joined in 1942 as engine fitter, 11 OTU Wellington, 243 Sqn Dakota, pilot training, Meteors at 211 AFS, 203 AFS, 231 OCU Canberra, 138 Sqn Valiant, CFS, 10 Sqn VC10. Retired 1974 and joined CSE at Kidlington.

With further contributions from Alan Colman (Chapter One) and Derek Davies (Chapter Three).

LEARNING TO COPE WITH JETS
At the end of the 1940s and into the early 1950s, the rapid onset of a large increase in demand for pilots came at a time when the flying training system was still feeling its way around how best to teach people to fly jets and indeed, where to find the numbers of experienced instructors required. This, coupled with the particular

demands of mastering the Meteor's asymmetric flying characteristics, was material in bringing about the very high number of accidents and fatalities suffered in the early years of the jet AFS system. **Alan McDonald** was to learn something of the problem even before he started flying them.

> "My first brush with the Meteor came before I actually started my flying training. I joined the RAF at the very end of 1951, but because there was a shortage of initial training school (ITS) spaces due to a lot of expansion then (they actually opened up Cosford as an ITS just for two courses), my course was sent to Driffield for a month 'on hold'. There was an atmosphere at Driffield that was hard to define – it was fear; you could almost touch it. It was an active AFS but the pilots on the courses in training seemed to be a bit afraid of the Meteor. It soon became apparent why – we did four funerals in the month that we were there and about three of the cadets on my course decided that it was all too dicey and actually opted out of flying training before we started. There were an awful lot of crashes and fatalities in the Meteor in those days. Although the jets had been going then for several years, a lot of people were still flying them like a piston-engine fighter. I also think the standard of instruction at times wasn't very good; a lot was assumed – you were shown what to do and then you tried to do it. Sometimes you needed to be shown how to do it!"

Opinions about the reasons behind the accident rate are many and varied, but the two biggest issues that are voiced time and again are the standard of instruction and the procedures adopted when teaching asymmetric flying. In the latter case, a major factor was the initial requirement to practise asymmetric handling by shutting one engine down completely; this was subsequently changed to allow the training to be done with one engine simply throttled back. There also seems to have been a noticeable difference in the accident rate between some of the AFSs which is not easy to explain, even allowing for the frequently mentioned perpetually poor visibility at Worksop.

THE ASYMMETRIC ISSUE

There is little doubt that the Meteor could be something of a handful when being flown on one engine, especially so when low and slow in the circuit. Thus, teaching new pilots how to handle the situation was always a key aspect of learning to fly the type. **Alan Colman** described how he was taught when he was training at 205 AFS and 226 OCU in 1951.

> "In Training Command we had been in the habit of shutting down engines, stop-cocking them in order to do practice single-engine flying – or to save fuel at low level. When I got to Stradishall they said, 'If you're in one state of emergency by being short of fuel, for Christ's sake don't create

211 FTS Worksop aerobatic team July 1957. From L to R: Terry Bollands, Alan Colman, Benny Bennett and Les Harrison. [Alan Colman]

another one by shutting down an engine'. There was a fuel-saving case for actually shutting down an engine if you were critically lost and at low level, but the argument against just throttling back during asymmetric training was that it still left you with residual thrust, which meant that you were always in a slightly worse handling situation if you shut the engine down. There was also the feeling that you weren't going to take asymmetric flying seriously if you knew you had a 'good' engine, which would be immediately available if you cocked things up.

"When I was under training at 205 AFS it was the normal procedure to shut down an engine completely to simulate engine failure. So, on 16 April 1951, I was undertaking a sortie in an F.4 (VW259), where I was authorised to do just that – a few normal two-engined landings followed by a single-engined overshoot and then a single-engined final landing. Unfortunately, I slightly misjudged my single-engined circuit and instinctively selected airbrakes out to correct my height on finals. The tower then ordered me to go round again as there was traffic on the runway, thus prompting me to start an overshoot 'on one' – but with those airbrakes still out – and forgotten. Before I discovered my error, I have vivid memories of the top of the flagpole outside station headquarters passing just a few feet below as I struggled. The Meteor would not 'go round again' on one with the airbrakes out! I am here because I discovered my mistake just in time. A student on a later course was not so lucky and crashed fatally into the officers' mess."

THE PHANTOM DIVE

A highly undesirable characteristic of the Meteor manifested itself if it was being flown with the airbrakes out and the undercarriage was then lowered without first retracting the airbrakes, an issue briefly referred to in Chapter Two. This could and often did, result in a loss of control and came to be known as the Phantom Dive, which killed many pilots. Opinion clearly suggests that not all marks were susceptible to it; the T.7 being most prone based on the accident statistics. **Alan Colman**:

"The existence of the Phantom Dive characteristic was hotly disputed by many pilots with considerable experience on the aeroplane – as was the final conclusion that it was a feature unique to the extended-fuselage versions, like the T.7. I did have a fright though following a formation break in an F.8; it suddenly fell out of the sky sideways on the downwind leg and I had to level the wings and apply power in a hurry to avoid the topography. When you dropped the gear on a Meteor the left leg always came down first, causing a sudden yaw. In a tight break onto the downwind leg the airbrakes would be already out, the throttles closed, the speed around 140 knots and there would be nearly 90 degrees of bank applied as you banged the gear down. Asking for trouble maybe, but that sudden sideslip only caught me out once!"

Landing weight to the debate about whether or not the T.7 was the only Meteor variant to suffer from this phenomenon, **'Moose' Davies** tried to get an F.8 into a Phantom Dive – at a safe altitude – while he was flying with 616 Sqn.

"A safety trick in the Meteor was when turning onto the final approach, you put your left hand forward in open position and checked that you could feel three levers. Touching three meant you had landing gear down, full flap and importantly, speed brakes in. Only feeling two meant something was wrong. The Meteor had a bad reputation known as the Phantom Dive and there were quite a few fatalities. It occurred when downwind and lowering the gear; the aircraft suddenly dived to the ground and pilots were too low to recover. It was suggested that it was due to having speed brakes out at the time of gear lowering. Due to hydraulics not being symmetrical, one wheel lowered before the other, or one started going back up for a time from half-way down. This, with speed brake out, could cause dramatic alteration in the airflow above and below the wing. Eventually we were teaching downwind 'Speed brake in, gear down' and making the physical action of the left hand pushing the lever even if already at the 'In' position. I tried many times at safe height to bring about a Phantom Dive but never succeeded. I think it more of a training thing in the T.7 as it seemed very rare in the F.8."

F.4 VW255 O 205 AFS Middleton St. George, 1951. [Alan Colman]

Mike Read was a QFI on both the Meteor and the Vampire and had strong views about both the Phantom Dive and in the general characteristics of the two types.

> "I began Meteor flying at 202 AFS Valley, then went on to CFS qualifying as a Meteor QFI. I instructed on T.7s at 210 AFS Tarrant Rushton from its formation in November 1952 until it closed in April 1954. There were two squadrons: No.1 using the Meteor T.7s and Vampire FB.5s, which I instructed on and No.2 with Meteor T.7s and F.3s. I ferried an F.3 into Tarrant Rushton at the start and thought it was rubbish compared to the Vampire. The following April, I had another go which confirmed my original impression, so there was no incentive to try again. After completing my flying instructor tour at Tarrant Rushton, I was posted to 233 OCU Pembrey to learn to be a fighter pilot on Vampires.
>
> "As far as the Phantom Dive was concerned, I believe all marks would have been affected. At low speed, 160 knots or so, if a yaw was induced, a very high rate of descent built up c. 6,000 feet per minute, which when you were halfway round the finals turn or even downwind at 1,000 feet, gave no time to recover. The yaw could be induced by asymmetric power, the undercarriage lowering one leg at a time, a boot-full of rudder by

mistake, or any number of reasons accentuated if the airbrakes were out. At AFS, we used to demonstrate the Phantom Dive at a safe height. The emphasis was always to 'watch the ball' of the turn and slip indicator until it became second nature and make sure the airbrakes were in. I believe the absence of a ventral tank may have worsened the situation – we normally flew with them. Of course the night fighters had long canopies too, but I can't remember any differences between the marks. The main aim was to avoid getting into such a situation, no matter what."

GETTING TO GRIPS WITH THE METEOR

Following his unfortunate introduction to the problems the Meteor fleet was experiencing at Driffield, undeterred, **Alan McDonald** found himself getting his hands on the aircraft.

"I was posted to 211 AFS at Worksop for jet conversion onto the Meteor at the beginning of May 1953. I was just 19 years old and it was all a big adventure. Worksop was a strange base; it was an old wartime airfield made up entirely of wooden and Nissen huts. It was very spread out and the first thing that you got on your arrival was your own bicycle. They were all air force blue and numbered but I have no idea how we found

Alan Colman over the north Norfolk coast at 35,000 ft in F.8 WE936 13 of 4 FTS Worksop, 12 December 1955. [Alan Colman]

our own machine with the hundreds that were lying about everywhere. The other thing about Worksop was the visibility – it was awful all the time. It was before the Clean Air Act and we were east of Sheffield, south of Doncaster and, if the wind swung around, we were to the west of Scunthorpe. All these towns, plus all the many local coal mines, were belching out smoke and the visibility at Worksop was sometimes so bad that you could not see the other end of the runway when you lined up for take-off! One day I actually said to control, 'Is it clear to go?' and they said, 'Yes, it'll be clear by the time you get back' – and we only had about 40 minutes duration. As a means of helping us to line up with the runway on finals, three great big lights were placed on the Ranby roundabout on the A1 road in a sort of an arrow. We didn't have GCA so all we had was the old QGH (a descent through cloud approach) as a landing aid. It was all a bit crude really and was not the ideal spot for an AFS full of very inexperienced pilots. But, the atmosphere was so different from Driffield – there was no fear of the aircraft and we did not have a single accident in the whole time I was there.

"No.211 AFS was an 'all weather' AFS and we did more night flying and instrument flying than the other similar units. We were lucky too, in that we had brand new F.8 single-seat Meteors as opposed to the older F.4s on the other AFSs. The dual flights were still on the T.7 but the F.8 was a revelation, single-seater, ejector seat, pressurised and we had the latest version with wide intakes and duplex burners, just the same as the front-line fighters of the day. When I first flew it, it left me trailing; I thought I would never catch it up. The Harvard could do 200 knots in a dive if you pushed it, but the Meteor did 500 knots plus and it took me time to catch up with the rate of acceleration. My first trip was with a Sgt Greenhead and I hardly caught it at all. It was not the easiest thing to fly and was a bit unforgiving if you got it wrong, as many pilots found out to their cost, especially on one engine, but I must admit I got to like it very much – it was a great adrenalin rush. It was a dodgy aeroplane really, it killed an awful lot of people and it was no respecter of you if you did something wrong. But it was fast and furious and I enjoyed it. I particularly liked the F.8; it was a real pleasure to train on it.

"As usual though, there were a few hairy moments. Not too long into the course I was flying an F.8 solo and was doing aerobatics at about 25,000 feet. All was going well until I got too ham-fisted and enthusiastic with my throttle handling and both engines flamed out. The Meteor was not known as much of a glider and the earth seemed to be rushing up as I tried to relight the motors. This was not the easiest thing to do and you needed four hands and to hold the stick between your knees! You had the relight button on the end of the HP cock and you had the throttles to operate as well. After a short time I got one engine going, but despite all my best efforts, the other one would not start so I called base for an emergency landing and duly landed on one engine. I couldn't taxi off the end because with one motor you went round in circles, so they towed me in. There was some concern that I had only managed to relight the one engine so the engineers investigated the problem and discovered that it would never have started – the relight button was not connected properly. I was glad it was not the same on both sides.

"Later on in the course I had another sortie that made the heart pump a little. I was flying with a new QFI who had only just joined the squadron and we were doing general handling plus some GCAs at Linton-on-Ouse. We did one and I said to the instructor that it was time to go back to base as fuel was getting a bit low, but he replied that he thought we could do one more so I went round the whole pattern again. At this stage, we were getting short of fuel and as we headed back to base I asked if I should shut down one engine. The answer was 'yes', so I duly closed one down but I was still worried about our fuel reserves and enquired whether or not we should land at Finningley and refuel. My instructor thought we could make it home so off I went. When we got back to Worksop, we were *very* low on fuel and I thought it was probably time he took over, but there was no word and I called for a priority landing only to be told that the runway was temporarily blocked and could I go round again. There was no option but to do this so, sweating buckets, I went round again with a whiff of fuel left in the tanks! Still no word from the back about taking control. After we landed (to my great relief), we had to be towed into the dispersal and a voice from the back said, 'How many hours have you got on the Meteor, Mac?' I said about 50 and he answered, 'I thought so, I have only got 20!' It turned out he had been a QFI on Oxfords at Moreton-in-Marsh and had only done a quick Meteor conversion at CFS before coming to Worksop. I was about his second flight with a student. I was, to say the least, a little worried – we had a smell of fuel in that aircraft, much less than the usual '20/20 minimum' left – I think it was nearer 10 and zero! I can't imagine anything like that happening in this day and age, but it was the sort of thing that went on in the rather chaotic early '50s. In his defence, I have to say that he became a very good QFI and many years later we were both captains on the same Valiant squadron.

"There were other memories too, including the first time I pulled a contrail – sounds silly now but at the time, it was a big 'first'; I went round in circles looking at it, never seen one before from up there. The Meteor was a first for me in many ways – the first jet, the first twin, the first single seat, the first ejector seat and even the first tricycle undercarriage. It was, for me, a giant leap in my flying experience. Another thing that has stuck in my memory for all these years was during night flying. It was a lovely dark summer's night and I was sat at about 35,000 feet over the Midlands, you could see all of England laid out from that position; it was magnificent. The visibility was so good that I could see the lights of London and all the big towns to the south almost down to the south coast and Manchester right up to Newcastle in the north. What a sight, which started a long term liking for night flying that lasted right through my career.

"I duly completed the course but many others did not. Only eight of us finished of the 18 who started, although some were transferred to the multi-engine AFS at Swinderby to go on to Transport or Coastal Command. However, most of us who did qualify did not end up on night fighters as we expected, because the Canberra was just coming into service and we were destined for that. My time on the Meteor was not quite over though. We had to wait for a slot on the Canberra OCU at Bassingbourn and so we all went up to Driffield (again) for a month on a holding course. It was like a step backward in time for, far from our brand new F.8s, we flew some very elderly F.4s, they really were rattle-buckets and they were really crude in many ways. I am glad I had the chance to fly them, but I am glad I did not train on them. Driffield was a day fighter AFS and they weren't keen to do night flying, so we almost had to drag them in the air at night because we thought that was part of our job – we still didn't know where we were going then."

Gordon Webb began his RAF career during the war as an apprentice – a Halton Brat – before starting his flying training some years later. He too was sent to Worksop for his jet conversion.

"My introduction to the Meteor was at the All Weather AFS Worksop in 1953. I was thrilled to be moving into the jet world, though I was not destined to fly the Meteor in squadron service. However, like all who did, I never forgot the introduction to its asymmetric characteristics. I think the very strongest amongst us found his knee tested as the speed was allowed slowly to decay until directional control was lost. The fact that the resulting speed was measurably above unstick certainly kept one alert during take-off. I thought it a delight to fly with its amazing rate of climb and its handling at heights far above the existing airways structure, to say nothing of the absence of mixture controls and constant speed units; just fuel cocks and a pair of throttles. Who wouldn't want to fly it?

"My lasting memory of Worksop itself was of constant bad visibility, of groping around the circuit hoping to see the 'sodium' at the end of the downwind leg...all weather training! I flew the Meteor again at AFS Driffield where I was joined by some old hands converting from pistons. To my knowledge there were a couple of instructors who would not 'shut one down' on asymmetric exercises and I realise now that they were probably old Meteor hands who knew the aircraft's recent history. We never dwelt on the matter.

"I remember Driffield mainly for a few moments of excitement. One clear day after reaching altitude, a wisp of smoke curled from behind the gunsight, obscuring the windscreen. It slowly intensified as a horn sounded and the cockpit filled. Still on approach frequency, I put out a PAN call and was immediately given a QDM (magnetic bearing to a station), which was good thinking but didn't seem to matter much at the time. I began a descent to a level at which I intended making my next move when magically, the smoke began to subside. By this time, the duty pilot was on the R/T. Another QDM was followed by his assurance that the horn was nothing to worry about, 'It's only the Angel Gabriel'. The humour had its desired calming effect and I landed without further incident. I gathered later that the problem was something to do with a fuel vapour leak into the cockpit from the ventral tank system, but I learned no more than that, except that if your luck is in, you certainly can have smoke without fire.

"It was on a later staff tour at Little Rissington that I was to be reminded of the Meteor, almost 25 years after Britain's first jet aircraft with its powerful new engines had been catching and tipping up 'Buzz Bombs' bound for London. One day, I was privileged to meet two gentlemen who knew the Meteor inside out, having been part of the design team that brought it into service. They were guests of CFS and I was invited to accompany them to the small CFS museum which housed a Derwent. Of course I leapt at the opportunity to spend time in the company of such venerable men; they had been at Glosters since the beginning of the war. They would have known Frank Whittle, who was a fellow, albeit a much senior entry ex Brat and might even have been involved with the E.28/39. They were the very architects of modern aviation history – this was my lucky day. It was a delight to share their company as they spent a while reminiscing about the Derwent, which they also knew inside out. I reminded myself that these were the very men who had worked against time to build a fighter platform powered by two such engines. Sometimes they simply recalled shared memories; I was enjoying every moment of it. It was an unforgettable day."

Bill George was another National Serviceman who, after being trained to fly Meteors, did not go on to fly the type operationally. He ended his brief RAF career primarily because he didn't feel he fitted in with service life and he wanted to find another career.

"After learning to fly Tiger Moths at Kirton-in-Lindsey and Chipmunks at Booker, it was either Oxfords or Harvards as far as the air force was concerned, and if you trained on Harvards you went on to Vampires. I went to Pershore on Oxfords (10 AFTS). I found the Tiger Moth and Chipmunk were quite easy aircraft to fly, but the Oxford was a testing aircraft. I think that's really the sort of thing you should learn on, because it sorts the men from the boys. I got my wings in May 1953 and went on to Meteors at Full Sutton. I was then 19, a teenager flying jet fighters at a time when we didn't drive motor cars and I think the Meteor was a more glamorous aircraft to fly than the Vampire, so I was well pleased.

"Some of our lot went to Worksop and from there they tended to go onto night fighters, but all the clever chaps went to Worksop and they all failed. Whereas me, the lowliest of idiots, went to Full Sutton and survived. I was good at things like formation flying and aerobatics, but not very good at keeping plus or minus five knots, plus or minus 200 feet and that sort of thing. As well as the T.7s we still had F.3s and F.4s. The F.3 had a smaller jet-pipe than the F.4, you could tell when you walked out to the aircraft what it was, but to get up and climb in they were more or less identical; the one thing they didn't have was ejection seats. I absolutely enjoyed the Meteor and, if I had stayed in the air force, I would have gone straight on to F.8s I think.

"I had a few exciting moments and the worst one was my fault again. We were flying formation in vic more or less into sun. The leader, who was an instructor, was going to turn starboard and I'd be looking at him with the sun behind, so he told me to go echelon port. I was getting cocky by then thinking I knew it all. You'd normally drop down, go about half a mile away and pull up from 50-100 yards to come back in, but I thought, 'No, I'm clever enough now, I'll go down and come up quick'. Well I did that and I thought I was there and I looked at this aircraft at my level and thought, 'That's my mate Pete'. I started to pull up alongside him and I suddenly realised it was the leader and I was coming up under Pete; the aircraft were being sucked together. I was kicking on the stick and we were destroying lift for both of us and were losing height rapidly. I knew what the trouble was but Pete didn't know what the hell was going on. I could see the rivets and read the writing on the underside of his aircraft and my head was sort of level with his ventral tank, probably only about a foot or so clear. I was pushing hard to go down and it wouldn't go, but eventually it did and I must have lost 1,000 feet – Pete lost 500 feet. When we got back on the ground he asked me, 'What was going on there?' and I told him, but I think that was the only incident I had on Meteors.

"After I completed the course, that was the end of jet flying for me, because they knew that I wasn't going to sign on, and I wound up with 288 Sqn at Middle Wallop on Balliols – stooges for the radar school there."

THE INSTRUCTOR'S VIEW

Following his tour on 74 Sqn at Horsham St.Faith and like so many others, **Alan Colman** was sent to CFS to become a QFI. He then found himself instructing at Worksop and during his time there, he had quite a few exciting moments.

"At the end of the CFS course in January 1955, because I'd already flown a full tour on the Meteor, I was posted to 211 FTS Worksop as a Meteor QFI. At Worksop I was riding with another instructor, my very good friend Benny Bennett, in a Meteor T.7 and he was demonstrating manoeuvres that he thought might be useful in a forthcoming aerobatics competition. During his enthusiastic demonstration one of my lap straps broke and I fetched up lying in the canopy of the T.7, which was then upside down (I was in the front!) It required some fairly delicate manoeuvring by me – and he had to turn the thing the right way up very carefully, so that I didn't fall on the flying controls. We both thought the episode was hilarious.

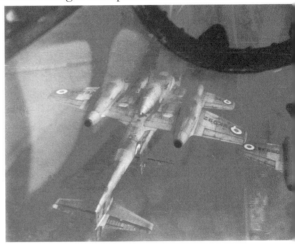

"On 8 July 1955, I was carrying out a pre-final handling test revision flight with a pilot officer student. He was in the front seat of Meteor T.7 WL475 and I was in the rear. On our return to the circuit at the end of the sortie, I quietly stop-cocked one engine – whereupon the student started his engine failure checks and instantly shut down the other engine. I was able to call 'Downwind on None'

Impromptu formation by instructors at 211 FTS Worksop led by Benny Bennett, circa 1956. [Alan Colman]

to the tower as I took control and did a frantic relight on one engine. I then handed control back to the student and ordered him to go round again, regaining circuit height and then carry out a single-engined landing. After that fright, I made a point of always reaching down to wedge the other HP cock in the down position before shutting down an engine when a student was in the other seat! That sort of thing wouldn't happen today because engine failure is always simulated by throttling back. That, of course, is less effective, as the student notices the throttle move so he does not have to recognise from the instrumentation and aircraft feel which engine he has lost. There were no simulators in which to practise emergencies in those days.

"We used the disused Gamston airfield as a relief landing ground and once I had to grab control and carry out a single-engine go-around from the flare when a flock of sheep suddenly ran onto the runway. The teaching was that a landing was compulsory once speed had been reduced below 150 knots, but, if you were lucky and very careful not to apply more live-engine power than you could balance with rudder, such a manoeuvre was possible provided that the 'good' engine (I think it was the port one that ran the hydraulic pump) still provided hydraulic power so that the gear and flaps could be retracted. The best other example was when Pete Stonham had an engine disintegrate (the turbine carving chunks out of the runway) during a night roller landing in a Meteor at CFS Little Rissington. He had just got airborne and still had full flap down, but he somehow managed to fight the thing, disappearing down into the valley at the end of the Rissington runway and then reappearing to complete a normal single-engine circuit and landing. Brilliant flying!

"I was in the rear seat carrying out an instrument rating test (IRT) on a student near the end of his course. At Worksop the QGH procedure involved homing to the overhead at 10,500 feet, then descending outbound a few degrees off the runway reciprocal to half that height and then turning and descending inbound, guided by cathode ray direction finder (CRDF) bearings from the tower, down to (if I remember correctly) 400 feet or until sighting the runway approach lights. On an IRT, a student was required to perform this manoeuvre on 'limited panel' (no artificial horizon) and, usually, on one engine. On this occasion, the student misread his altimeter and descended to 500 feet overhead the airfield (instead of 10,500 feet), at which height we were skimming the tops of a layer of low stratus which was partially covering the ground. In his attempt to turn onto the outbound leg the student 'lost it' and rolled the Meteor inverted and fell into the cloud top. Time for me to grab control and sort it out before we hit the deck! Not surprisingly, the student failed that IRT (and would have had to sit it again another day).

"On 7 January 1957, I was up in T.7 WH129. By this time the practice of fully shutting down engines had been banned and the student, a Flt Lt Campbell, was carrying out a simulated single-engined landing with one engine throttled back. All appeared normal, but as we touched down, I felt the starboard wing drop and the starboard undercarriage light flashed red. Without thinking, I grabbed control and banged full power onto both engines while keeping the starboard wing up with aileron. We made a successful go-around and then observed that the starboard undercarriage light indicated normally green the next time the gear was lowered. A low and slow pass over the tower was arranged and I was advised that the undercarriage appeared to be normally extended. However, on the subsequent landing, the starboard undercarriage light again changed to red as we touched down and very soon after, I felt the wing begin to

T.7 WH192 W-75 206 AFS Oakington, late 1952. [Peter Bogue]

drop. I held it up as long as possible until, pursued by fire engines and ambulances, WH129 executed a gentle slew to the right, off the runway and onto the grass. There we stopped in the middle of the airfield, shut down the engines and evacuated in some haste. A subsequent search found a broken downlock pawl lying on the runway – its condition subsequently diagnosed as 'fatigue failure'. The aeroplane had damage to the skin on the underside of the starboard engine nacelle only – and was quickly repaired.

"In fact WH129 was a 'rogue' and needed to be avoided if you were taking a student up to demonstrate the effects of engine failure on take-off (this would be his introduction to asymmetric flight). This exercise involved level flight at 5,000 feet with gear down, reducing speed to about 130 knots, then applying full power on both engines and suddenly throttling back one. If the pilot did nothing, the dear old Meatbox would yaw violently towards the failed engine then snap upside down. A very frightening demo that was calculated to impress upon the student that an engine failure on take-off was something that needed instant, corrective action – or you went into the overshoot upside down. Only WH129 didn't do that! It would yaw violently and stagger about the sky – but it didn't roll upside down – and so most of the point of the exercise was lost. Needless to say, experienced instructors avoided taking WH129 if they were intending to give that demonstration!"

By the early 1950s, the Meteor F.4 was ousted from the squadrons in favour of the much-improved F.8 and relegated to a training role. Perhaps surprisingly, by the middle of that decade there were still a good number of these, by now rather tired, airframes in use in the AFS/FTS training system, even though F.8s had started to replace them as the squadrons moved on to more advanced types. **Bill Gill** found himself in a particularly difficult situation in an F.4 which, as a result and with the impending disbandment of the unit, was written off.

"In 1955, I was instructing on Meteors at 12 FTS (formerly 209 AFS) Weston Zoyland in Somerset. On 28 April, I took off in a Meteor F.4 (VZ392) to carry out some staff continuation training formation flying practice with a fellow instructor, also in a Meteor F.4. After about 15 minutes practice to the east of Weston Zoyland we decided to return to base with the other instructor taking the lead. I formated on him in the number 2 position on his right-hand side. There was continuous low cloud beneath us with occasional openings so we had a good idea of our position (I thought). Being a thoroughly instinctive fighter pilot I followed him, relying on his knowledge of the area to lead us back to base. He signalled airbrakes out and we commenced a descent at the normal speed of 230 knots.

"As we came down through the cloud, I became aware that it was slowly dissipating and as it cleared, my leader suddenly pulled up so violently that I could not stay in formation with him. He had miscalculated our position and we were in fact on top of the Mendip Hills! I looked ahead and found myself confronted by a stone wall. I banked right and pulled up but could not avoid the aircraft striking the wall just under the starboard wing. The Meteor began shaking violently as I climbed back up in the cloud, but this stopped just as I came back into clear skies at about 3,000 feet. The shaking ceased, but the aircraft was flying as though one engine was not working, i.e. in asymmetric mode. This was strange because both engines were indicating the same power setting. I found out later that the starboard jet-pipe had fallen off, but this was not apparent to me looking out to the right from the narrow confines of the cockpit and the wing looked okay.

"I realised I was in trouble and put out a Mayday call. I did not fancy baling out as the Meteor F.4, which had no ejection seat, had a very high tail and pilots had collided with it trying to escape the machine. Whilst under training one of my fellow students had been killed trying to do just that. With this in mind I cruised around, did a stall check, which was at a lot higher speed than usual and contemplated my options. Both engines appeared to be operating normally but the aircraft was still behaving as though one was out, so I knew something was amiss. Whilst having these thoughts I suddenly saw a gap in the cloud and miraculously an airfield

F.4 VT225 M-19 1 Squadron 206 AFS Oakington, November 1953. [Peter Rogers]

appeared. I selected the undercarriage lever and was surprised when the gear locked down quite normally. Another stall check indicated about 30 knots above normal. I got below cloud and circled the airfield which turned out to be Bristol, then all grass. I managed to get the aircraft down after a very fast approach and came to a halt about 80 metres short of the boundary fence. I got out of the beast, kissed the ground and surveyed the damage. Whilst doing this, a rather pompous official drove up in a Land Rover and to my surprise berated me for landing without a clearance. When he saw the damage to the aircraft he was somewhat chastened but still didn't apologise. Weston Zoyland was informed and they flew a light aircraft over to pick me up.

"The sequel to this was that I appeared before the station commander who told me off for blindly following the leader. It turned out that he had flown bombers all his life and had no idea how fighters were operated. I was exonerated at a later date when, after the accident investigation, a 'green' endorsement was put in my log book. It also bears witness to the amazing strength of the Meteor airframe for staying in one piece after hitting a brick wall at 265 mph! The aircraft was not repaired, however. There were an awful lot of Meteor prangs in those days. I personally lost 12 mates in Meteor accidents. One wonders why."

WZ.RAF. 312.C. || 30.4.55 || DAMAGE TO A/C. NO VZ 392 || RESTR

12 FTS F.4 VZ392 63 after hitting a stone wall during a let-down, 28 April 1955. [Bill Gill]

After suffering such a horrendous accident rate in the early 1950s, the situation at the Meteor-equipped schools did improve considerably as both instructor and jet experience, together with revisions to some of the teaching methods – especially with regard to asymmetric training – made their mark. By 1955/56 the Meteor had all but disappeared from Flying Training Command, only the Worksop unit (by now renamed 4 FTS) soldiering on with the type until it too, went in June 1958. For jet training, the Vampire T.11 now reigned supreme, but as we shall see in the next chapter, the Meteor was to make an unexpected, albeit brief, return to the advanced flying training system.

SECOND WIND –
AIRCREW TRAINING INTO THE 1960S

THE BOYS

Flt Lt John Batty

Joined in 1956. 6 FTS, 5 FTS, 231 OCU. Meteors on SRF, 229 OCU and 54 Sqn Hunter, SRF, 43 Sqn Hunter. Left the air force in 1968 and went into corporate flying.

Sqn Ldr Robin Chandler

Joined in 1954. Flying training at Cranwell, and 7 FTS. Meteors on 4 FTS, BCBS, 231 OCU and 16 Sqn Canberra, Kinloss Shackleton, CFS. Retired 1975. Flew Chipmunks with air experience flights, then joined the Civil Aviation Authority (CAA).

Sqn Ldr David Jackson

Joined in 1961. Flying training at Cranwell, then 3 FTS. Meteors on SRF, 229 OCU and 20 Sqn Hunter, CFS, instructor on 3 FTS Jet Provost, ETPS, Avionics Flt RAE, OC Aero Flt Bedford, 4 FTS Hawk, MoD. Retired 1997.

Wg Cdr George Lee

Joined in 1957, trained as radio observer. 1 ANS, Javelin OCU, 89/85 Sqn Javelin. Retrained pilot '62/'63. 2 Sqn Hunter, CFS QFI Jet Provost, Hunter, Meteor, Vampire, Gnat. 79 Sqn Hunter, Meteor. MOD Jaguar, Hawk. Retired 1989. BAe 146 Captain '90-'04. Currently Pathfinder Flying Club Wyton.

Sqn Ldr Mike Sayer

Joined in 1961 as a navigator. 2 ANS, Meteors on 1 ANS, 242 OCU and 267 Sqn Argosy, 511 Sqn Britannia, Air Transport HQ Upavon, 10 Sqn VC10, Episkopi. Retired 2010.

Sqn Ldr Colin Wilcock

Joined in 1963. 6 FTS, Meteors on SRF. 229 OCU Hunter, 5 Sqn Lightning, 228 OCU, 6 and 14 Sqns Phantom, 226 OCU Jaguar, ETPS, RAE. Retired 1989 and test flew for BAE, later joining British Regional Airlines.

A RETURN TO MAINSTREAM TRAINING

By the late 1950s, the Meteor had almost completely left mainstream Flying Training Command, although it stayed on for refresher flying for pilots coming off ground

tours. But within a few short years, it was back to the fore again in two guises; one
of which was completely unforeseen. In late 1962, the Gnat T.1 entered service as
the RAF's new advanced training aircraft to replace the Vampire T.11. However,
in the following year, it ran into technical problems which forced the cancellation
of two pilot courses at Valley and a decision to send all the students to Strubby
where the School of Refresher Flying (SRF) Meteors were to be used instead; **Colin
Wilcock** was among them.

> "On completion of basic training at 6 FTS Acklington in August 1964, I
> was lucky to be given enough leave to go home to Nairobi. As my flight
> departed from Lyneham in the morning after the Wings Ceremony, the
> station commander arranged for two Jet Provosts to get me and my suitcase
> down in time to catch it. After my holiday, I expected to go to 4 FTS at
> Valley to complete my advanced flying training, but I was told that I was
> to go to Dishforth on the Student Pilot Holding Flight (SPHF) instead.
> On arrival, I found other members of my Acklington course. The SPHF
> was used to hold pre-FTS pilots and was set up for marching etc. We said
> that we'd done all that and for a couple of days, we were allowed to watch
> films whilst we were re-assigned. I was to go to SRF at the College of Air
> Warfare Manby on the Multi-Crew Refresher Squadron. When I arrived
> there, I went onto the Varsity as a co-pilot which allowed the students to
> get their captain flying. I spent a couple of months thus employed until
> I was re-posted to the Meteor at Strubby (a satellite of Manby) to carry
> out my AFS training. I finished flying the Varsity on 14 November and
> started on the Meteor on the 26th – the intervening time must have been
> Ground School!
>
> "I was on one of about three courses sent to the Meteor and Vampire
> (at Linton-on-Ouse) to offload 4 FTS where the Gnat was suffering
> serviceability problems. We all really enjoyed the AFS at Strubby as we
> usually got to fly single-seat aircraft when solo and the Meteor was an
> interesting aircraft to fly – especially on one engine! During the course
> I did 58 hours on the T.7 and 15 on the F.8, finishing on 24 April '65.
> However, to start with, we all found it a handful on one engine because
> the instructors insisted on us flying at the minimum speed and in the
> T.7, you couldn't trim out all the foot-loads below about 250 knots or
> thereabouts and this gave a very, very heavy foot-load in the circuit and
> on instrument approaches. If you spent a lot of time on one engine you
> ended up getting what we called a leg-trembler – i.e. when you got out
> of the cockpit, your leg trembled as you tried to walk. Being young, this
> physical problem was soon resolved after a reviving cup of coffee. The
> Meteor had a bit of a notorious reputation on one engine although we
> did not suffer any accidents in my time on them.
>
> "An early exercise was to establish your personal 'critical speed' – the

minimum speed at which you could maintain control on one engine. We had to work out our own critical speeds which involved flying very slowly (about 105 knots) and then applying full power and letting the aeroplane accelerate – the instructor then pulled an engine on you and established the minimum speed at which you could maintain control. There was a safety speed (now called V2) at which all pilots could control the aircraft, but the critical speed depended to a large extent on your size and strength. Large, strong guys had a lower critical speed than those of smaller stature. From memory, whilst the safety speed was 150 knots, my critical speed was around 135 knots and this was tested many times during the course. When doing instrument flying, we had to sit in the back seat, which was interesting to say the least. To prevent us looking out when not in cloud, the rear seat was blanked at the front and the glass sides of the canopy were covered with furniture polish and so we couldn't see out at all. So you'd sit in the aeroplane, the hood would close, the engines would start, you'd taxi around a bit and then the instructor would say 'you have control', so you knew you were on the runway. Off you'd go and as soon as you started rolling, the artificial horizon would start to topple and the directional indicator (DI) would precess (change direction of rotation) because they were early air-driven instruments – this left only the turn and slip for keeping straight. You knew that when you got to about 150 knots you would lose an engine.

"Apart from that, I think we all enjoyed it, especially the F.8; it was delightful to fly. Aeros were fun as there was plenty of power. One trick we all tried was to assist stall turns by closing the inboard engine to idle first. What we forgot was that the secondary effect of yaw is roll and the ailerons were not powerful enough at low speed to stop this roll so the stall turns all became very untidy. High speed runs were always a game as you'd accelerate the aircraft up to Mach 0.8 and see what happened. Because they were all different (and bent from many years of mishandling) and did different things one had to remain on one's toes; they would often tuck under or go over the top as they were all fairly well bent by the time we got to

Sqn Ldr Colin Wilcock 6 Squadron, 1969. [Colin Wilcock]

fly them. I remember coming back from an F.8 sortie and saying to my instructor 'every time I stall this aircraft it flips upside down' and he said, 'well have you looked at the back?' I did and the rudder was twisted over to one side instead of being perfectly vertical, which explained why it wouldn't stall properly without flipping upside down. There was a lot of asymmetric work, instrument flying, night flying and formation. I expect that the course followed the standard exercises as flown by the guys on Gnats. Except for asymmetric the Meteor was a delight to fly. All of us managed to get back to our old FTSs on a solo land-away in an F.8 and we didn't behave too badly.

"I can't remember any major problems with the Meteors. I don't think anyone on the course had a real emergency as the aircraft remained very serviceable, no-one got the chop and there were about 12 to 15 of us. Our engineers were from Airwork and all the ground crew were civilians. We used to drive round the peri-track to get to the squadron. I remember the boss being very cross one day when he was in his Mini and he couldn't catch one of us because the student was taxying too fast for the boss to catch up. It was quite a long taxiway and you could get to quite a high speed down the straight towards our pans. We lived in wooden Nissen huts and the mess was a Nissen hut with three spurs off for sergeants, officers and airmen.

"I finished the course at the end of March '65. We had another month at Strubby and then took the aeroplanes away to storage at Kemble. I was in two of the T.7s that we delivered and my last flight was on 21 April. After this, there were no Meteors left at Strubby and I think that the only ones left flying were those at Chivenor. At the end of the course, three of us got posted to Lightnings, one Hunters, one Canberras and the rest were posted to V-bombers. The boss, Sqn Ldr John Scambler asked if anyone was not going on holiday. I answered that I probably would not. So I went to Binbrook on 85 Sqn – Meteors again – and did my first flight there on 30 April.

"Flying there was mainly with F.8s for the Fighter Controller Training School at Bawdsey. We had a ventral tank with two drop tanks on doing practice interceptions for the student controllers. We'd take off as a pair and climb to somewhere up around 35 or 40,000 feet and spend about an hour and a half up there. The students would control us to intercept one another. One of us would be the fighter and one the target and the students had to control the 'fighter' into about one mile line astern of the 'target' and this was considered a successful intercept – we would take turns in being fighter and target. I have memories of these sorties ending up with the inside of the cockpit icing up as the conditioning provided little warm air at 40,000 feet. We were provided with glycol sponges to wipe down the windscreen so that we could see out to land safely. I stayed on 85 until 16 July and then I went to the OCU at RAF Chivenor where I started flying Hunters on 5 August. Here we met up with students who had been Gnat trained. It amused us Meteor-trained pilots to find that the Gnat guys felt they were making a retrograde step from the integrated OR 946 instrument display of the Gnat to the traditional Hunter instrument display, whereas we were impressed as we were moving up from air-driven instruments with all sorts of error to the Hunter's modern electrical-driven instruments. I started on 5 Sqn Lightnings on 22 April 1966."

David Jackson was another student on the same course as Colin and has similar fond memories of his Meteor flying at Strubby.

"I was entirely neutral about not going on to the Gnat, I just wanted to get on with my training and the Meteor was actually super fun. So I wasn't sad at all and I flew the Gnat later on. Certainly, the transition Jet Provost to Meteor, Meteor to Hunter was very straightforward so I didn't feel it compromised my future at all. In fact because I'd done a lot of asymmetric on the Meteor, it actually helped me later in life anyway. I became quite a senior instructor later in my life and I have to say that the more basic the flying of an aeroplane is, the more the basic skills get into the person learning. Nowadays and even on the Gnat, you are thinking about the aircraft systems a lot more. I appreciate there is a serious role for that, but I do wonder sometimes how much of the basic instinctive reactions

T.7 R of School of Refresher Flying Strubby taxying in at Kemble on delivery for storage.
[David Jackson]

to funny things are being picked up.

"A bit of a shock was that the Jet Provost and all the other aeroplanes I had flown had illuminated cockpits, but the Meteor didn't, it had fluorescent instruments. It was quite different looking at instruments in a black hole if there was no moon or anything and it was a very black night. One had the feeling, although it never happened to me, that there was a possibility of becoming somewhat detached from the world around you and disembodied, more so than if you had the red or white lighting that modern cockpits have. The general flying was really just taken for granted, we had very little fuel and when I came back to the Meteor I was very conscious of that, but at the time, you accepted that was the way life was. We used to rush around the railway lines in the March area as part of our low flying area up there, so navigation at low level was hardly a challenge as you had something to follow.

"In the Jet Provost, if you wanted to go fast, you just shoved the throttle forward. If you did that in the Meteor you regretted it because it over-temperatured, there was no fuel control system sophistication of later engines. One learned to walk the throttles forward and the initial part of the first trip was on the ground being shown how to open the throttle, so that was new; you had to learn the discipline. If the jet-pipe temperature went too high, the engine grumbled and you didn't get any thrust, so basic engine handling on the Meteor was a good thing to have learned. The people off big pistons had learned that a long time ago because of the torque. A lot of the Meteor accidents were during practice asymmetric; the death from real asymmetric was negligible compared with practising for it and the Meteor T.7 had no bang seat.

"My first solo was on the F.8. I climbed in, switched on and there was no sound in the headphones because I'd never flown a single-seater before. So I called out to the ground crew, 'Is this radio broken?', which of course it wasn't. That took a bit of getting used to for a young, impetuous lad who'd done all his flying with multi-seat aeroplanes. We did real shutdowns and relights in the air, solo – which was very good for building your character. Sod's Law struck of course and I had one that wouldn't relight after I'd shut it down. Strubby had a reasonably long runway, but they were very careful with young lads in aeroplanes so I was sent to Waddington to land there. We'd done umpteen asymmetric landings so it was a non-event really; I think it was the only serious excitement during my time there.

"The east coast was prone to sea fog and one morning we struggled through it to get into the Met room for briefing (at least those that got there very early did). When we got inside the coke-stoved Nissen hut the windows were all steamed up. In those days, the Met Office did a cloud-time diagram on the chalk board – a work of art really. He told us that about lunchtime, the fog would disperse and then it would be a nice day with puffy cumulous at first – a lovely day for flying. After he'd finished, the Wg Cdr Flying got up, put his arm around this guy's shoulder and said, 'Are you ready for this?', walked him to the window, wiped off the condensation and he could see for hundreds of miles! The fog had cleared at about a quarter to eight."

John Batty had two stints on the SRF. The first time was after he was taken off a Canberra course at Bassingbourn and then, after a tour on Hunters and then a ground tour, it was back to Meteors at Strubby again.

"I finished second in my wings course and I should have gone onto Hunters, but for various reasons I didn't; I was really hacked off about that. But my flight commander on the Canberra OCU at Bassingbourn said, 'You're in the wrong place here, you should be on Hunters. I think I'm going to talk to the Wg Cdr, we'll fail you from here with a strong recommendation that you go to the Hunter force.' So that's what he did, it was a bit of a risk obviously. Because I'd failed the Canberra course, they put me on a twin-engine refresher at Strubby just to see if I was all right with asymmetric; apart from the Canberra I'd only flown single engines. I arrived there the first time on No.165 All Weather Refresher Course in February 1959 and left on 1 May 1960 after my final handling test on 30 April. Obviously, I was a bit apprehensive but I had confidence enough to know that it wasn't actually my asymmetric that had been a problem at Bassingbourn. After that, I went down to 229 OCU at Chivenor and from there I was posted to 54 Sqn at Stradishall and did a full tour.

"When I was tour-ex on 54 Sqn, I did a short ground tour and then in October 1964 I went back to Strubby. The course didn't seem to have changed at all, in fact I think there were still some of the same people there. I did three trips with Ray Hanna and 'Bugs' Bendell was my instructor; I flew most of my trips with him. Sqn Ldr White was the CO; he did my final handling test. I had absolutely no problem with the asymmetric flying, there was always this talk about the Phantom Dive but I found as long as you kept the speed up and didn't do anything stupid, you didn't have to put a lot of power on the good engine. Of course we only ever did asymmetric with the 'bad' engine throttled back – in the early days of the Meteor they used to shut it down, which created a lot more drag. I thought the Meteor was a great aeroplane, I really loved it. The F.8 was a much nicer aeroplane than the T.7, a real joy. It had a much nicer cockpit; the T.7 seemed all sort of angular with that big canopy, all frame and glass.

"On 14 November, I went off in the morning in an F.8 to do my revision for my final handling test. I'd heard about this guy Jan Zurakowski who used to do this loop with a stall turn (essentially a vertical cartwheel) and

I thought I'd practise that. I started at about 10,000 feet and it wouldn't do it; I made several attempts and it would just flop out of the sky and I got myself in what I thought was a spin. I tried the standard spin recovery, stick fully forward, full opposite rudder and nothing happened. By now I was down to 7,000 feet – 6,000 – 5,000 and in those days, you were supposed to bale out if you hadn't recovered at 7,000 feet I think it was. I was still going down at 4,000 feet and I thought, 'Bloody hell what's gone wrong?' then I looked down and saw the throttle split. I had full power on one engine and no power on the other – I was in a spiral dive. I just pulled the full power engine back and I just flipped straight and level and climbed out from about 3,500 feet – that was a scary moment. At that point I decided I'd better go back, land and face my final handling test. I did 40 minutes with Sqn Ldr White and passed. I then went back to Chivenor to do the Hunter short course before going out to Aden on 43 Sqn."

LEG STRENGTHENING

Colin Wilcock talked about the problems of the amount of leg strength required to keep a Meteor straight when flying asymmetrically. **Robin Chandler**'s experience of the type came when he was sent on No.36 Asymmetric Course at Worksop, which was better known as the Leg Strengthening Course! In addition to a lot of general handling during the course, Robin flew five asymmetric circuit sorties and made no fewer than 23 throttle back landings (TBL), so his leg strength must have improved enormously!

"I came out of training on the piston Provost and Vampire at Cranwell. If you went on to Canberras, as so many people did, the Meteor was the link between the single-engine Vampire and the twin-engine Canberra. You did 25 hours or so on the Meteor at Worksop and it was called the Leg Strengthening Course because you spent a lot of time on one engine; it was basic asymmetric flying. On one engine you had to put a geometric lock on your leg to establish the critical speeds. When I got there in 1957 they weren't shutting down engines anymore, they were doing TBLs. You did your 25 hours, split between the T.7 and the F.8. I enjoyed the Meteor; the Vampire, especially the single-seat Vampire, was a bit twitchy and a bit light, but the Meteor felt like a proper aeroplane. I liked the F.8 very much, that was good fun. But the thing that was banged into you was that you'd got to be downwind to land with 40/40 or whatever the gallonage was because the Meteor drank fuel like it was going out of fashion. We had ventral tanks and were doing about 35 to 40-minute sorties; the longest I think I did was an hour. The T.7 was claustrophobic with the glasshouse canopy, but the F.8 was a delight.

"The other thing was the danger of misreading the altimeter which had three pointers (hundreds, thousands and tens of thousands). On one of my trips, I think we were cleared down to 1,000 feet and the QFI said, 'Look up now' and there we were hurtling across the Nottinghamshire countryside at 100 feet! Easily done, at least I made that mistake with somebody on board. Eventually of course, they came to a digital readout. Gamston was our relief landing ground (RLG) just down the A1 and the orderly officer had to go and check the security of the control tower at midnight. So you were solemnly driven down the A1 from Worksop to Gamston and then you had to open up this elderly control tower, it was spooky.

"I enjoyed my time at Worksop – nice weather, nice aeroplane and I learned a lot. We were let out of Cranwell with all the limitations that it had, out into the real air force – just got on with the job. We were lucky in that we were there in May and June so the weather was not bad at all really, but I would hate to have been there in bloody February, with all the industrial muck around the Nottinghamshire area. After that, I did a short Bomber Command Bombing School (BCBS) course at Lindholme to learn the mysteries of the Mk.14 bomb sight flying around bombing ranges in Varsities, then I went to 231 OCU at Bassingbourn. Then I went to Germany on Canberra B(I).8s with 16 Sqn at Laarbruch."

NAVIGATOR TRAINING

The second new training role for the Meteor came when it was recognised that navigators – especially those destined to join the Javelin force – needed to have jet experience as part of their training. This recognition was fortuitous for the Meteor's future as significant numbers of NF.14s, not long since withdrawn from operational units, were being held in storage – mainly at 33 MU Lyneham. At that time, the only jets being used for navigator training were a few Vampire NF.10s at Thorney Island and the Meteor was felt to be better suited to the job. The modification for the training role was quite simply a case of removing the AI radar and adding some other equipment to aid navigation – the variant was thus designated NF(T).14. **Mike Sayer** learned his fast-jet navigation skills on Meteors in 1963, but on completion, found he was destined for the somewhat slower transport fleet.

"I had already been selected as a navigator and offered a commission while I was an air cadet at school. Although I had a private pilot licence from the age of 17, I didn't pass the RAF eye-sight test for pilot so they offered me navigator and I took it because I wanted to get into the air force one way or the other. We were officer cadets at South Cerney and then became acting pilot officers at 2 Air Navigation School (ANS) Hullavington, where we stayed from April to December '62. There were Valetta flying classrooms which were used for teaching equipment like GEE and astro navigation, so that one instructor could teach perhaps 10

A very smart NF[T].14 WS774 D of 1 ANS Stradishall, 4 October 1964. [Richard Ward]

or 12 students; then we went on to Varsities.

"In December '62, I moved on to 1 ANS at Stradishall for the advanced phase of training which again started on Varsities, in which we did a fair amount of astro navigation and some low level coastal navigation. We then had the Meteor phase which comprised some 11 hours flying. This phase was designed to introduce and select people for fast jets. The Meteor was the first jet I'd flown in – I remember being strapped in for my first flight on 25 March 1963 in WS788 C for Charlie. We did eight exercises in total, which usually started with climbing up to a departure point on the North Sea coast near Cromer. You climbed up into the 30 thousands and did an exercise which might be just straight navigation or a timing exercise. There was also low level where you took the pilot basically around Norfolk, map reading and turning at low level and with a bit of timing involved. The NF.14s had GEE navigation equipment fitted, which was a system that looked at time differences between different radio stations, usually a master and three slaves. The time differences were printed on a chart as a hyperbolic lattice. The operator lined up blips on a scope in the aircraft, the set displayed the time differences and these were plotted on the lattice to get a fix. There may also have been Rebecca, which was a range-measuring transponder and I'm sure there was a radio direction finder of some sort. Apart from the eye-ball navigation – it had a big clear canopy so you could see very well – it was GEE we used most. They'd taken out all the night fighter stuff, including the radar and there was reputed to be a concrete block in the long nose

Fleet Requirements Unit TT.20 WD785 at Hurn on 15 August 1967, with a Rushton towed target under the rear fuselage. [Adrian Balch]

Javelin-equipped 29 Squadron retained a few Meteors for target towing including this F.8 WF654 W, seen over Cyprus in 1964. [Adrian Balch collection]

Llanbedr's last D.16 WK800 Z landing unmanned in its final heavily-modified form. [RAE Llanbedr]

Above: Rolls-Royce-owned NF.14 G-ASLW flying from Hucknall in 1963. [George Webb via Richard Andrews]

Below: RRE Pershore's NF.11 WD790, still fitted with a TSR2 nose cone from earlier trials, taken in 1971. [Adrian Balch]

Above: 'Slippery Six' formation of two Meteors and four Hunters, 229 OCU Chivenor, 23 August 1969. [Stephen Wolf]

Top to bottom, right: Trio of F[TT].8s of Nicosia TTF including WK946 D. [Jeff Peck]; WL180 & WE876 F[TT].8s of 1574 Flight over Singapore, 12 December 1970. [Adrian Balch collection]

Above: Both Martin-Baker Meteors in a rare formation over Chalgrove. WL419 in the lead flown by Andy Gent, with Dave Southwood in WA638. [Martin-Baker via Dave Southwood]

Below: CFS trio of T.7s WF791, WA669 and Vampire T.11 XH304 near Leeming in April 1986. [Adrian Balch collection]

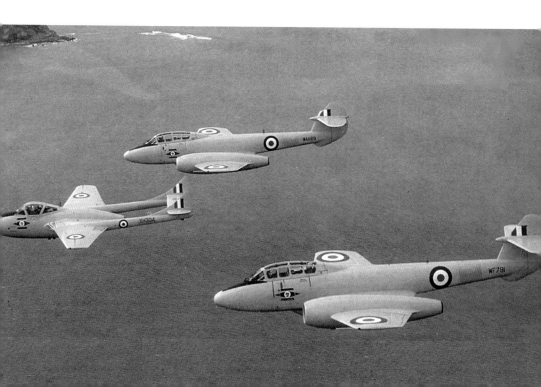

Above: F.8 A77-851 VH-MBX of the Temora Aviation Museum. [Darren Crabb]

Below: One of the handful of Meteors still flying, NF.11 WM167 [G-LOSM] at Coventry on 4 July 2015. [Adrian Balch]

THE BOYS TODAY

Les Millgate, May 2015. [Steve Bond]

Alan McDonald, May 2015. [Steve Bond]

Bill George, June 2015. [Steve Bond]

Norman Tebbit, June 2015. [Steve Bond]

Gordon Webb, June 2015 [Steve Bond]

David Jackson, June 2015. [Steve Bond]

George Lee, December 2015. [Steve Bond]

Robin Chandler, May 2015. [Steve Bond]

Pete Sawyer, 2002. [Steve Bond]

Darren 'Buster' Crabb crewing in the Temora Aviation Museum F.8 A77-851 VH-MBX 23 February 2007. [Darren Crabb]

Dave Southwood, 9 January 2016. [Steve Bond]

to restore the centre of gravity.

"I did three exercises in March and five at the beginning of April; there was one which I will always remember. On 1 April in WS774 (now in the Malta Aviation Museum), I flew Navex J7 which was a diversion exercise. That meant that you took off from Stradishall and climbed up to the entry/ exit point over the sea and the pilot told us to divert to somewhere. You had to get the direction obviously and the range, do a mental re-plan and divert. All of my contemporaries seemed to have been diverted to places like Middleton St.George, Horsham St.Faith, Coltishall and Wattisham, all those places up and down the southern and eastern coast. At the top of our climb, my pilot Flt Lt Kent said 'Lossiemouth'. Now this was something of a blow because, thinking we would be diverting somewhere in the south-east quadrant of the UK, I had not got a very good map of the whole of the UK. What I'd got with me was a set of GEE charts which each covered a transmitting chain, so you had Southern England, South Eastern, North Sea, Midlands, Northern, Scottish – I probably had quite a few of these tucked away in the side of the cockpit. I thought, 'Well, Lossiemouth's in Scotland isn't it, so I'll steer north'. So I steered north off Cromer and I was working out times and things, but from the charts, I couldn't get the whole picture because I didn't have the whole picture of England, I only had segments of different areas up the east coast.

"It wasn't until we'd been going for some considerable time that it dawned on me that in fact if you look at the map, England and Scotland don't go south-north, they go south-east – north-west. So we ended up some distance east of Lossiemouth out over the North Sea. Whether it was Flt Lt Kent or myself that broke the news, I'm not sure. I might have said, 'You're probably a bit far off Lossie, turn west', which he duly did – he was probably giggling to himself, but no doubt keeping a good eye on the fuel as well. It was a one and a half hour flight, a fairly long slog in from the North Sea and we got a bearing to steer which homed us in on Lossiemouth. We descended and the next exciting thing was the cockpit completely misted up, due to us being up high and cold for some considerable time and it being warmer and humid down at low level. The pilot had to yaw the aircraft to look through little bits that he'd cleared on the sides of the canopy; happily, we landed safely and taxied in. You felt fairly proud in a Meteor because you could roll the canopy back (the nav had the main button for it) and just sit there – it was like flying a light aircraft really – and wave to people, very immature. We went into the wardroom (Lossie was a navy station in those days – HMS Fulmar), had lunch and flew home again – more directly!

"The next flight on 2 April was in a Varsity and that was a night astro exercise for four and a quarter hours. I then did three more Meteor trips on 3, 4 and 5 April which were one to one hour 30 minutes duration;

NF[T].14 WS797 O from 1 ANS Stradishall at Benson, 19 September 1964. [Steve Bond]

one was low level and the others were normal medium to high level nav exercises. That brought the navigation training to an end. Despite mistaking the orientation of the United Kingdom, at the end of that course in the middle of April, I graduated and was awarded the top nav prize and a cup for being the best navigator! I don't think that was to do with the Meteors; I think it was probably because I was steady at routine navigation in the Varsity and particularly enjoyed astro navigation. After nav school, I asked to go to the Comet, very presumptuous for a spotty, first tourist but I wanted to do long-range, high speed navigation from A to B, preferably where B was somewhere warm and overseas. However, together with three others, I was selected to go to the Armstrong Whitworth Argosy, then new in service but hardly long range or high speed."

THE CFS 'TRAPPERS'

Although many Meteor Boys have described how much they tried to avoid being sent to CFS Little Rissington to become instructors, some did find they ended up enjoying the role. **George Lee** had started his RAF career as a navigator with a tour on Javelins before opting for pilot training. He then completed a Hunter tour before going to CFS to become a fast-jet examiner.

"I didn't go near the Meteor until very late; I converted to it in 1971. I was on the last Hunter operational squadron in Germany, 2 Sqn and the Phantoms came in in the fighter-recce role to replace us. My posting was to CFS as an advanced jet 'trapper' examiner, which didn't impress me very much as I'd only escaped from Training Command three or four years before. However, when I got there, to my absolute surprise the boss of Exam Wing said to me, 'By the way, you'll mostly be spending your time trapping on Hunters and Gnats plus any foreign fast jets that we do when we go overseas on visits. But, obviously there are no Gnats here at Little Rissington, it's a bit tight and Hunters even more so, but don't worry about it because there's a Vampire T.11 and a Meteor T.7 and they're yours. So you can use them to go where you want.' This was a bit of an eye opener. I hadn't flown either one other than sitting in the back or at the side as a nav, but the chap who I replaced was posted off to Lightnings (with a big grin all over his face having escaped), and gave me a quick check out on both aircraft. The only other people who flew the Meteors was a real old pilot who happened to be boss of Exam Wing at the time, Pat Lewis, and Wally Elsgood who was boss of Advanced Standards Sqn of which I was part, but they didn't fly them very much.

"I was told: 'There's the odd Meteor still in service down at Chivenor on 79 Sqn for target towing, so you're going to have to be rapidly converted as a full QFI on the aircraft.' So having only just got used to the front seat, they promptly stuck me in the back. I had to do quite a lot, which was nearly all asymmetric because of the problems. On quite a lot of occasions, I've had conversations with people in bars and messes saying they flew Meteors and you could always tell whether they had flown one or not. Every Meteor pilot knows one thing – port pneumatics, starboard

CFS T.7 WA669 leading 3/4 CAACU Vampire T.11s up from Exeter. [George Lee]

hydraulics – the port engine had the pneumatic pump on it (mostly for the brakes), the starboard engine had the hydraulic pump for undercarriage, flaps and air brakes. When you thought about it, if you were asymmetric, you had to think about what services were no longer available to you before you attempted anything. So a lot of the training that I received to become a Meteor QFI (and I think I was the last one ever trained), was concerned with making sure that whenever asymmetric turned up you knew exactly what to do, because it killed an awful lot of people. Mostly they never would obey the one rule that was dinged into me right at the beginning, never let the speed get below 140 coming round the corner and when you get to 600 feet, if you're asymmetric you make a decision. You assess it and either land or go round. Whatever decision you make, you stick with it because if you've got to do a go-around, when you open up the live engine at that speed, you've got a hell of a load of asymmetry power on the rudder to hold. You must keep going down to get your speed so the rudder will operate fully before you get anywhere near full power – you're going to need full power to go around. On at least one occasion, I had decided on landing and some idiot in air traffic lined-up somebody in front of me, but I'd got no choice, I was going to land. I just transmitted to the other aircraft, 'Stay where you are on the end of the runway, I am landing over the top of you'. Later on, we had a few words with the air trafficker concerned.

"The other situation was the engine failure on take-off. You had a safety speed depending on the configuration, the weight and all the factors that come in, but there were circumstances where you had to lift off because the end of the runway was coming up, but you were below safety speed. If you lost either engine at that point, you had to throttle the other one back, even if you wanted just a chance of survival; if you left full power on you rolled in. Then there was the famous Phantom Dive. Pilots trained in the '50s were taught basic handling on aircraft, which, although they were good trainers, they still required pretty careful handling. The air force accepted an accident rate that was quite high but wasn't at all concerned about chop rates of 50% on pilots' courses.

"I used to go down from CFS to Chivenor quite regularly to fly the Hunter. Part of that was because they were very short of fighter-recce instructors and I was straight off the last Hunter fighter-recce squadron. So I would do some instructing to help out the staff and I also liked to get hold of one of the single-seat Meteors, because I'd never flown a single-seater and they had three. An old mate of mine was boss of the squadron, Johnny Houghton, who said to me, 'OK mate, you're the expert on Meteors. Our QFI is the very busy Hunter standards man and really has no time to spare for the Meteors – you're ours, take the single-seat.' So I gaily read up the Pilot's Notes just to make sure I knew what I was doing, jumped in, fired it up, and took off. What I thought was going to be a nice, gentle bumble around North Devon, the moment I got airborne, there were Hunters falling on my tail, left and centre – I was straight into combat. In those days, out of Chivenor, you were an idiot if you didn't look over your shoulder, somebody was going to bounce you and there were 50-odd Hunters all around the place, so I didn't have too much time to sort it out before I was back and landing. That gave me an introduction to the single seat and then they let me tow a banner a few times, which helped them out because they were always short of pilots. Apart from that, the odd trip I did down at Chivenor was normally in the back seat of a T-bird checking out the guys who normally flew the Meteors as well as the Hunters, but just doing the target towing.

"I had just short of a year at CFS and was promoted to Sqn Ldr but, presumably because I was Hunters, Meteors and a few other things as well, what popped out of the woodwork for me was OC 79 Sqn. So with a big grin I shot off to join the boys down at Chivenor. That meant I took over all the Meteors as well as the Hunters and a couple of Chipmunks that we used for training forward air controllers. So then I got much more involved with the single-seat Meteors because one of them, WH291 was quite different from the other two we had. They both had the small intakes, WH291 had deep breathers – big intakes – and spring tab ailerons, the other two didn't; it was much the nicer aeroplane. Rejoicing in the power of a brand-new squadron commander, I gaily directed my engineers to strip it of everything to get it as light as possible for a bit of fun. All the guns came out – they muttered about taking the bang seat out – I told them to wind their necks in! But lots of other bits and pieces came out that weren't necessary. I had it as a sort of one-off, which caused a little bit of scratching of the head by OC Eng Wing, but he wasn't a bad guy and I knew him from some time back and he fixed whatever was necessary up the line. He also helped in another way because the aircraft didn't appear on the RAF inventory anywhere. They'd got a new computer for spares and it didn't appear, there were no spares for Meteors, we didn't have any! So to get spares we used to raid the ones at Kemble. If you wanted a piece, you went up there and took a piece off, unless somebody had got one hidden in a shed somewhere. It was a joke, but they were very, very serviceable.

"With WH291 now quite light, the restrictions on speeds for asymmetric and what have you were probably too restrictive for it, because certainly it went a lot better – it went fast enough to bounce Hunters. One of the things that we always liked with youngsters going through the course was to use dissimilar types to bounce them, so I could use that Meteor. It looked a bit funny; this thing would keep up with a Hunter up to about 400-odd knots. Of course they soon learned that all they had to do was to open the throttle and they soon saw me coming and learned to scoot for the horizon. But it was nice, I could have some fun with it.

"My Meteor time really lasted up until I finished my tour in 1975 as boss of 79 Sqn and I said goodbye to it at that point. In total I suppose I flew it for less than 200 hours. I never had a problem; they were simple. The only other thing I remember about the Meatbox was you had HP and LP cocks down behind you on the bulkhead at the back. The two were different tactilely so you didn't get the wrong one, but you had to be very careful when you started the engines up. They were spun up by an electric starter motor with the LP cock on and when you got to about 15%, you opened the HP cock very slowly to about a third to a half. Then you didn't do anything, you watched the turbine gas temperature (TGT) and when it lit you very, very slowly eased the HP cock forward. If you went too quickly, you over-fuelled it and you got horrible vibration and then you eased back a bit hoping that the TGT wouldn't go through the red line. As long as you did it slowly you were OK."

With Strubby having ferried all its Meteors to Kemble for storage and subsequent scrapping in 1964, the last Meteors in regular use at training establishments were the NF(T).14s at 1 ANS Stradishall (which also had one or two T.7s). With the advent of the replacement Dominie T.1, which had the advantage of being able to take several students at a time, the Meteors were finally withdrawn in February 1966, leaving just a handful of target tugs at Chivenor and the CFS example to soldier on for a few more years with the RAF.

CHAPTER NINE
TARGETS AND TAXIS

THE BOYS

Flt Lt Rupert Butler
Joined in 1958. Flying training Cranwell, Provost and Meteor. SRF, 231 OCU and 45 Sqn Canberra, CFS, instructing on Jet Provost at Church Fenton, Manby, instructing at 231 OCU, RAE Llanbedr. Retired 1978. Chipmunk flying with air experience flights.

Chief Tech David Curnock
Joined as a Halton apprentice in 1955. Engine fitter. Shackleton ASF Gibraltar, 229 OCU Hunter and Meteor, 64 Sqn Javelin, 24 Sqn Hastings and Hercules, 48 Sqn Hercules, Lyneham, Akrotiri, Lyneham. Retired 1977 and worked as a technical author.

Flt Lt John James
Joined in 1955. Flying training Ternhill and 8 FTS, 4 FTS. 99 Sqn Hastings, Levant Comms Flight Nicosia Meteor, 152 Sqn Twin Pioneer and Pembroke, CCCF Anson and Valetta, 267 and 105 Sqns Argosy, 99 Sqn Britannia. Retired 1974. Flew IAS Britannias and DC-8s.

Flt Lt Peter Macintosh
Joined in 1959. Flying training Provost, Vampire and Varsity at Valley. 48 Sqn Hastings, 1574 Flt Meteor, Manby Jet Provost, CFS, instructing on 7 FTS and 3 FTS, 'Red Arrows'. Retired 1971. Secretary F1 Constructors' Association, '72-85.

Flt Lt Peter Sawyer
Joined in 1953. Flying training Cranwell, Chipmunk and Balliol. 8 FTS, 233 OCU Hunter, 16 and 94 Sqns Venom, APS/TTS Sylt Meteor, 229 OCU Hunter. Retired 1978.

With further contributions from Alan Colman (Chapters One and Seven), George Black (Chapter Two) and Peter Bogue (Chapter Four).

TARGET TOWING
Although the Meteor was replaced in the squadrons by more advanced types, it remained in demand for a wide variety of other uses for some considerable time. Even when still in front-line use, it became common for F.8s especially, to be used to tow banner targets for air-to-air gunnery practice by fellow squadron pilots

and at armament practice stations (APS) at home and abroad. This role was to continue throughout the remainder of the type's RAF service and in fact the very last Meteors to be withdrawn (from 1 Tactical Weapons unit [TWU] at Brawdy), were still primarily employed towing targets for the resident Hunters.

'HEAVEN IN DEVON'

The Hunters and Meteors had moved to Brawdy from Chivenor, an airfield long associated with the target tugs and in Chapter Eight George Lee described his flying there as a CFS trapper. Engine fitter **Dave Curnock** served on 229 OCU's Target Towing Flight at the Devonshire station.

> "After graduating from Halton in 1958, I was posted to North Front, Gibraltar, where I was employed in Shackleton Aircraft Servicing Flight. Apart from servicing and rectifying the Old Grey Lady, we had the additional task of providing second-line support to Station Flight. Here, among several others, resided a Meteor F.8 which was used for towing sleeve targets for ground-based anti-aircraft gunners to practise, although this type of activity had almost finished before my arrival on the Rock. The Meteor was subsequently used as a bit of a plaything for those qualified to fly it. My somewhat limited involvement included an engine change (assisted by my engine trade chief!) and some scheduled servicing.

229 OCU F(TT).8 WK941 flying at Chivenor's open day, 23 August 1969. [Adrian Balch]

"In early January 1961, I was posted to Chivenor, a peach of a posting that was known as 'Heaven in Devon' and which lasted for me until mid '64 when I was posted away to work on Javelins. For the first couple of months I was working on the Hunter F.4 first line and second line. One day the chief came into the crew room with someone I didn't recognise, pointed at me and asked, 'Would you like to go with Sgt White?' He was the engine NCO in charge of the Target Towing Flight (otherwise known as 'F' Flight of 2 Sqn, 229 OCU) and he wanted another engine man – I was a J/T at the time. Here I happily spent the next 3 ½ years and renewed my acquaintance with the Meteor, of which type we had four F.8s (VZ467 and VZ567, WH286 and WK941) and a T.7 (WL360). The Cpl and I split them between us for day-to-day stuff, general servicing, before flights, turn rounds, after flights, that sort of thing. On non-flying days we mucked in together in the hangar doing the scheduled servicing.

"Your aircraft was a matter of personal pride trying to keep it serviceable. They were sort of falling apart – basically they were knackered and nobody else wanted them. In fact VZ467, which later became 'Winston' and ended up in Australia, was one of the worst. Fortunately, it wasn't one of mine; I looked after VZ567 and WK941. But they weren't bad in terms of serviceability. WK941 was very popular, because it was the nominated aerobatic ship and it wasn't normally fitted with external tanks. Everybody liked it, especially the instructors off the OCU who used to ring us to keep their currency on multi-engines during their lunch hour, a nice little 70 or 75-minute sortie and that aircraft wasn't used so much for target towing. Although it was an easy life we were still quite busy and the other engine man was never there. He was a Command sportsman so he was always off playing some sport or other. It was a great job, apart from the annual AOC's inspection and one occasion, when the Station Flight safety officer burst a mainwheel tyre when landing at 16.50 on a Friday afternoon – 'sorry chaps', he said – having just messed up my weekend arrangements.

"There was also an Anson communications aircraft. Additionally, 'F' Flight performed the duties of a station flight, which included the refuelling and servicing of visiting aircraft; these often arrived in batches of two or four around lunchtime as their crews dropped in to Chivenor for their lunch while on a cross-country navex and we were nicely tucked away between the hangars and the railway line. Among these visitors were Meteor NF.14s from the Air Navigational School at Stradishall which required fuel and a quick look around.

"Our T.7 WL360 had, at some time before its arrival at Chivenor, been involved in an incident with a vehicle that had collided with it from the rear, causing damage to the rudder and (so the story went) the fin stern post. We had a picture, taken from a flight safety magazine, on the crew room wall that showed the vehicle embedded in the back end of the aircraft. Following the repair, the aircraft displayed a characteristic that was not shared with others of its type in that, it performed a slow roll to one side if flown 'hands off' the controls. Apparently, this fault had been partially 'fixed' by making some rather unusual adjustments to the trim tab systems; being an engine man, I can't recall the exact tweeks. After a servicing, our riggers checked the control system and reset everything to the correct rigging datums. On the post-servicing air test the pilot reported this strange slow-rolling effect and after several attempts at adjusting the trim, followed by air tests, the aircraft was eventually persuaded to fly in a fairly straight and level manner. The same aircraft was coming round Baggy Point on finals when a herring gull hit the leading edge of the wing and smashed up against the aileron control rod. The pilot was Tony Haig-Thomas, later of Aden Hunters and Shuttleworth Trust fame and he managed to get almost full deflection of the aileron on the other side to hold the aircraft level. He'd lost his airspeed indicator as well; luckily there was another aircraft in the circuit, as the bird had taken out the pitot system. The other aircraft led him in on approach and he got it down fine, but the guy in the back was as white as a sheet when he came back in.

"I had just one trip in the T.7. It still had the small diameter air intakes and the mod programme had long since finished. The boss had located a set of the deep breathers – the large intakes – in the MU at Lyneham and got permission to 'acquire' them. We flew up there, taxied up to the hangar doors and one of the MU guys gave me a hand to swap the intakes over and we flew back. That was the sum total of my fast-jet flying.

"There were about 14 of us ground crew, a nice little outfit, including those who worked in the banner section; here they made up the targets and recycled what remained of the 'flags' after an air-firing sortie. When they were doing air-to-air firing, we were very busy and had to anticipate the scheduled servicing around those periods on the OCU. One sortie from us would probably look after two pairs of Hunters or sometimes even more. These men were sometimes supplemented by the occasional random tradesman during busy periods. The banner section staff usually did the runway duties, laying out and hooking up the banner to the aircraft prior to take off and collecting the banner after it had been released by the Meteors following the air firing that took place over the Bristol Channel, near Lundy Island, with a typical routine 'drag' sortie lasting for around 1 hour 25 minutes. We had quite a relaxed turn round time in terms of fighters and no need to bust a gut, because there was usually a second aircraft available anyway. We had five or six staff pilots and then the odd guy would come up from one of the squadrons, usually a Hunter instructor, the Station Flight safety officer, or one of the guys out of the simulator. These pilots were generally all OK guys and included a couple of master pilots.

"None of our target tugs had winches; instead, a fitting on the target rope was attached to an electro-magnetic release unit (EMRU) fitted to a bracket on the aft end of the ventral fuel tank. During an air firing programme, the start-up ground crew performed a check that confirmed correct operation of this unit, which required the EMRU to first be manually cocked, then tested by exerting a tensile load by physically pulling on the hook, then signalling the pilot to operate the release button on the top of the stick. A 'thumbs up' signal sent to the pilot confirmed satisfactory release, at which point he proceeded to taxi to the runway. We didn't do night flying as a scheduled thing although the Hunters did. But every now and again, they'd stick a night sortie on for us and then you'd have to do an extended shift for about four hours in the evening.

"From an engine man's point of view, the Meteor was a fairly reliable aircraft. Apart from routine servicings and component changes, there were fairly few problems during my time on the Meteor; among these were a couple of torch igniter plug failures on start-up, a cracked oil tank, a barometric pressure control (BPC) failure and the occasional fuel leak. One such 'fuel leak' was caused by one of our staff pilots attempting to taxi into the hangar after the last flight of the day, in order to save us time. Unfortunately, he contacted a short concrete fence post situated on an adjacent bulk fuel storage area with the port drop tank that was, fortunately, empty at this stage of the sortie. The resulting drop tank change was my first and only experience of that particular procedure."

SYLT

RAF squadrons in Germany frequented Sylt in Schleswig-Holstein, where an APS was based, for them to hone their air-to-air gunnery skills. Following a tour on a Venom squadron, **Peter Sawyer** found himself posted to Sylt as a staff pilot in September 1957.

"I was flying Venoms with 16 Sqn and when it was disbanded in 1957, I seem to remember I was the only pilot posted to Sylt from Celle. Sylt was the APS for 2nd TAF and was situated about two miles off the west coast of Jutland, just south of the Danish border. It was an ideal place in many ways as all the ranges were out over the sea. However, it was not easy to get to by road. The island was connected to the mainland by a causeway with only a train crossing it. So everything had to be loaded onto the train to travel to and fro. Other supplies and heavy equipment came in by sea. The weather factor was also an issue. Sylt was subject to frequent sudden fog and low cloud which rolled in off the North Sea, even in the summer. This made flight programming difficult and accurate Met was very important to avoid having to recover large numbers of aircraft in a panic.

Pete Sawyer climbs aboard F[TT].8 WF715 TTS Sylt 1957. [Peter Sawyer]

"All the 2nd TAF fighter squadrons came up, usually twice a year, for about three weeks to carry out their live air-to-air firing. The firing ranges themselves were out to the west over the North Sea and were covered by a GCI radar unit positioned on the station. The radar basically had two functions; one was to track the tugs and attacking aircraft to keep them within the confines of the particular range areas, which varied in position and height; the other was to ensure that any shipping in the area wasn't fired upon. I don't think there was any requirement for ships to be in contact with the radar unit and certainly not with the aircraft. So this is where the resident Target Towing Squadron came in. TTS, as it was known, operated 26 Meteor F.8s and two T.7s. Its function was to provide tugs to tow the banners for the visiting aircraft to fire at and to provide continuous shipping searches whilst the ranges were active. It was also responsible for carrying out periodic weather checks. In addition, there was a flight of Vampire T.11s to provide PAIs for the benefit of visiting pilots not familiar with the procedures. By comparison with 16 Sqn, TTS was huge. It still had a Sqn Ldr as boss and operated on a two-flight system. Most of the pilots were older and well experienced. There was a large number of Flt Sgt pilots as well, known as 'old hairies'. All they wanted to do was play cards in the crew room so there was plenty of flying available.

"I found the Meteor a very pleasant aircraft to fly and after doing a conversion on the squadron with the QFI on the T.7, I was let loose on the F.8. It was quite a large aircraft after the Venom and felt really solid with a nippy performance. A good comparison might be a Mini Cooper to an Austin Healey. The single-engine safety speed was 150/155 knots, I seem to remember, but each individual pilot had his own critical speed, which was generally below the safety speed depending on the take-off weight. However, being a light weight then, I expect mine was actually above it. Asymmetric circuits were flown with the simulated failed engine throttled back and not shut down and we were only allowed to practise rollers off asymmetric landings when dual with a QFI. This meant that you flew the asymmetric landing with the entire rudder trim applied. Then as you applied full power on both engines to take off again, the poor old QFI in the back had to rapidly wind all that trim off, so you were back in trim as full power was reached on both engines.

"The target banners were streamed off the side of the runway. They were about 30 feet or so long and about 5 or 6 feet deep. To stop them spinning when airborne, there was a heavy weight attached to the bottom of the spreader bar. If this was shot off, as frequently happened, the sortie had to be abandoned. If this happened at the end of the sortie, the first attackers lost their scores! The ground party laid the towing cable out along the side of the runway and the tug aircraft taxied forward so that the cable was fully extended when attached to it. I can't remember the length of the cable, but it must have been about 100-150 feet. Once you got the all clear from the ground party and ATC, you opened up slowly to take up the slack and to ensure the banner, or flag as it was known, was secure. Then a slow rotate to climb away steeply to get the flag airborne. Sometimes it came un-hooked, so you had to land again to have another go. The take-off was quite critical if you lost an engine. Climbing with flag was at about 160 knots, i.e. just above the single-engine safety speed. Once airborne, we were directed onto the range by the GCI controller and when there, set up a tow under his direction. This was at about 180 knots and you continued until he told you to turn onto a reciprocal track. Depending on the attackers' exercise, the height of the tow varied, but was usually at 5,000 or 10,000 feet. The attacking pair would be directed to intercept you by the GCI controller and they would then set up a quarter attack pattern, one from each side in turn, usually from about 2,000 feet above and off to one side. They would then call 'turning in live' to track the flag with the gunsight down to a firing range of about 250 to 200 yards. The ideal approach angle was at 30 degrees; sometimes their 'angle off' as it was known got well below this and became a bit hairy for the tug! Once their attack was complete, they would break up over the flag to position themselves on the other side for a further attack after their playmate had made his attack.

"Once your attackers had completed their sortie and usually there were two pairs on each flag, the GCI took them and you back to the airfield. We joined to run in alongside the active runway at 800 feet and 150 knots to drop the flag before turning downwind to land. This would be followed by a cup of coffee and sometimes a nervous visit to the loo! Each attacking pilot had the ammunition in his aircraft colour coded. The bullet tips were painted red, blue, green or yellow and if the bullet hit the flag it left a paint mark. Scores varied and ducks were not unknown.

"Each hour, a Meteor would be put up to check the sea below the ranges under the direction of the GCI again. You were directed on a search pattern at low level at around 1,000-2,000 feet. Once over a ship, you advised the controller of its estimated speed and direction and the controller would plot its position on his screen. An hour later, the next aircraft would update the position so that a continuous plot of all ships in the range area could be kept. I can't remember there being any incidents of ships complaining or being damaged. Shipping searches usually took an hour, but some of the far ranges took one and a half hour sorties. Frequently these involved flaming out one engine once airborne, then relighting it to re-join and land. The attacking aircraft varied in types. By this time, all the Venoms had gone, so there could be Hunters, Swifts, Meteor night fighters, Belgian F-84s and Javelins. Also the German air force was being re-equipped with the F-84F and I seem to remember them being a bit hairy on the flag!

"Sylt was a very busy airfield and with the large number of different aircraft and squadrons, life was very exciting. Mess life in particular was hectic too, as all the visiting pilots lived in. Parties abounded and after one particularly heavy night, I was up at the crack of sparrows to do the weather check and to act as radio relay for the shipping search aircraft. The weather was gin clear, so there I was, orbiting at 10,000 feet waiting for the sortie to end. The next thing I was aware of, was that I was in a gentle spiral dive at 5,000 feet having 'dropped off'!

"The boss decided that he would like to lead a formation of all 28 Meteors in the form of the letters 'TTS'. The idea was that each letter would practise until proficient and he would then end up leading the whole formation over the airfield for a photograph. This proved to be difficult. Firstly, days had to be arranged when there was no range flying. Next was the task of ensuring that all 28 aircraft were serviceable and available and finally, there was the weather. Somehow the individual letter formation practices were achieved. I seem to remember I was somewhere in the middle of the 'S'. Then came the day when we would all join up. There was a massive briefing and we all got successfully airborne, which was an achievement in itself, to join up into the individual letter formations. After some difficulty, we then formed up for the first fly-by as 'TTS'. It was OK, but it was decided we should have another go. It was like trying to manoeuvre a 1,000 bomber raid! Then it happened.

Fog was rapidly coming in off the sea. However we all landed safely; the last aircraft disappearing into the fog on the landing roll half way down the runway. There were no further attempts! After eight months at Sylt, I was posted back to the UK. I had spent about two years enjoying 2nd TAF and was sorry to be going home. Although I had completed the Hunter OCU at Pembrey back in 1956, I was told that, yes, I was to be posted onto Hunters, but I would have to go through the OCU again. This time it would be at Chivenor as Pembrey had been closed as part of the cutbacks."

SINGAPORE

In similar fashion to the target-towing facilities in the UK and Germany, Meteors were stationed in Singapore to support the quite extensive range of units based there. Originally established in 1951 as the Towed Target Flight, the unit eventually became 1574 Flight and soldiered on until being disbanded in March 1971 as the RAF forces in Singapore were being drawn down. Following his service on UK-based Meteor night fighters, **Peter Bogue** was posted to Base Flight Seletar, where the flying involved more than just target towing.

Singapore flypast by 1574 Flt marking the end of TT.20 operations, WD591, WD629, WD641, 12 December 1970. [Tony Robinson]

"I went out to Singapore, where I joined Base Flight Seletar when they still had Beaufighters. We were in part a fleet requirements unit and our job was to attack ships basically, or try to. They worked up as ships do and then had an Admiral C-in-C inspection; they would hold a meeting with all the departments and say, 'Right, we'll put her on notice to steam at 02:00, out to sea at 05:00'. We'd be told she'd be at a specific location at a certain time and all the time we were doing this, presumably the guys who were monitoring what was going on in the ship were making sure everyone was doing the right thing. The Beaufighters were not happy in the hot climate. You had to do the heavy twin experience before you could fly them and I was going round the circuit at Changi in a Valetta. On the last circuit before I went solo, as we were downwind, a fellow called Pike in a Beaufighter coming in on one engine, lost it and went into the Straits. From then on, they stopped flying the Beaufighters. They sent a test pilot from Boscombe Down out to Singapore with a Beaufighter. He landed, refuelled, took off, cut an engine, did a roll on one engine, landed and said, 'No use out here' and that was it. I never got to fly one, but I taxied the last one to the scrap heap on 15 October 1958. After that it was Meteor T.7 training, then on to the F.8.

"The Beaufighters had really been used for towing sleeve targets for the navy, but with the Meteors we were literally beating-up ships. We were left well alone and we had a lot of fun with the navy because we got to know them, as you can imagine! Around six months before I left, we got the TT.20. It had a dirty great air-driven winch hung under the starboard wing and allegedly, you had four targets and you could change the targets if one got shot off, which was very rare. I had the job of trying the first one out and the first thing that happened, was the cable broke and wrapped itself round the tailplane. Not a very happy situation, but it unwrapped itself and no harm done. It was an NF.11 basically, with the radar removed and ballast in the nose I suppose, although I never looked. All the radar racking was still there in the back cockpit, which had the controls for the winch as well.

"It was quite interesting, because there was 6,000 feet of steel cable and the droop on that was quite considerable. I got one in the sea; I got too low and the whole thing stopped – I was on full power and the cable was supposed to break, which it never did. We used to go up to a place called Ulu Tiram up in Malaya where the army used to shoot. A friend of mine went up there in the early morning; like most of the Far East you get very low cloud in the morning. He was scraping underneath the cloud and he decided to stream his drogue. There was an aged Chinaman cycling along a path, there was a hissing noise and a red drogue went past at about 120 knots! So it had its moments. When I came back from

Singapore, I first did the Junior Commanders' Staff School. Then I went to Ternhill to train on helicopters. I was not very happy about moving until I actually got on the things, then I realised how intriguing they were and what you could do with them."

Peter Macintosh also flew with 1574 Flight, albeit via a rather more circuitous route at a time when the Meteor even found itself being placed on standby to resume its original fighter role.

"I was posted onto the worst transport aeroplane, the Hastings C.1. But the good side was that we were given our choice of posting – I opted for Singapore needless to say. I was a co-pilot on 48 Sqn; it was a brilliant aeroplane for doing a job; it was just a bloody awful aeroplane to fly, very difficult to land. In Christmas 1963, the Indonesian Confrontation started, which initially was a kind of sponsored rebellion and then became an all-out thing with the Indonesian army, mainly in Borneo but also anti-terrorism stuff in Singapore Island and the mainland of Malaya. Because of that, the powers that be thought it would be a good idea, since 1574 Flight had moved from Seletar to Changi where I was (they were right next door to our squadron building), to arm the F.8s of which I think they had four, as an additional operational possibility. So it was actually an operational squadron and up to then, the F.8s still had the cannons fitted, they were just not used. Sometimes, they'd have two aircraft on stand-by first thing in the morning. Eric the boss and 'Smudge' Smith, a master pilot on the unit would sit in the aircraft and after about an hour and a half, they'd get out and have breakfast. To my knowledge, they were scrambled a couple of times because we had, for example, Indonesian guerillas or military who landed on the beach at Changi. They'd come across in disguised fishing boats or something. Next door where my 48 Sqn was we had a Bofors anti-aircraft gun on the roof and one of the co-pilots was officer in charge (OIC) of that – I had no idea how it worked!

"In '64, they said that since they were going to be doing a bit of standby quick reaction alert (QRA) stuff at Changi with the Meteors, they could do with a couple more pilots who would mainly take part in the target-towing work, which would free up the boss and another couple of the guys to do the QRA.* So they asked if there were any co-pilots who would like to do this as a part-time job. I managed to sprint to the door and knock everybody else down and got top of the list! I was then in the wonderful position of flying to all these lovely places like Hong Kong in the Hastings and when I got back, I didn't do much in the way of continuation training or local flying. I used to leap off to the Meteor Flight next door."

* As the Indonesian Confrontation continued, towards the end of 1966 a number of 1574 Flt's Meteors were detached to Tawau Sabah in Borneo for a further period in the QRA role.

"I hadn't got much jet time up to then. I had a copy of the Pilot's Notes given to me to read through the night before. The boss was a Flt Lt with about nine aircraft in his command, an amazing Scotsman called Eric Stewart, a total extrovert like something out of the Battle of Britain. He just said to me, 'Right lad, get in the front seat of the T.7 and we'll go and have a whizz round' and that's what we did. That afternoon he told me to have a whizz round on my own. I thought the Meteor was much better than the Vampire, it was more powerful, quicker and you could do more with it in my opinion. On the Vampire T.11 when I was at Valley, they re-introduced and I actually did, a couple of spins in one; it was all a bit iffy, whereas on the Meteor it was more rugged, you could be pretty rough and it was quite an honest sort of aeroplane. Having said that, the T.7 didn't have a great view, because it had the old canopy which used to be shut and closed by the ground crew which, at Singapore, often meant sweltering inside it for any more than a few minutes on the ground. I thought the F.8 was wonderful – the first single-seat 'plane I flew. The Meteor was much easier to land and much easier in the circuit than the Vampire – trim changes were quite marked on the T.11 certainly. The Meteor had the trailing arms wheels and you could land it from 10 feet with 10 degrees of bank on and it just sort of collapsed onto the runway.

"The TT.20 was an NF.11 with a socking great winch on the starboard side between the engine and the fuselage. That was diabolical; the drag of the winch affected performance. We always flew them with underwing and ventral tanks and a winch operator in the back, so they were at maximum all-up weight. In the heat in the Far East, it didn't have much performance; in comparison between it and the F.8, it was like a different aeroplane. We used to do navy, army and air force target facilities. The most boring job was trundling up and down in a ten-mile straight line over the navy base while somebody twiddled around with a radar on one of the boats and calibrated it. We'd do a run at 220 knots, then at 280 knots – intensely boring; that was at one end of the spectrum. When we were doing army stuff we fitted the TT.20s with a big target out the back, went to China Rock range and ground forces would fire at the target. That was also pretty dull and generally just involved a straight pass down the range. We did the same thing with the T.7 and F.8 for the RAF towing flags off the runway for air-to-air, that was for 20 Sqn Hunters and 60 Sqn Javelins, obviously at higher altitude.

"Much more interesting was a thing called Exercise Maxbus, which was a multi-aircraft simulated attack on whatever naval forces they decided to stick out into the South China Sea. That could be a carrier with two destroyer escorts, or all kinds of stuff; I remember doing attacks on HMS *Centaur* for example. That was great fun; often by three F.8s or two or three F.8s and maybe even a T.7 and we'd all try and come from different directions. We'd fly very, very low to attack the boats – I'm not sure what height we were supposed to be at but it was below 50 feet. They would fire blank break-up shots from their guns, which you could feel in the aircraft as you went past. For a kid like me in his early 20s, never having flown a twin-jet before, it was all very exciting. I was obviously tail-end Charlie initially, but we did some of those with just one aircraft where we'd go and attack a couple of boats, but the Maxbus ones were our versions of a maximum effort.

"I was doing a dummy attack on HMS *Vampire* one day. There was an inflatable seal on the F.8 canopy, when it shut, it motored forward and this thing inflated and sealed the pressurisation. Just as I shot past the boat, it failed, which caused quite a bit of dust and crap in the cockpit. I was doing about 440 knots at the time and didn't really know what had happened, so that was a bit exciting! I pulled the stick back instinctively, zoomed up to about 5,000 feet and wondered what the Hell was going on. I quickly worked it out, but then I looked down and the *Vampire* had done a sort of split-arse turn and was launching a boat. The boat came up on the radio saying, 'Are you all right?' and I said, 'Yes, the canopy just moved back an inch or so'. The trouble is, when that happens, the airflow moves your hand a bit so initially, I didn't know what was going on. They used to do some flag towing for 28 Sqn in Hong Kong, tracking Labuan – Philippines – I can't remember the exact route. There was a very unfortunate incident at Kai Tak airport. The guy bringing the target flag back dragged it over the roof of one of the high-rise buildings by mistake, that didn't go down too well. There was an airfield called Kuantan up the coast that we'd occasionally go to when there was an exercise. We'd go as a detachment with Canberras from 45 Sqn.

"Originally, we had two T.7s and I was told that one got metal fatigue and/or rust in the lower fuselage and it actually split down the middle. It was just taken away and dumped. The F.8s and TT.20s seemed remarkably serviceable and most of the time we had more aircraft than pilots. There were small differences between individual aircraft and certainly the 7s, 8s and 20s were all markedly different. But with the four F.8s, I didn't notice major differences because of my inexperience. One of the features of the Meteor was that if you did high speed runs at high altitude, it would accelerate reasonably well, lots of buffet would set in at about Mach 0.8, there'd be lots of buffeting, then at about Mach 0.82-0.83, the controls would just stop working. It would just start a very gentle roll or go down and you could move the stick to all four corners of the cockpit, it wouldn't make any difference. If you then throttled back and put the airbrakes out, as you decelerated below 0.82, it was as though somebody turned the power controls back on – it was bizarre – you definitely knew you were going too quick. The T.7 at high altitude, particularly out there, was quite unpleasant. You had no pressurization and they tended to get lots of water vapour, so it used to mist up. It didn't have much in the way of heating so it got bloody cold at altitude as well.

"I stayed on the flight until early 1965 after about six or seven months, having done a good amount of flying. Eric used to give us an aircraft for our last trip when we were going back to the UK. I was leaving on the Friday and on the Wednesday, he said, 'Get airborne, you can wire all the Singapore airfields – Seletar, Paya Lebar and Tengah – to say goodbye'. Everybody did this at the end of their tour. When I came back to Changi, we had a Royal Navy squadron there with Buccaneers, 801, they'd weighed in with what was going on as well, so my low run at Changi was done with a Buccaneer on each wingtip – that was fun.

"I then got posted back to the UK and was going to do the CFS instructor's course. They told me, 'You've been on Hastings so you're definitely not qualified to fly the Jet Provost. You've got to go to Manby and do a jet refresher.' I said, 'Actually I've been flying jets and a jet that's a bit quicker than a Jet Provost' and they just said, 'We don't believe you. Don't be silly, pleasure flights don't count.' 'But I've been doing hours and hours on three different versions of the Meteor'; 'No. no, off to Manby'".

TARGET DRONES

In addition to streaming banners for other people to shoot at, a further use was found for the Meteor in which it was destined to always come off worse – as a target drone to be shot down by a guided missile. The release from service of large numbers of F.4s and later F.8s, provided the ideal platform for a relatively high speed, unmanned, expendable aircraft to be sacrificed to fighter pilots practising target tracking and missile release and over 200 were converted by Flight Refuelling at Tarrant Rushton. Operating primarily from Llanbedr in North Wales over the Cardigan Bay ranges, the Meteors were also used to shepherd other drones and were therefore still often flown normally by a pilot until the time came for them to join all the others at the bottom of the bay. Other examples were flown by the Royal Navy from Hal Far in Malta and by the RAAF at Woomera. **Rupert Butler** spent some time flying the drones at Llanbedr.

"I entered Cranwell in the autumn of 1958. The third year was the advanced flying training from Cranwell's south airfield. This training ought to have been in the Vampire T.11, but it had been long established that a lanky chap like me could not safely eject from the Vampire. So three of us in my year had to fly the course on the Meteor. Between us

RAE Llanbedr's Meteor line in the early 1970s, with T.7 WA662, NF.11 WD790 and three D.16s.
[Hywel Evans]

we had five aeroplanes to play with, it was altogether a rather splendid way of doing things. Much later, after a Canberra tour, I went to CFS and taught on Jet Provosts. I enjoyed instructing, but my QFI tour was finished early; I was taken off the role to be aide-de-camp (ADC) in a big HQ. That did not work out, so I was effectively un-promotable. They would have given me whatever posting I might have reasonably asked for. I was intrigued by and went for the No. 1 GD Aero Systems Course at Manby, a slightly revised version of the specialist navigator (Spec N), which the navs could no longer fill. Being a year's course, it partly matched the ETPS course so I, as a pilot, was doing the theory that the chaps were doing at Farnborough and Boscombe Down, but not the flying. We did do trials-type flying and exercises, but essentially as boffins or back seaters. I eventually did a tour as a Vulcan captain and then got sent off to 231 OCU to be a flying instructor on the Canberra. I was not enjoying it, so a trials station was a natural thing really and they found a slot for me at Llanbedr in April 1976.

"Llanbedr was an RAE station on Cardigan Bay. It was a target facilities base for the much larger station at Aberporth. It might have seemed that I was really going to use my knowledge at last, doing trials work. In fact the job was just flying – as a jockey following other people's plans, making really no trials input of my own. The main target facility that we offered was the Jindivik drone, two-thirds the size of a Jet Provost with a short-life version of its Viper engine. This was flown by a committee of old aviators, each in charge of one control input. I had nothing to do with the Jindivik – my business was mostly to fly Llanbedr's Meteors.

"Of our Meteors, just one was a T.7. Late in my tour, we acquired an NF.11 (WD790) as a sort of hack. It had no radar to play with, presumably carrying ballast instead. I flew it a few times, once just to say hello to my future AEF flight commander at Finningley in preparation for my retirement the following April. Finningley was the station nearest to our house in Lincolnshire with a resident Air Experience Flight. I wanted to join the flight when I left the service in the following April, for which the CO's welcome was essential. In those days, one could just take an aircraft and 'pop over to…' with little official concern. There were also two trips 29 October and 1 November 1976. My family were still in Lincolnshire so I could show them 'my' aircraft, but the object was for me to attend a college old boys' guest night; most attending had to come by road – hah!

"The main Meteor fleet was made up U.16s, effectively F.8s modified so they could be flown as drones. Their main role was to shepherd the Jindivik drones. If a Jindivik had been shot at and was wobbling a bit, could we see if we could dare bring it back over land? So you'd rush up to it and you'd get into the rear left quarter, rear right quarter and have a nose around to see if you could see an aileron flapping around or something like that. If you told them it looked fine from the outside, they'd bring it home. If you saw something like an aileron hanging off, they would just send it out to sea. I never saw one like that, because if they wanted to shoot it down, the trials weapons were more than capable of doing so and because on all other occasions, the Jindivik would trail a drogue as the target and it would come back having had only its drogue shot at. What they were sometimes afraid of was, if the sort of barrage that they threw at it should wander up the string a bit and find the Jindivik. They could not risk a damaged Jindivik getting out of control over land.

"I was conscious that these lovely, clean, perfectly good Meteors were sooner or later going to be put up to be destroyed, perhaps to clinch a Middle Eastern sale. That was why it was a drone, but it was only ever a real drone once I think, when it was going to be shot down. I was never aware of one being launched unmanned with the intention of recovering it. We would occasionally be tasked as a drone to prove the system, sitting in the Meteor to bring it home if everything wasn't working properly. I was never asked to let the ground controllers land me. Of course the aircrew were all experienced pilots. There were two of us blue-suit pilots, a Sqn Ldr and me. There were about ten old gentlemen controlling the Jindivik, all aged about 55 or 60. Mostly they were ex-aircrew but four of them were still qualified pilots, who had made their way to Llanbedr when their Meteor squadrons of the RAuxAF were disbanded. Those four operated turn and turn-about with us two, always aware that the powers-that-be could reduce the maximum flying age and rob them of their innocent pleasure.

"A secondary role for our Meteors was familiarisation with destroyers in Cardigan Bay who wanted to play anti-aircraft. So we would rush at the destroyer and generally beat it up – probably the beating up bit was unnecessary, but rushing at it was what their air defenders wanted to see. We would have a lot of fun doing that. I should not be the only one to mention what a splendid undercarriage the Meteor had. Every landing was a good one. I never knew if I made an authentic greaser landing, because the undercarriage cheerfully absorbed all of the others. On the other hand, with the big flaps and the low ground profile, perhaps ground effect meant that one could not do a bad landing. Brakes were good too.

"Towards the end of my time, we collected a Sea Vixen from Tarrant Rushton, where Flight Refuelling did all the drone engineering. The Vixen was to replace the Meteor (for no other reason than that they had lots in a hangar at Farnborough). Such a hairy aircraft was a bit *de trop* after the Meteor and there never was a dual-control version; so I could not justify my being converted to type before I left. I was on a 38/16 commission (denoting the age of 38 or 16 years commissioned service if later). My last flight at Llanbedr was on 16 March 1978 and I retired on my 38th birthday two months later. As soon as I could, I started flying Chipmunks in an air experience flight and kept that up for over twenty years. I was given one medal for my time in Singapore and twice that for flying cadets about!"

The drone Meteors even managed to outlast the Brawdy target tugs, with the final one (Korean War veteran WK800) being flown to Boscombe Down and into preservation on 11 October 2004. It is now on display at the Boscombe Down Aircraft Collection at nearby Old Sarum.

TAXI!

As yet more Meteors became available for second-line duties, a good number found work as general 'hack' and communications aircraft with a variety of units. Many were attached to station flights, with others being on the strength of various communication flights and squadrons. Surplus F.8s also found favour with station commanders and officers of air rank as their semi-official personal transports. **George Black** managed to make use of a number of such Meteors with both the Royal Navy and the RAF.

"I left 263 Sqn in 1955, posted to Lossiemouth for a tour with the navy. Unusually, the navy operated two Meteors T.7s at Lossiemouth. When

Dark khaki overall, F.8 WK827 was the personal mount of AM Sir Henry Paterson Fraser AOC 12 Group at Newton, July 1957. [Steve Bond collection]

they found out I was qualified on type, they said, 'Oh well, you can fly the Meteor any time you like, they belong to Station Flight'. Then it wasn't the same rules and regulations as now, so occasionally I would go and borrow one and in fact, I flew quite a few chaps from my Aberdeen ATC Sqn. You could authorise the flights, because you were qualified on the type with more than 200 hours. You just rang up and said, 'Any chance of a Meteor tomorrow morning?' 'Oh certainly', so you'd get in and away you'd go. I could land back at Aberdeen, have a cup of coffee with the auxiliary squadron, back into the Meteor and return to Lossiemouth. They also said things like, 'The Captain wants to go to Lee-on-Solent a.m. tomorrow, would you like to take him down there?' So I was current on the Meteor and on their Sea Vampire T.22 two-seater, because I was also the instrument rating examiner for 802 Sqn. Then I ended up going to the deck with the Sea Hawk and got involved with carrier operations. Alas, that sadly ended Meteor flying with the navy.

"After that tour, I went to CFS instructing on the Vampire. I went from there to 74 Sqn with the first Lightnings and we had two Meteors on Station Flight at Coltishall. When I was posted to Fighter Command as a staff officer, we still had a Meteor T.7 at Bovingdon which was used for communication flying. The FCCS was a great asset for staying current,

Royal Navy T.7, WL350 of 776 FRU landing at Hurn, 12 November 1968. [Adrian Balch]

so I used to book the T.7 and do a staff visit to a station. It brought back memories of 263 Sqn days, when you could take an F.8 Meteor away at weekends, fly up to Dyce and return south again on the Monday morning. No problem, nobody asked any questions. Great times with many happy memories."

Like Peter Macintosh, **John James** was a Hastings pilot who found an opportunity to get some jet flying in courtesy of the Meteor.

"I was a second pilot on 99 Sqn Hastings, having gained my wings at Swinderby (Vampires) in July 1957. I was lucky enough to get the only Hunter posting with a course at Chivenor starting in December, I was detached to Valley to fly their Vampires. Then the Duncan Sandys axe struck and my Chivenor course was cancelled and I was allocated a Hastings second pilot 'course' at Dishforth. I turned into a bitter young Plt Off! In July 1958, a large force of Hastings and Beverleys was despatched to RAF Nicosia to take part in an arms airlift to Amman. A second pilot friend on Beverleys knew Flt Lt Mick Kendrick, the CO of the Levant Communication Flight and talked himself into a quick Meteor T.7 check-out. I followed him, was given a set of Meteor 7 and 8 Pilot's Notes and passed an aural

F[TT].8 VZ467 of 229 OCU Chivenor, Abingdon 14 September 1963. [Steve Bond]

test a few days later. After the test, Mick Kendrick fitted me out with a bone dome and told me that the WF795 was ready. I was sitting in the crew room waiting for him to lead me out for a bit of dual, when he poked his head through his office door and said, 'I have authorised your flight, what are you waiting for?' I signed the authorisation book and headed for the flight line. The ground crew helped me strap in, I completed the checks and pressed the port engine starter button. Nothing happened! An airman climbed up outside and pointing at the throttles, indicated to fully close them. They were slightly open, enough to disengage the start solenoid. The rest of the flight went smoothly and enjoyably. After one more trip in a T.7, I flew the F.8. All my Meteor flights were over lunchtime in August when it was too hot for the 54 Sqn Hunters to operate out of Nicosia and AHQ wanted some sort of fighter presence over Cyprus as Nasser was making warlike noises. I think Levant Com Flight had four or five Meteor T.7 and F.8s and two Pembrokes. I flew two of their T.7s, WF795 and VW482 and always flew the same F.8 – WK952. I only enjoyed 14 hours in those Meteors, but it did go some way to repairing my self-esteem after my full time job of raising and lowering Hastings undercarriages and flaps.

"My later Meteor experience consisted of a couple of rides in the back seat of a 216 Sqn T.7 at Lyneham. In the late fifties Transport Command used second pilots in Comets, Hastings and Beverleys, who were not qualified on type and in order to retain flying pay had to log 50 hours a year 1st pilot time. 216 Sqn had two Meteor T.7s and 99 Sqn had two Chipmunks and an Anson for second pilots to play with. I did two local circuit flights at Lyneham on 27 Jan 1959 in a T.7. That was my last trip in a Meteor and I didn't fly a pure jet again until 1976 after converting from Britannias to DC-8s."

Nicosia Station Flight F.8s at 35,000 feet over Ethiopia during the first non-stop transit from Khartoum to Aden in 1953. WK946 nearest the camera. [Michael Fopp]

Alan Colman, who we met in Chapters One and Seven, also had some later involvement with the Meteor in some more out of the ordinary roles, including display flying and Comet pilot conversions with 216 Sqn.

"I was posted to the Ferry Training Unit (FTU) at Benson. They employed Meteor QFIs and had T.7s. To my delight, they also had an aerobatic team, which I quickly became involved in. The leader was George Gill, I was number 2, Butch Hamer number 3 and Ray Hoggarth number 4. While there, I travelled up to Kirkbride on 13 December 1957 to collect a Meteor U.15 RA432. This was a radio-controlled conversion of a Meteor F.4 for use as a missile target. Preparing to fly it manually was a slightly odd experience, as the links from the radio control system to the flight controls all needed to be disengaged. In flight, it just felt a little heavier on the controls compared with a normal Meteor.

"In the summer of 1958, the FTU had begun to run down prior to disbandment. I was posted to 216 Sqn at Lyneham, which had recently re-equipped with the Comet 2. Again to my delight, I was detached back to Benson on several occasions to fly with their Meteor aerobatic team, which was preparing for a Battle of Britain display. Also, as a QFI and IRE on the type, I was frequently required to fly the Lyneham-established Meteor T.7s (VZ644, WH215 and VW472) which were used by 216 Sqn to aid jet conversion of aircrew new to the squadron. Similarly, from January to July 1960, I performed the same checking functions after being posted to 51 Sqn at RAF Watton, often flying the Station Flight Meteor T.7 WN314. However, my final experience of the Meteor was in late March

1962 – when, as a Comet captain temporarily detached to RAF Akrotiri in Cyprus, I was invited to fly four sorties in their target-towing Meteor T.7s (WA721 and WL378). I remained in the RAF until April 1976, but never flew a Meteor again."

Eventually, as the RAF continued to contract, the heady days of station flights operating their own aeroplanes and of dedicated command communication squadrons, faded away and by the late 1960s, were almost completely gone and with them, some very shiny Meteors.

CHAPTER TEN
AIR DISPLAYS AND EARNING THEIR KEEP

THE BOYS

Air Cdre Alan Clements RAAF
Joined RAAF in 1985. 1st tour HS.748, CT4 instructor, MB.326H instructor, 2 OCU, 75 and 77 Sqns F/A-18, CO 77 Sqn, officer commanding 78 Wing. Currently serving as commandant Australian Defence Force Academy. Flies Meteor F.8 for Temora Aviation Museum.

Captain Darren Crabb
Joined Canadian Air Force in 1980. CT-114 Tutor instructor, 419 Sqn CF-5, 410 and 321 Sqns CF-18, instructor on CF-18. Retired 1995. Joined RAAF 1996. Instructor on 76 Sqn, 77 Sqn F/A-18. Retired 1999. Now flying corporate Gulfstream. Director of Flying Operations Temora Aviation Museum, Vampire, Canberra, A-37B, Meteor F.8 and Sabre.

Sqn Ldr Bruce McDonald
Served with the Royal Navy as a seaman. Transferred to the RAF, trained at 6 FTS and on Meteors at 205 AFS in 1950. 1st tour 66 Sqn Meteor and Sabre, Kenya, CFS, instructor 1 FTS, CFS, 2 Sqn Hunter, 226 OCU Lightning, CFS, 226 OCU Jaguar, CFS. Retired 1990.

Sqn Ldr Dave Southwood
Joined in 1976. Cranwell, 4 FTS, TWU. 237 OCU and 208 Sqn Buccaneer, A&AEE, ETPS, RAE, ETPS. Retired 1999. Now a tutor at ETPS, flies Hunters for Hawker Hunter Aviation, warbirds for The Fighter Collection and the Martin-Baker Meteors.

With further contribution from George Lee (Chapter Eight).

THE METEOR TODAY
In 2016, although a considerable number of Meteors survived as museum pieces, just five remained in flying condition worldwide, four in the United Kingdom and one in Australia. Three of these were maintained purely for display purposes and comprised a T.7 (probably the world's oldest airworthy jet aircraft) and NF.11 in England and an F.8 at the Temora Aviation Museum in New South Wales. By contrast, the remaining pair of flyers (both basically T.7s) were still hard at work earning their keep with Martin-Baker.

The prospect of any more examples getting air under their wheels again was remote, since at least two other projects in the fairly recent past had foundered because of a lack of serviceable Derwents.

DISPLAY FLYING

The Meteor's use as an air display aircraft goes back a very long way and in the 1950s most operating units had their own aerobatic team. In the early 1970s, at the twilight of its RAF career, CFS at Little Rissington brought it back to the public's attention with T.7 WA669 as one half – with Vampire T.11 XH304 – of the 'Vintage Pair'. **Bruce McDonald** was instrumental in putting the team together and was a part of it until 1986.

"I first came across Meteors in October 1950 at Middleton St. George. I then went to 66 Sqn on Meteors, then Sabres. Then I went to Kenya for a while, came back and did the CFS course. I went instructing at 1 FTS Linton-on-Ouse, then back to CFS on the staff and started to fly the Meteor again. Then I went to Germany on a fighter-reconnaissance squadron (2 Sqn) and flew the Meteor when we were target towing. After that, I went on the Lightning OCU as an instructor, then back to CFS Examining Wing. After that, came the Jaguar OCU and back again to CFS for 14 years as the fast jet 'trapper'.

"We had the Meteor and Vampire established and we used to examine Llanbedr as trappers on the Examining Wing. We also used to examine the Civilian Anti-Aircraft Co-operation Unit (CAACU) at Exeter and they used Vampires, so we kept a Meteor and a Vampire so that we could stay current and go and examine them. When the CAACU packed up, we had this bright idea of keeping the Meteor and the Vampire and doing a show. It was quite well received as well; nobody put up any big objections at all. The big thing was we got them repainted in this new polyurethane grey, which was a very hard-wearing finish and kept them very clean; the old original finish on the Meteor was an absolute sod to keep clean. So that was how it came about and why we had the aeroplanes at Little Rissington.

"Roy Johnson did the first year with me on the Meteor and then a chap called Bill Shrubsole. He was the unit test pilot at the time and he had flown Meteors many years before. The thing was, everybody who started on the Vintage Pair in the early days had all flown Meteors or Vampires before. We weren't actually starting from scratch with anybody for some time until we had to begin converting people who hadn't flown the aeroplane before. Preferably, we were looking for people with a multi-engine background and had some asymmetric experience; anybody who had flown Canberras was fine. For the Vampire, we were still fortunate because people had been trained on them.

"All told, I was involved for about 17 years; I handed over just before the accident at Mildenhall. By then we had got T.7 WF791 back, which had more fatigue life left on it; as everything was governed by that, it was the biggest problem we had with the aeroplanes. As far as spares were concerned, we used to get onto Carlisle and most spares were still stored there; if ever we asked for anything, we got it. The only thing we couldn't get was a Vampire nose-wheel tyre, so we had to use a Devon tyre, which was the same size. As for engines, we certainly had a Derwent that came out of a snow blower and went into one of our Meteors. We tried to get our hands on the Martin-Baker aeroplanes, but that was not on. So we pulled '791 back into service and the last thing I did before I left CFS, was to check out the next Meteor pilot as a QFI.

"I last flew a Meteor in 1988. I did about 1,200 hours and can honestly say, I never had a troubling moment in one. The only time was when the brakes failed and I overshot the runway, but that was it. That was late on in 66 Sqn when I was the squadron aerobatic pilot; I carried on doing that when the Sabre came in. That was a great aeroplane, much better than the early Hunters, but once you got to the Hunter FGA.9, it was a much better aeroplane."

George Lee was with Bruce McDonald at Little Rissington and was also heavily involved in getting the Vintage Pair started. He had an interestingly different view about how some of the Meteor spares were acquired!

"I had just short of a year at CFS and another pilot was posted in as a fast-jet examiner, Bruce McDonald, ex-Lightnings. He was an old Meteor man and he started in the spring of 1972. In those days there were long programmes in the spring, summer and autumn of air displays all over the place and a lot of people were asking if the Meteor and Vampire that we had could come to this and come to that.

CFS Little Rissington's Vintage Pair T.7 WA669 and Vampire T.11 XH304. [George Lee]

So Bruce and I sat down together and invented the Vintage Pair and unlike today, we were encouraged. The commandant of CFS was Air Cdre Roy Crompton at that time and he thought this was great. This was CFS showing the flag – which reflected on him – so we had no trouble at all, except for engineering support; of course 5 MU at Kemble was just down the road from us, so we could go down and pinch anything from the Meteors sitting out in the fields, nobody bothered. OC Supply didn't want to know – we probably never asked him. The station commander at Kemble was a Wg Cdr, a very nice chap, who basically gave us what we wanted.

"Throughout that summer, Bruce and I did probably about 15 or 16 weekend displays all over the country; very nice, we enjoyed ourselves. It became a bit of a joke; the pair of us were these two Sqn Ldrs (I had just been promoted) who wandered around in these old aeroplanes that were older than us."

The Vintage Pair came to grief in a mid-air collision during a display at Mildenhall on 25 May 1986, with the loss of Flt Lt Andrew Potter and Cpl Kevin Turner in the Meteor, the Vampire crew ejecting. After a time, CFS's second T.7 (WF791) re-appeared on the display circuit as a solo aeroplane. However, this was not to last long as in a tragic repeat of so many earlier Meteor accidents, it fell victim to the Phantom Dive during a display at Coventry on 30 May 1988, killing the pilot Flt Lt Peter Stacey. The MoD Accident Summary outlined the circumstances.

"The display followed the normal sequence for about three minutes until a wingover to the right, which was intended to bring the aircraft back along the display line with undercarriage and flap extended. However, although the manoeuvres up to this point seemed normal, the Meteor had been flown throughout the sequence with airbrakes extended, contrary to normal practice.

"As the pilot started the wingover, flaps were at about ¼ and airbrakes were extended. The undercarriage appeared to lower normally as the Meteor climbed to the highest point of the wingover to the right. As the aircraft began the descending turn back to the airfield, the roll rate appeared faster than on previous occasions, the bank increased to 45 degrees and the nose dropped. The aircraft turned rapidly through 90 degrees to the right and settled into a dive, with the nose some 45 degrees below the horizon and the wings approximately level. This attitude remained fairly constant, apart from small variations in bank, until shortly before impact, when a roll to the right developed. The aircraft crashed into an area of open ground close to the airfield and was destroyed." *

The report goes on to confirm the cause as a Phantom Dive. This then brought an end to any further involvement by the military in displaying Meteors. This job was first taken on by Jet Heritage with NF.11 WM167, later passed on to what became

---

* MoD accident summary 23/88, 14 December 1988.

Classic Air Force at Coventry, where it was joined by T.7 WA591.

Probably the most famous of the Meteors still flying is Temora's F.8, better remembered in the RAF as VZ467 'Winston' at Chivenor, later Brawdy before being sold off. After a brief flying career with Kennet Aviation at Cranfield, it was sold to the Temora collection and arrived in Australia in 2001. **Darren 'Buster' Crabb** is now the Meteor's chief pilot.

Darren 'Buster' Crabb with the Temora Museum F.8 A77-851 VH-MBX. [Darren Crabb]

"My first flight in the Meteor was on 19 August 2001 and in the subsequent years of display and proficiency flying, I've amassed 109 hours of flying time in it. While that may not sound like much, each sortie is about 15-18 minutes. For the first seven years, I was the only pilot flying the only airworthy Meteor F.8 in the world; it was a unique privilege and honour for me. To ensure redundancy and the continued display of the Meteor, I endorsed Al Clements in June 2008 and most recently, Guy Bourke in June 2014. So, due to our busy schedules outside of the Temora Aviation Museum, one of us is available to cover the flying weekends and air shows. My Meteor training was conducted by Rod Dean who was the last F.8 display pilot in the UK (in the same aircraft). He conducted my ground school and systems training at Bankstown Airport, Sydney. Due to the built-up nature of Sydney, it was agreed that Rod would fly the Meteor out to Temora where I would do my flying training. So, when I completed schooling I went to the museum, where a relatively large crowd had congregated to meet the arrival in Australia of the Meteor F.8.

"Just like the Second World War pilots, my first flight was solo. After a thorough briefing by Rod, I strapped in for the first time. The cockpit is quite cramped by modern standards, keeping in mind that the pilots of yesteryear were a bit smaller. That said, the side rails touched my shoulders and numerous switches had to be reached by feel. As with the Spitfire, the control stick is hinged at the base of the grip for left and right movement over my knees, with the column hinged at the floor for full fore and aft movement. The start requires a bit of contortionism to reach the low pressure and high pressure cocks. During start we feed raw fuel in via the HP cock. Too slow and she won't start, too fast and you induce a reverberating compressor stall (just raise the handle until the reverberation stops and then feed it in slower) and just right sees the Derwent engines nicely come to life.

"Rod stood on the step to watch my first start, then jumped down and watched his protégé taxi for take-off. I had a detailed sequence of training exercises to conduct over two trips before being qualified on the Meteor. Taxying is a different treat when you're used to modern jets. The Meteor has a 'floating' rudder bar with pneumatic brakes, actioned by the front stick grip. To turn, you move the rudder bar to where you think it's required and squeeze the stick. This apportions the measured percentage of braking to each wheel brake. This makes for interesting crosswind take-off and landing techniques. As well, on the ground the brake reservoir has a limited number of applications, so you plan ahead to minimise brake usage. Differential throttle is also used to assist in taxi direction. To stop straight ahead, you hold the bar neutral and apply the brakes. Braking degradation is most noticeable during landing on hot days, and of course, anti-skid was not invented at the time.

"As it is only the pilot controlling the amount of fuel to the engines, we teach the technique of 'walking' the throttles and avoid any slam accelerations unless in an emergency situation. For take-off, I'd hold the brakes while setting 14,100 rpm, release and finish pushing up to 14,700 rpm – a couple of fine-tuned braking actions until the rudder becomes effective at 60 knots. The acceleration is positive with each engine producing 3,500 pounds of thrust. One of the critical items for these early jets is the take-off safety speed, or the minimum speed at which you can control the aircraft with full rudder and a small amount of aileron, if you suffer an engine failure just after lift-off. For the Meteor, we use 160 knots. What this means is that at full power, below this speed, the jet has a tendency to roll over on her back very low to the ground, which is less than ideal! So, while the Meteor can be rotated at 90 knots, the time to get through 160 knots is excessive. To mitigate this, we rotate at 125 knots, which has us in the 'dead man's curve' for only about four seconds.

"The controls are well balanced, so she rotates nicely and flies very stable. As she has conventional controls, you get a feel through the stick as to what's happening. After lift-off, we squeeze the brake handle to stop tyre rotation and select the gear up. As speed increases, we have to trim off control forces via the trim wheel located on the lower left cockpit quadrant. The Meteor flies best in a 250-300 knots band. Above 300 knots, aileron stick forces increase and below 200 knots, she starts to feel a bit mushy. I have flown a formation photo shoot behind a T-6 Harvard at 140 knots. I had full flap selected and good throttle response, but had to be quite delicate with control inputs and had briefed that if she was going to go I would let her depart, regain flying speed and then reposition. This happened once as we slid down and away, but once a few more knots were on the airspeed indicator, she regained control easily.

"The Meteor is a thirsty girl. Internally, she holds 380 gallons of fuel and we use 80 gallons as minimum fuel. When we first started operating it, the engines burned 10 gallons per minute, so you had only 30 minutes total flying time with a full tank. The Temora engineers refurbished the engines, which improved consumption to 7 gallons per minute. For transits, we use a ventral fuel tank that holds 175 gallons, giving an additional 20 minutes and if required, we have two wing tip tanks for an additional 180 gallons, or 20 minutes. All three tanks are capable of manual jettison, which was a requirement for our engine failure after take-off considerations.

"My display routine is a low-g, low stress one, designed to showcase the graceful lines of the Meteor and the high speed passes to bring to life the 'blue note'. This is the distinct sound the Meteor makes, generally above 320 knots and best about 360 knots. The sound is generated by the wind flowing over the gun shell casing ejector ports under the fuselage. I fly my display at 2.5-3g only to keep the Meteor below our 4g limit and I don't use any looping manoeuvres, as this requires excessive speed and the mere chance of an over-g on pull out.

METEOR DISPLAY
Minimum 500 feet above ground level (AGL), verticals 3,000 feet AGL
Take-off and reposition
Topside pass – 200 knots
Reposition – Derry turn
Level 360-degree turn (200 knots)
Reposition – Derry

Slow roll (away) – Derry
Oblique 8
Reposition – Derry
Topside pass – 200 knots
Reposition – Derry
Low level high speed pass
Reposition – Derry
Initial/pitch up – Derry – downwind 1,500 feet

> "In addition to the take-off safety speed, there are two more critical areas
> for the Meteor and both pertain to the landing phase. The first is the
> well-known Meteor Phantom Dive. On early variants, if you tried to land
> with the speed brakes deployed (upper and lower wing surfaces between
> the engine nacelles and fuselage), they would blank out elevator control
> effectiveness, causing an unrecoverable loss of control or stall in the
> landing phase. Even though ours is a later version, with a re-designed tail
> to avoid such a dilemma, we never land with our speed brakes deployed.
> We do however, practise this up at altitude to feel control effectiveness
> and recognise that we can do it. Secondly, the early jet engines have a
> slow throttle response time, should full power be required anytime during
> landing. As such, we adhere to a minimum of 8,000 rpm until landing is
> assured. This allows for a shorter spool-up time for engine response, in
> case a go-around manoeuvre is required. The Meteor lands wonderfully
> due to the nature of its trailing link landing gear. She kisses the runway
> and softly sticks every time, without any bounce. The rudders are effective
> down to about 60 knots for directional control, and then judicious use
> of the pneumatic brakes during slow speed control. It can be a bit un-
> nerving to feel the brake control handle fully depressed and no apparent
> sign of deceleration for the first bit of landing."

Al Clements supports Darren flying the Meteor. His experience of converting to and
displaying it are very similar, but as one of the few Meteor display pilots anywhere,
it is worthy of repetition. There are also some interesting comparisons to be made
with the experiences of those who flew the type in its heyday.

> "After first trialling the Meteor F.3 in 1946, the RAAF operated over 100
> F.8 and T.7 variants in the 1950s. While the aircraft were in service from
> 1951 through to 1959, they are most notably remembered for replacing
> the P-51D Mustang in 77 Sqn during the Korean War. The first 15 of
> them arrived in Iwakuni (Japan) transported by HMS *Warrior* on 24
> February 1951, with the remaining 20 on 23 March. After training for
> both aircrew and ground crew was complete, a comparative analysis was
> conducted against an F-86 Sabre and the aircraft modified to include a

The RAF's last F.8 VZ467 01 'Winston' of TWU Brawdy, 30 April 1976. Now flying in Australia.
[Steve Bond]

radio compass, it was decided that 77 Sqn would re-commence operations in Korea on 27 July 1951 as interceptors. This role would change over the course of the war and by the time of the armistice signing on 27 July 1953, the Meteors had flown 4,836 missions (around 15,000 individual sorties), destroying six MiG 15s, over 3,500 structures and some 1,500 vehicles. About 30 Meteors were lost to enemy action in Korea – the vast majority having been shot down by anti-aircraft fire while conducting ground attack.

"My first flight in a Meteor was on 16 July 2008 and by the end of 2015 I had completed 71 flights and 49 hours in F.8 VH-MBX. The vast majority of flights have been display flights with the occasional transit to another airport for an air show. Darren Crabb, who had flown the aircraft since it was imported in 2001 from the UK by the Temora Aviation Museum, conducted my Meteor training. At the time of my conversion, I had been flying the Vampire T.35 for the museum and was therefore reasonably familiar with the idiosyncrasies of older jets, particularly the engine handling. This, combined with my F/A-18 Hornet time and also heavy twin-time having flown HS.748s early in my RAAF career, meant the transition to the Meteor went smoothly. All my Meteor training was conducted at Temora and of course, my first flight was solo.

"My training began with several hours of briefing by Darren on the aircraft systems and procedures. I spent a lot of time in the cockpit going through normal and emergency procedures to ensure my hands, eyes and brain were synchronised and I would react appropriately to anything that may transpire. After I was satisfied with all the procedures, I had my first practical lesson; starting the centrifugal flow Derwent engines. With Darren standing on the step outside, I worked through the start checklist (everything is always done via checklist – not memory – due to reduced recency in the aircraft) and then started both engines. Originally designed in the early 1940s, the cockpit is quite narrow by modern standards, but the seating position is far more comfortable than the Vampire. The cockpit is obviously less advanced ergonomically than modern fighters and you have to twist sideways to operate some of the switches on each side. Much of the instrumentation and controls are the same as aircraft of the day such as the Spitfire, even to the point where the control stick is hinged both half way up for left and right aileron control and at the base on the floor allowing fore and aft movement to control the elevator.

"With the low pressure fuel cock open the start is commenced by pressing the respective engine start button to get the engines rotating and activate the igniters. When the undercarriage lights dim, but less than five seconds, you open the HP cock half way and then watch the exhaust gas temperature (EGT) and listen carefully. There is no automated engine start system so you slowly open (lowering the handle) the high pressure fuel cock matching the increase in RPM. It requires a bit of finesse to operate, as too slow from the half open position and it won't start, too fast and the over fuelling induces a reverberation and overheating in the engine (just raise the HP cock until the reverberation stops and then feed it in slower). If you get it just right – the centrifugal flow Derwent engine comes to life with its distinctive sound clearly audible.

"After starting and then shutting down both engines, Darren and I had a quick chat about my first sortie and I strapped in to the jet. There is one harness for the parachute and one for the fully functioning (at the time) Martin-Baker Mk.2B ejection seat. Strapped in with the detailed training exercises on my kneepad, I again started the engines and prepared to taxi. Taxying the Meteor is a different experience compared to most modern aircraft. The amount of rudder deflection plus how hard you squeeze determines how quickly you turn or how hard you brake. With no prop wash over the rudder, it doesn't become effective until about 60 knots, so differential braking is required with crosswinds.

"After mastering the taxi technique, I arrived at the end of runway 23 to take off and lined up on the centreline. With the brakes applied, I advanced the throttles to 14,100 rpm, quickly checking the engine was within limits and the canopy was locked (a green light comes on above 14,000 rpm). I released the brakes and pushed the throttle to 14,700 rpm.

After a couple of small brake applications to keep straight, the rudder became effective around 60 knots. While nothing like the 32,000 lbs thrust of an F/A-18, with each engine producing 3,500 lbs of thrust, the acceleration is positive. Being a twin with widely spaced powerful engines, one of the critical items for the Meteor is the take-off safety speed. With full power on the live engine, full rudder and a small amount of bank into the live engine, we use a conservative safety speed of 160 knots. Go below this speed and the aircraft will yaw (no more rudder to stop it) and then it will ultimately roll and lose control. During take-off and a go-around this is less than ideal.

"Once positively clear of the ground and climbing, I apply the brakes for four seconds and raise the gear. Priority is to get above 160 knots, check gear and flap are up and accelerate to the 280-300 knots climb speed. For the first mission I climbed to 5,000 feet AGL and commenced a sequence of manoeuvres that would familiarise me with the handling characteristics of the aircraft. To get an initial feel for the aircraft I did general handling, stalls, asymmetric handling and some upper air circuits. The Meteor controls are well balanced below 300 knots however, she does exhibit some Dutch roll (seen as snaking), which is exacerbated in turbulence. Through the conventional direct linkages and manual trim (e.g. cables, bell cranks and push rods), you get a good feel for what the aircraft is doing. The Meteor really flies best in a 250-300 knots band. Above 300 knots the controls are not as well balanced with aileron stick forces increasing and consequent poorer roll performance and while the elevator stick force is heavier, I find the aircraft more sensitive in pitch making it easy to over-g the aircraft. Below 200 knots all controls are a bit mushy, however this really is only an issue when flying in formation with dissimilar aircraft with different response rates. I vividly remember one particular display, flying in echelon number three on a Spitfire and Mustang. With the speed around 180 knots, the Meteor control effectiveness was low causing me an elevated heart rate particularly during turns, descents and climbs as I bounced around in the same piece of sky with a Spitfire!

"The Meteor is definitely a thirsty aircraft using 2 gallons per minute on the ground and then up to 10 gallons per minute airborne. The Temora engineers have done a fantastic job in maintaining the aircraft and engines, which has also improved the fuel consumption. Therefore, with 380 gallons of internal fuel, the flight endurance can be quite short at high RPM. I use 8 as minimum fuel when manoeuvring the aircraft due to inaccuracies in the fuel gauges and for transits, I normally use a ventral and two wing tanks. Interestingly, the flight manual states that shutting down one engine will increase endurance. While the aircraft is capable of greater than 40,000 feet and is fitted with an oxygen system, we are limited to 18,000 feet due to Civil Aviation Safety Authority (CASA) regulations. Up until 2015, the Mk.2B ejection seat provided an ejection capability, however Martin-Baker has withdrawn support for historic seats worldwide due to their safety concerns and the seat has been made non-functional.

"The Meteor lands wonderfully and it will hide a multitude of errors on touchdown due to the trailing link landing gear. After touchdown, I aerodynamically brake (including the speed brake) to below 70 knots before lowering the nose and using the wheel brakes. The rudders are effective for directional control down to about 60 knots followed by judicious use of the pneumatic brakes during slow speed control. My display routine is low-g and low risk designed to showcase the graceful lines and distinctive 'blue note' sound of the Meteor.

"As a past commanding officer of 77 Sqn (2005-06 on the F/A-18), to fly the only airworthy Meteor F.8 in the world is a unique privilege and honour. I will be forever grateful to David Lowy and the Temora Aviation Museum for the opportunity to fly such an important aircraft in both aviation and RAAF history."

MARTIN-BAKER – THE WORKING METEORS

Ejection-seat manufacturer, Martin-Baker have become the longest continual operator of Meteors by a very wide margin. They first used one for seat testing in

Martin-Baker's modified T.7 WA638 flying from Chalgrove in October 2003.
[Adrian Balch collection]

T.7 WL419, now the standby aircraft for Martin-Baker carrying out a seat-firing test in 1990. [Adrian Balch collection]

1945 and in 2016 are still flying two modified T.7s from their base at Chalgrove in Oxfordshire, mainly flown by chief pilot Andy Gent. It was recently decided that having a second pilot available would be a sensible thing to do, so well-known displayer of vintage aeroplanes, **Dave Southwood** has taken on the job.

"I went to Cranwell in 1976, did Jet Provost there, Hawks and Hunters at Valley and the Hunter Tactical Weapons Unit at Lossiemouth. I then went to the Buccaneer, followed by ETPS and a lengthy tour at Boscombe Down and RAE until I left the air force mid '99. After a short period of airline flying I went back to ETPS as a tutor in 2002 and I'm still there. I started flying warbirds in 1988 with Charles Church and now mainly fly for The Fighter Collection. I fly Hunters for Hawker Hunter Aviation out of Scampton, fly the Martin-Baker Meteors and some Tornado test flying as one of two Tornado test pilots on 41 Sqn. Flying in old aeroplanes is my first love really. I've flown 10,000 hours and about 150 types. My favourite is the Hunter, without a shadow of a doubt, but the Meteor really has become one of my favourites. There have been a few aeroplanes that really stand out from the others and the Meteor is one of them, I think – Meteor, Tomcat, Viggen, Mirage III, those sorts of things. The Meteor is certainly a fascinating aeroplane; it is absolutely delightful.

"Martin-Baker, from the early days of the company, have always used the Meteor as their aeroplane for airborne testing. For the actual ownership of the aeroplanes you'd have to delve down into the histories, but I think the Ministry of Supply owned them originally. They were always military registered, effectively owned by some part of UK MoD, but then back in 2001 when QinetiQ was formed, there were quite a few of these aeroplanes that flew on what was the Ministry of Defence Procurement Executive (MoD PE) fleet; I think the Meteors were part of that fleet. Those aeroplanes were then basically gifted to QinetiQ; the Hawks, Alpha Jets, Andovers etc. at Boscombe Down and the Meteors were rolled into that and QinetiQ leased them to Martin-Baker.

"They were military registered, so the airworthiness aspects of them were covered by QinetiQ and the regulation of flying was covered by MoD. In one of their audits of the documents, they said that they really wanted an independent assessment done of the aircraft document set. So it was the flight reference cards, the aircrew manual, tied in with the QinetiQ aircraft release document. It came down through Boscombe airworthiness and they knew of my interest in and experience of, old aeroplanes. So they asked if I would be prepared to do a review of all the document set, as requested by the regulator's audit – absolutely! By then Andy Gent was the chief pilot at Martin-Baker and we had known each other for years, so I discussed it with him and we did it between us. Obviously, I was quite conscious of not wanting to come blundering in never having flown the Meteor at that stage, with all sorts of edicts that were totally inappropriate for what was, by today's standards, quite an unusual configuration of aeroplane.

"I discussed this with Andy all very amicably and it was just some rationalisation in some ways, with modern phraseology and modern procedures, but also with the fact that the aeroplanes then had Mk.10 ejection seats. So, whereas the original documentation was based on sitting on a manual parachute and therefore if you had an engine failure after take-off and were below safety speed, you had to just close the throttle and land in whatever direction you were pointing, you'd now got the eject option. A lot of it was just tidying up on wording and procedures; there was nothing fundamentally inconsistent at all. Andy said it would be great if I could come up and actually fly them and then I could validate and give more credibility to it all – 'Yes, I'd be delighted!' I was sort of hoping that offer might come along.

"That was it and I think it carried on, because Martin-Baker tended to operate a bit in isolation with just one type-qualified pilot and it's always good to have somebody there to bounce ideas off and do a sanity check. Jim Martin was quite happy and I've flown them very little but just a bit, really to give support to Andy. It helped certainly when they were still QinetiQ-owned aeroplanes that I was a bit of a bridge between the QinetiQ airworthiness side and had the understanding of the procedures there, and with the Martin-Baker side who understood the aeroplane. From the QinetiQ point of view, they then had one of their employees who was a subject matter expert on flying the Meteor, albeit on a very few sorties. There was a big safety case written for it and then at least I could go through and review the safety case for applicability to what was relevant to the aeroplane. So that was how I got involved.

"From Andy's point of view he knew me; I'd got a lot of fast-jet time, had the experience of aeroplanes with a significant asymmetric thrust problem – a lot of time on the Andover – and teaching asymmetric certification testing. I was familiar with 1940s-style cockpits and the logic and layout there. Obviously they are single-seat aeroplanes and at the time, the Classic Flight NF.11 was going, but the T.7 wasn't. There was no option, it was a case of a briefing, go off and fly it. So to have a background of similar vintage aeroplanes and a broad spectrum that covered all of the quirks, it was relatively straightforward to go and do it.

"It was then a case of a set of Pilot's Notes, a set of flight reference cards, an essential knowledge quiz, ground school, brief with Andy and go and fly the aeroplane. As it turned out, the first sortie I did was on 16 June 2008. Andy had taken both the aeroplanes down to Kemble for static display on their open day, so I brought the black one WA638 back on a transit from Kemble to Chalgrove, one hour and five minutes. That was the majority of my conversion flying, of just getting used to the aeroplane. We tend to save the wheels and tyres, we don't do touch and goes, just do low approaches, all the basic handling stuff. We only fly them day, visual meteorological conditions (VMC), clear of cloud, because of the age of the instruments. We have got a full instrument fit, but it's just prudent and best practice to avoid flying in cloud if you can.

"We obviously had to get the approvals from the Military Airworthiness Authority (MAA) for me to go and fly it. Most of the things I needed to do in fact I'd covered on the first sortie, the only thing really I hadn't done, was to do an in-flight engine shut down and re-start. That's always one of those things you have slight trepidation about with its asymmetric reputation. One of the things is that the systems aren't crossed over, so one engine does not supply all of the systems. You have pneumatics for the brakes one side and hydraulics the other and the thing with the hydraulics is that you've got an accumulator. There's enough in that to have one in-selection of the airbrakes, one down-selection of the gear and flaps, whereas if you're using pneumatics, you may need multiple applications which depletes the accumulator. Quite an interesting thing I've found, is that it's a really straightforward aeroplane to fly but on landing, because of the bag brakes, we don't want to glaze them so you have to be very careful with your braking technique. It's probably the one thing I have to put more conscious thought into than anything else. If we had lots of bags, it probably wouldn't be a problem to change them, but now with a fairly limited life we're quite circumspect with the braking.

"The next time I flew it was 17 March 2010, when I went off and finished the conversion, which was the engine shut-down and relight, did some more circuits and then did another trip the same day. That was the conversion to the Meteor done really. The asymmetric characteristics of it are interesting with these; they're T.7½s with a big fin and rudder, so you don't have the Phantom Dive problem that you do with the small fin and rudder T.7s. But what I found was that the force displacement gradient on the rudder is steep, so that if you do slow right down on one engine the rudder forces are really high, but you're nowhere near full rudder deflection. It's just the aerodynamic balance characteristics of the rudder; it's not like some aeroplanes where you can end up with the rudder up against the stop. I actually found it is totally manageable if you understand how to fly it and keep the speeds correct. Whereas with a lot of aeroplanes where you have big asymmetric yawing moments, it's because you've got big propellers blowing air over the wings, then you've got roll aspects, which obviously in the Meteor, you don't. It is quite unusual to have a jet with that amount of asymmetric yaw. These do have spring-tab ailerons, so they are to the last build standard. The only difference is WA638 is an earlier one with the small diameter intakes.

"On 15 May 2011, it was the 70th anniversary of the first British jet flight, the E.28/39 from Cranwell. As the Meteors were two of the oldest jets still flying, we took them up there for a flypast, it wasn't publicised as a display; we took both the aeroplanes and flew them in formation. We had a practice sortie at Chalgrove on 18 April. It's an interesting aeroplane in formation – these two have rarely been seen like that – and if you go into close line astern then the downwash off the wings gives you quite a pitch trim change. So when you go behind into formation, you need quite a bit of nose-down trim because of the high-set tailplane. It is something with high T-tail aeroplanes, but other than that, it is a delightful aeroplane in formation.

"When we took them to Cranwell Frank Whittle's son, Ian was there, as were two people who had actually seen the first flight of the E.28/39. One was Eric 'Winkle' Brown who just happened to divert in because of bad weather the previous day, before he knew anything about it; the other one was a sergeant engine fitter. When I did the ETPS course in '85, we had a visit to Rolls-Royce at Derby and that day there was a visit from Frank Whittle, so we had a course photograph taken with him; that was one of those really special days and special photographs. I did feel a strong affinity for the whole thing, so it was delightful to be able to take the Meteors up to Cranwell and fly them there.

"Andy did a few trips the year after, but then there was a change in the regulation, the setting up of the MAA – there were lots of things going on. Martin-Baker still had a need for the aeroplane and they decided the way ahead was to try and purchase them and put them on the UK CAA register; it took a while to go through the process of doing that. There was a lot of work in the company on the Mk.16 seat for the F-35 Joint Strike Fighter (JSF) and so the plans are to keep them going as G-registered permit to fly aeroplanes. Hopefully they will appear at the odd air show for static or flying. We are really careful to maintain the fatigue life, WA638 is the primary flying aeroplane with WL419 as a back-up. The annual utilisation for each of them is about 10-15 hours a year because they are short sorties. The seat-firing tests are usually done at Chalgrove between 200 and 1,000 feet, the medium altitude ones are done down at Cazaux in France. Other than that, it is just purely pilot proficiency flying and air tests to keep the life usage down. Even with the ventral tank on it's quite a short endurance aeroplane, about one hour is the longest sortie other than on high level transits. They've got a good spares supply, it's just maintaining that and we've got a reasonable supply

Coventry-based T.7 WA591 FMK-Q [G-BWMF] in its original 203 AFS markings, Duxford 23 May 2015. [Keith Hawes]

of engines. During my time at Boscombe Down, the Meteors were still going up at Llanbedr and that was all part of the same fleet, so I think some of the spares from there were acquired and the engines. Even when the airframes were owned by QinetiQ, the engines, avionics and ejection seats were still owned by Martin-Baker.

"I can't think of anything I don't like about the Meteor; it's quite an intuitive aeroplane to fly in many ways. There are five knots between unstick and single-engine safety speed, but frankly I was used to 20 knots on the Buccaneer on a blown take-off, so it is not a concept that is new to me. The rudder forces are high asymmetric but you know about it, it's manageable. I do like having a Mk.10 ejection seat in something like that! The stall characteristics are very benign; we only fly them to 3.5 g to conserve fatigue, so we do gentle looping manoeuvres. I think the one thing – and it's like it with a few other aeroplanes – is the use of brakes on the landing roll. We will touch down, aerodynamically brake, put the speed brakes out and then just blip the brakes for about two seconds a time and release them to prevent glazing on the bags. Normally we fly from Chalgrove and we've got a 6,000-foot runway, so it's not a problem. But there are other aeroplanes, like the Tornado, that have got very good brakes, but if you use them above 80 knots you will turn off with hot brakes and have fire trucks following you back. If I haven't flown a Tornado for a while, I have to consciously think about braking technique, rather than just landing and braking like I do in most aeroplanes. But there's nothing I dislike about the Meteor in the slightest. I think probably it's just the fact that the systems aren't on both sides. I haven't done a seat firing yet, but I hope I will do one soon."

Thus, the Meteor's long story goes on with no immediate sign of the Derwents being finally silenced. Its extraordinary career has seen it operating in many different guises, while both challenging and exciting – occasionally infuriating – those who have found themselves either crewing it or working on it. Almost to a man, they have said they enjoyed the experience and still have a soft spot for the aeroplane as these two quotes about flying Meteors 70 years apart well illustrate.

"The Meteor was fantastic. It was tremendous, a wonderful aeroplane." Paul Holden, 74 Sqn 1946

"There have been a few aeroplanes that really stand out from the others and the Meteor is one of them…a fascinating aeroplane, it is absolutely delightful." Dave Southwood, Martin-Baker 2016

APPENDIX

In addition to the numbered operational squadrons, flights and the supporting training establishment detailed below, Meteors served in a vast number of support units, communication/station flights, etc.

Royal Air Force

Squadrons

This includes those which had some Meteors on strength concurrently with other types e.g. for training or target towing. Dates shown are the earliest and latest with the type, regardless of variants shown, when operated as main equipment, unless there were separate periods of Meteor operation (e.g. 29 Sqn). Meteor-equipped squadrons also commonly had one or two T.7s on strength.

1	Tangmere. F.4, F.8. Jun 48 – Oct 55
2	Bückeburg, Gütersloh, Wahn. FR.9, PR.10. Dec 50 – Jun 56
3	Gütersloh (Vampire). T.7
4	Wunstorf, Jever (Vampire). T.7
5	Laarbruch. NF.11. Jan 59 – Jun 60
6	Deversoir (Vampire). T.7
8	Khormaksar. FR.9. Jan 58 – Aug 59
11	Geilenkirchen. NF.11. Jan 59 – Feb 60
13	Kabrit, Abu Sueir, Akrotiri. PR.10. Dec 51 – Aug 56
14	Fassberg (Venom). T.7
16	Cell (Vampire). T.7
19	Church Fenton. F.4, F.8. Jan 51 – Jan 57
20	Ahlhorn (Sabre, Hunter). T.7
23	Coltishall (Vampire, Venom). T.7
25	West Malling, Tangmere. NF.12, NF.14. Mar 54 – Jun 58
26	Wunstorf, Oldenburg (Vampire, Sabre). T.7
28	Kai Tak (Vampire, Venom). T.7
29	Tangmere, Acklington. NF.11, NF.12. Jul 51 – Jul 58. Akrotiri (Javelin). T.7, F(TT).8 – Nov 65, the last Meteors attached (in a supporting role) to a front-line fighter squadron.
32	Shallufa, Deversoir, Kabrit, Nicosia (Vampire, Venom). T.7
33	Leeming. NF.14. Sep 57 – Aug 58
34	Tangmere. F.8. Aug 54 – Dec 55
39	Kabrit, Luqa, Nicosia, Luqa, Nicosia, Luqa. NF.13. Mar 53 – Jun 58
41	Church Fenton, Biggin Hill. F.4, F.8. Jan 51 – Jul 55

43   Tangmere, Leuchars. F.4, F.8. Feb 49 – Sep 54

45   Butterworth (Vampire, Venom). T.7

46   Odiham. NF.12, NF.14. Aug 54 – Feb 56

54   Odiham. F.8. Apr 52 – Mar 55

56   Thorney Island, Waterbeach. F.4, F.8. Sep 48 – Jun 55

60   Leeming, Tengah. NF.14. May 59 – Aug 61

63   Thorney Island, Lübeck, Thorney Island. Waterbeach. F.3, F.4, F.8. Apr
       48 – Jan 57

64   Linton-on-Ouse, Duxford. F.4, F.8, NF.12, NF.14. Dec 50 – Sep 58

65   Linton-on-Ouse, Duxford. F.4, F.8. Dec 50 – Feb 57

66   Duxford, Linton-on-Ouse. F.4, F.8. May 48 – Apr 54

67   Gütersloh, Wildenrath (Vampire, Sabre). T.7

68   Wahn, Laarbruch. NF.11. Feb 52 – Jan 59

71   Wildenrath (Vampire, Sabre). T.7

72   North Weald, Church Fenton. F.8, NF.12, NF.14. Jul 52 – Jun 59

73   Nicosia, Kabrit, Idris, Nicosia (Vampire). T.7

74   Colerne, Fairwood Common, Bentwaters, Colerne, Horsham St.Faith,
       Acklington, Horsham St.Faith, Lübeck, Horsham St.Faith, Tangmere,
       Acklington, Horsham St.Faith. F.3, F.4, F.8. May 45 – Mar 57

79   Gütersloh, Laarbruch, Wunstorf. FR.9 Nov 51 – Aug 56

81   Seletar, Tengah. PR.10. Jan 54 – Jul 61

85   West Malling, Church Fenton. NF.11, NF.12, NF.14. Sep 51 – Nov 58.
       Binbrook. F(TT).8. Sep 64 – Aug 70

87   Wahn, Brüggen. NF.11. Mar 52 – Dec 57

89   Stradishall (Venom). T.7

91   Duxford, Acklington. F.3. Oct 46 – Jan 47.

92   Acklington, Duxford, Lübeck, Duxford, Lübeck, Duxford, Linton-on-Ouse.
       F.3, F.4, F.8. Jan 47 – Feb 54

93   Celle (Vampire). T.7

94   Celle (Vampire). T.7

96   Ahlhorn, Geilenkirchen. NF.11. Nov 52 – Jan 59

98   Fassberg (Vampire, Venom). T.7

100   Wittering (Canberra). T.7

111   North Weald. F.8. Dec 53 – Jun 55

112   Fassberg, Jever, Brüggen (Vampire, Sabre). T.7

118   Fassberg (Vampire, Venom). T.7

124   Molesworth, Bentwaters, Fairwood Common, Bentwaters. F.3. Aug 45 –
       Apr 46

125   Stradishall. NF.11. Mar 55 – Jan 56

130   Brüggen (Sabre, Hunter). T.7

141   Coltishall. NF.11. Aug 51 – Sep 55

145   Celle (Vampire, Venom). T.7

151   Leuchars. NF.11. Mar 53 – Oct 55

152	Wattisham, Stradishall, Wattisham, Stradishall. NF.12, NF.14. Jun 54 – Jul 58
153	West Malling, Waterbeach. NF.12, NF.14. Feb 55 – Jun 58
185	Hal Far, Luqa, Idris, Nicosia, Habbaniyah (Vampire). T.7
208	Fayid, Kabrit, Nicosia, Abu Sueir, Hal Far, Akrotiri, Ta' Qali, Nicosia. FR.9. Jan 51 – Mar 58
213	Deversoir (Vampire). T.7
216	Lyneham (Comet). T.7. 1956
219	Kabrit. NF.11, NF.13. Mar 53 – Sep 54
222	Molesworth, Exeter, Spilsby, Exeter, Boxted, Exeter, Weston Zoyland, Tangmere, Lübeck, Tangmere, Lübeck, Thorney Island, Leuchars. F.3, F.4, F.8. Oct 45 – Dec 54
234	Molesworth, Boxted. F.3. Feb 46 – Sep 46. T.7
245	Colerne, Fairwood Common, Colerne, Bentwaters, Colerne, Horsham St.Faith, Lübeck, Horsham St.Faith, Lübeck, Horsham St.Faith, Stradishall. F.3, F.4, F.8. Aug 45 – Apr 57
247	Odiham. F.8. Apr 52 – Jun 55
249	Deversoir (Vampire). T.7
256	Ahlhorn, Geilenkirchen. NF.11. Nov 52 – Jan 59
257	Church Fenton, Acklington, Church Fenton, Horsham St.Faith, Lübeck, Horsham St.Faith, Wattisham. F.3, F.4, F.8. Feb 48 – Mar 55
263	Horsham St.Faith, Acklington, Horsham St.Faith, Acklington, Wattisham. F.4, F.8. Dec 47 – Apr 55
264	Linton-on-Ouse, Leuchars, Acklington, Linton-on-Ouse, Middleton St.George, Leeming. NF.11, NF.14. Nov 51 – Oct 57
266	Boxted, Acklington, Boxted, Wattisham, Boxted, Wattisham, Tangmere, Lübeck, Tangmere, Acklington, Tangmere. F.3, F.4. Sep 46 – Feb 49
500	West Malling. F.3, F.4, F.8. Jul 48 – Mar 57
501	Filton (Vampire). T.7, F.8 – Mar 57
502	Aldergrove (Vampire). T.7 – Mar 57
504	Wymeswold. F.4, F.8. Oct 49 – Mar 57
527	Watton. NF.11, NF.14. Jun 53 – Oct 55. NF.11. Sep 57 – Nov 57
540	Wyton (Canberra). T.7
541	Benson, Bückeburg, Gütersloh, Bückeburg, Gütersloh, Laarbruch, Wunstorf. PR.10. Dec 50 – Sep 57
600	Biggin Hill. F.4, F.8. Mar 50 – Mar 57
601	North Weald. F.8. Aug 52 – Mar 57
602	Leuchars, Abbotsinch, Renfrew, Abbotsinch (Vampires). T.7 – Mar 57
603	Turnhouse, Leuchars, Turnhouse (Vampire). T.7 – Mar 57
604	North Weald. F.8. Aug 52 – Mar 57
605	Honiley (Vampire). T.7, F.8 – Mar 57
607	Ouston (Vampire). T.7, F.8 - Mar 57
608	Thornaby (Vampire). T.7, F.8 – Mar 57

609   Church Fenton. F.4, F.8. Jan 51 – Mar 57
610   Hooton Park. F.4, F.8. Jul 51 – Mar 57
611   Woodvale, Hooton Park. F.4, F.8. May 51 – Mar 57
612   Leuchars, Edzell, Dyce (Vampire). T.7 – Mar 57
613   Ringway (Vampire). T.7 – Mar 57
614   Llandow (Vampire). T.7, F.8 – Mar 57
615   Biggin Hill. F.4, F.8. Sep 50 – Mar 57
616   Culmhead, Manston, Colerne, Melsbroek, Gilze-Rijen, Kluis, Quackenbrück,
      Fassberg, Lüneburg, Lübeck. F.1, F.3. Jul 44 – Aug 45. Finningley, Worksop.
      F.3, F.4, F.8. Jan 49 – Mar 57

Flights
1574 Changi. T.7, F(TT).8, TT.20. May 64 – Mar 71
1689 Aston Down. T.7 1950 – 1953

Advanced Flying Schools (AFS)
202   Valley. T.7. Apr 51 – Jun 54 disbanded
203   Stradishall, Driffield. F.4, T.7. Jul 49 – Jun 54 became 8 FTS
205   Middleton St.George. F.3, F.4, T.7. Sep 50 – Jun 54 became 4 FTS
206   Oakington. F.3, F.4, T.7. Nov 51 – Jun 54 became 5 FTS
207   Full Sutton. F.3, F.4, T.7. Nov 51 – Jun 54 became 207 FTS
208   Merryfield. T.7. Nov 51 – Jun 54 became 10 FTS (Vampires only)
209   Weston Zoyland. F.4, T.7. Jun 52 – Jun 54 became 12 FTS
210   Tarrant Rushton. F.3, T.7. Aug 52 – Apr 54 disbanded
211   Worksop. T.7, F.8. Aug 52 – Jun 54 became 211 FTS
215   Finningley. F.4, T.7. Feb 52 – May 54 disbanded

Air Navigation Schools (ANS)
1   Stradishall. T.7, NF(T).14. Early 62 – Feb 66
2   Thorney Island. T.7, NF(T).14. Jun 59 – early 62

Conversion Units (CU)
1335 Colerne, Molesworth. F.1, F.3, F.4. Mar 45 – Aug 46 renamed 226 OCU

Operational Conversion Units (OCU)
226   Molesworth, Bentwaters, Driffield, Stradishall. F.3, F.4, T.7, F.8, FR.9. Aug
      46 – Jun 55
228   Leeming, North Luffenham, Leeming. NF.11, NF.12, NF.14. Jul 52 – 1960
229   Leuchars, Chivenor (Hunter). T.7, F(TT).8. Dec 50 – Sep 74
231   Bassingbourn (Canberra). T.7, PR.10. Nov 51 – Oct 56
233   Pembrey (Hunter, Vampire). T.7, F.8. Sep 52 – Sep 57
237   Benson, Bassingbourn. T.7, PR.10. Mar 51 – Dec 51, merged with 231
      OCU

238   Colerne, North Luffenham. T.7, F.8, NF.11, NF.12, NF.14. Jun 52 – Mar 48

Flying Training Schools (FTS)
4   Middleton St.George, Worksop. F.4, T.7, F.8. Jun 54 – Jun 58
5   Oakington. T.7. Jun 54 – Feb 62
8   Driffield. F.4, T.7. Jun 54 – Aug 55
12   Weston Zoyland. F.4, T.7. Jun 54 – Jun 55
211   Worksop. T.7, F.8. Jun 54 – Jun 56

Fleet Air Arm

Squadrons
700   Yeovilton. TT.20. Dec 59 – Jul 61
702   Culdrose. T.7. Jun 49 – Aug 52
703   Lee-on-Solent, Ford. F.3, T.7, F.8. Aug 48 – Aug 55
728   Hal Far. T.7, TT.20. Feb 55 – May 67
728B   Hal Far. U.15, U.16. Jul 59 – Nov 61
736   Culdrose, Lossiemouth. T.7. Aug 52 – May 54
759   Culdrose, Lossiemouth. T.7. Sep 52 – Apr 54
764   Lossiemouth. T.7. Dec 57 – Mar 58
767   Stretton. T.7. Feb 53 – Dec 53
771   Arbroath, Ford, Lee-on-Solent, Lossiemouth. T.7. May 50 – Mar 55
781   Ford. T.7. Apr 51 – Jun 54
806   Brawdy. T.7. Feb 53 – Apr 53
813   Ford. T.7. Mar 53 – Dec 53

Apart from station flights, the other principal operator of Meteors was the Airwork-operated Fleet Requirements Unit (FRU) at St. Davids, which flew T.7s from September 1953 until the airfield closed in 1958, after which it moved to Hurn, added TT.20s and finally shut down in May 1970.

Experimental, Research and other Establishments

Not part of the military establishment, the following organisations all used Meteor aircraft at various times and are an important part of the story.

Aeroplane and Armament Experimental Establishment (A&AEE), Boscombe Down. All marks
Blind Landing Experimental Unit, Bedford. F.4, T.7
Empire Test Pilot's School, Cranfield, Farnborough. F.1, F.3, F.4, T.7, F.8, NF.11, NF.14. Apr 45 – Nov 66
Institute of Aviation Medicine, Farnborough. T.7
Radar Research Flying Unit, Defford, Pershore. F.4, F.8, NF.11, NF.13, NF.14

Royal Aircraft Establishment (RAE), Farnborough, Bedford. F.1, F.3, F.4, T.7, F.8, NF.14. 1944 – 1973

RAE Test & Evaluation Establishment, Llanbedr. T.7, NF.11, U.15, U.16/D.16

ABBREVIATIONS

ADC	Aide-de-Camp	CASA	Civil Aviation Safety Authority
AF	Air Force	Cat	Category
AFC	Air Force Cross	CB	Companion of the Order of the Bath
AFS	Advanced Flying School		
AFTS	Advanced Flying Training School	CCCF	Coastal Command Communications Flight
AGL	Above Ground Level	CEng	Chartered Engineer
AI	Air Interception	CFE	Central Fighter Establishment
Air Cdre	Air Commodore		
AM	Air Marshal		
ANS	Air Navigation School	CFI	Chief Flying Instructor
AOC	Air Officer Commanding	CFS	Central Flying School
		CGS	Central Gunnery School
APC	Armament Practice Camp	Chf Tech	Chief Technician
APS	Armament Practice Station	CO	Commanding Officer
		Cpl	Corporal
ASF	Aircraft Servicing Flight	CRDF	Cathode Ray Direction Finder
ASI	Air Speed Indicator	CU	Conversion Unit
ATC	Air Traffic Control		
AVM	Air Vice-Marshal	D	Drone
		DFC	Distinguished Flying Cross
BCBS	Bomber Command Bombing School	DFLS	Day Fighter Leaders' School
BFTS	Basic Flying Training School	DI	Directional Indicator
BOAC	British Overseas Airways Corporation	DME	Distance Measuring Equipment
BPC	Barometric Pressure Control	DSO	Distinguished Service Order
BSc	Batchelor of Science		
BT	Baronet	EGT	Exhaust Gas Temperature
CAA	Civil Aviation Authority	EMRU	Electro-Magnetic Release Unit
CAACU	Civilian Anti-Aircraft Co-operation Unit	ESC	Ejection Seat Cartridge
		ETPS	Empire Test Pilots' School
CAS	Chief of the Air Staff		

F	Fighter	J/T	Junior Technician
FCCS	Fighter Command Communications Squadron	KCB	Knight Commander of the Order of the Bath
Fg Off	Flying Officer		
Flt	Flight	LAC	Leading Aircraftman
Flt Cdr	Flight Commander	LP	Low Pressure
Flt Lt	Flight Lieutenant		
Flt Sgt	Flight Sergeant	MAA	Military Airworthiness Authority
FR	Fighter Reconnaissance	MAP	Ministry of Aircraft Production
FRAeS	Fellow of the Royal Aeronautical Society	MEAF	Middle East Air Force
FRSA	Fellow of the Royal Society of Arts	MO	Medical Officer
		MoD	Ministry of Defence
FTS	Flying Training School	MoD PE	Ministry of Defence Procurement Executive
F(TT)	Fighter (Target Tug)		
FTU	Ferry Training Unit		
		Mph	Miles per hour
GCA	Ground Controlled Approach	MT	Motor Transport
		MU	Maintenance Unit
GCI	Ground Controlled Interception		
		NAAFI	Navy Army and Air Forces Institute
GEE	Radio navigation system (from 'Grid')	NATO	North Atlantic Treaty Organisation
GLO	Ground Liaison Officer	Nav	Navigator
Gp Capt	Group Captain	NCO	Non Commissioned Officer
HP	High Pressure	NF	Night Fighter
HQ	Headquarters	NF(T)	Night Fighter (Trainer)
IAS	Indicated Airspeed	OBE	Order of the British Empire
IFR	Instrument Flight Rules		
		OC	Officer Commanding
IRE	Instrument Rating Examiner	OCTU	Officer Cadet Training Unit
IRT	Instrument Rating Test	OCU	Operational Conversion Unit
ITS	Initial Training School		
		OIC	Officer In Charge
JC&SS	Junior Command & Staff School	ORP	Operational Readiness Platform
JSF	Joint Strike Fighter	OTU	Operational Training Unit

PAI	Pilot Attack Instructor	SPHF	Student Pilot Holding Flight
PAN	Declaring a problem, from the French panne – broken	Sqn	Squadron
		Sqn Ldr	Squadron Leader
PI	Practice Interception	SRF	School of Refresher Flying
Plt Off	Pilot Officer		
PR	Photographic Reconnaissance	T	Trainer
		TAF	Tactical Air Force
QDM	Magnetic bearing to a station	TBL	Throttle Back Landing
		TGT	Turbine Gas Temperature
QFI	Qualified Flying Instructor	TT	Target Tug
QGH	A descent through cloud approach	TTF	Target Towing Flight
		TTS	Target Towing Squadron
QRA	Quick Reaction Alert	TWU	Tactical Weapons Unit
RAAF	Royal Australian Air Force	U	Unmanned
RAF	Royal Air Force	U/S	Unserviceable
RAFG	Royal Air Force Germany	USAAF	United States Army Air Force
RAFVR	Royal Air Force Volunteer Reserve	USAF	United States Air Force
RAuxAF	Royal Auxiliary Air Force	VHF	Very High Frequency
RLG	Relief Landing Ground	VMC	Visual Meteorological Conditions
RN	Royal Navy		
RPM	Revolutions Per Minute	Wg Cdr	Wing Commander
		WO	Warrant Officer
R/T	Receiver/Transmitter	WRAF	Women's Royal Air Force
SAC	Senior Aircraftman		
SATCO	Senior Air Traffic Control Officer		
Sgt	Sergeant		
SHAPE	Supreme Headquarters Allied Powers Europe		
SOP	Standard Operating Procedure		

SELECT BIBLIOGRAPHY

Bond, S. J. *Meteor – Gloster's First Jet Fighter*, Midland Counties 1985

Halley, J. J. *Broken Wings – Post-War Royal Air Force Accidents*, Air Britain 1999

Jefford, C. G. *RAF Squadrons*, Airlife 1988

Rawlings, J. & Sedgwick, H., *Learn to Test, Test to Learn*, Airlife 1991

Shacklady, E. *The Gloster Meteor*, Macdonald 1962

Sturtivant, Ray. *RAF Flying Training and Support Units since 1912*, Air Britain 2007

Sturtivant, Ray. *The Squadrons of the Fleet Air Arm*, Air Britain 1994

INDEX

MILITARY ORGANISATIONS